Practical Thai

Publisher
Pranom Supavimolpun

Project Manager
Y. Lee

Text by
Suraphong Kanchananaga

Revised and Edited by
Sitala Navamanond

Cover, Graphic & Illustrations
H. Tun
Minual
W. Tun

Consultant
Catherine Gordon

ISBN : 974-8362-27-2

Printed in Thailand by
Amarin Printing and Publishing Public Company Limited

2220/31 Ramkhamhaeng 36/1, Huamark, Bangkok 10240 Thailand.
Tel: 66 (2)375-2685–6, 375-2692, 732-0243-5 Fax: 66 (2)375-2669

a communication guide
for travelers and residents

PRACTICAL THAI

Text by
Suraphong Kanchananaga

Revised and edited by
Sitala Navamanond

15th Edition 1995

FOREWORD

PRACTICAL THAI, the best-selling and first book of its kind in Thailand, has been compiled for the use of foreign travelers and residents in Thailand. Its object is to teach simple and practical sentences and phrases of daily Thai conversation that will enable travelers and residents with little or no knowledge of Thai, as well as beginning Thai language students, to express their thoughts in intelligible words and with proper style when speaking with Thais. The selection of words and phrases compiled in this revised 15th edition should enable the traveler to avoid misunderstandings when obtaining hotel or restaurant accommodations, when shopping, when ordering meals, or when trying to find his way. The book also provides a wide variety of tourist and travel facts, lifestyle tips and useful information. Romanized spelling is used throughout, and the use of confusing symbols is avoided.

Study of the preliminary notes should provide a guide to Thai pronunciation; upon reaching Thailand, however, acquire a better accent by listening carefully to the language spoken around you. If your listener doesn't understand, then you should repeat words or phrases until he does. The person you are trying to talk to will most probably help you pronounce it promptly and correctly. Remember that your purpose is to communicate. A slight mispronunciation is no embarrassment.

The author of this book, Suraphong Kanchananaga, is also the former editor of *The Siam Trade & Economic Review, The Commercial & Economic Progress of Thailand, All-in One Book of Reference & Guide, Handbook for Tourist & Businessman Visiting Thailand, Resources & Products of Thailand, All About Thailand,* and numerous other articles and publications about his fascinating country.

We would like to wish you a most enjoyable trip to Thailand, and trust this little phrase book will prove helpful and entertaining.

Contents

PRELIMINARY NOTES AND GUIDE TO PRONUNCIATION

Some instructions *vivâ voce* from a Thai is almost indispensable in the beginning. If you are among Thais, listen and imitate. If you are not, the following general hints may prove useful.

(a) Vowels

There are five basic vowels: a, e, i, o and u.

The vowels "a," "e" and "i" in Thai are equivalent to the sounds of French or Italian; i.e., similar to "a" and "e" in *café* and to "i" in *hit.* Other vowels and dipthongs are pronounced as follows:

aa อา	is pronounced like "a" in *barn*
ae แอ	is pronounced like "a" in *mat* or *tan*
ai ไอ	is pronounced like "i" in *high* or *fine*
ao, au, ow เอา	are pronounced like "ow" in *how* or *down*
aw ออ	is pronounced like "aw" in *paw* or "o" in *song*
ee อี	is pronounced like "ee" in *bee*
ei เอ	is pronounced like "a" in *able* or "ai" in *air*

eu เออ is pronounced somewhat like "u" in *suet,* and almost exactly like "eu" in the French word *feu.*
o โอ is pronounced somewhat like "o" in *more* or *vote*
oo, ou, อู is pronounced like "oo" in *soon* or "u" in *rule*
u อุ is pronounced like "oo" in *book* or "u" in *full*

When a vowel is repeated (as in **rawaang**), ระหว่าง the effect is to lengthen it to almost double the length of the single vowel. It is very important to keep the distinction between long and short vowels to avoid confusion (e.g., **rawang** ระวัง means "to be careful," but **rawaang** ระหว่าง means "middle" or "between.")

(b) Consonants

b, d, f, k, l, m, p, s, v, w, y. บ,ด,ฟ,ก หรือ ล,ม,พ,ส,ว,ย Normally, these are pronounced as in English.
ch จ a palatal, nearly as in *church, chat.*
sh ช pronounced as in *Shanghai, shell.*
d ด initial "d" like English "d"; final "d" like "t" in *cat.*
g ก as in *gun, get,* but not as in *gem* or *gin.*
ng ง as in *singing,banging,* never as in *tingle, sponging.* It is pronounced exactly like English "ing" with "i" cut off. Quite a few words begin with "ng", e.g. **ngo** โง่ (stupid), **ngarm** งาม (pretty) and **ngou** งู (snake).
th ท an aspirant, pronounced like English "t" in *tie,* not like the "th" in *thigh.*
ph พ another aspirant, pronounced like English "p" as in *pony,* not like the "ph" in *phony.*
r ร is often nearly silent, like the British "r" in *arm.*

(c) Tones

The Thai language is tonal with five primary tones. These tones can be indicated in this manner:

high tone (´)   rising tone (ˇ)
low tone (`)   falling tone (^)
middle tone (no mark)

No two tones are alike for the simple reason that no two people hear them exactly alike. Neither are any two voices absolutely the same, and while there is a similarity in trends of tone, there is great difference from person to person and region to region in the relative position of the lines representing tones. Pronunciation must therefore be learned by talking with Thais. One should pay careful attention in listening, as tonal differences can represent a significant difference in meaning. For example, the word for dog is ma:หมา horse is ma ม้า; and come is ma มา. Likewise, the word for the number five is ha ห้า while find is ha หา.

In speaking Thai, emphasis should be given on the overall sounds and rhythm in sentences rather than single words. It is not necessary to know the meaning of each part, but the memorization of many sentences and sounds is necessary in order to retain interest and increase the fluency of pronunciation.

It will help you to spend a little time in the study of pronunciation before you begin your study of the language. The better your accent, the easier it will be to understand what Thais say to you.

RUDIMENTS OF THAI GRAMMAR

The Thai language has a simple grammatical construction, a great paucity of word forms, a vivid, picturesque way of forming cumulative nouns from other words which describe the object; it also has a wealth of idiomatic expressions. These unique characteristics make the Thai language a very easy one to learn — except for the Westerner to whom its very simplicity makes it peculiarly difficult.

The key to speaking Thai is the art of simplifying one's English and then translating it. The beginner, whose limitations compel him to stick to simple sentences, is often better understood than the more ambitious advanced student who attempts to use conditional and relative sentences. Literary Thai has, of course, greater capabilities than the ordinary colloquial, but it demands prolonged study and is only understood by the best educated Thais.

(a) Articles

There is no article such as "a" or "the" in Thai. To indicate a definite object the demonstrative adjectives **ni** นี้ (*this, these*) and **nanh** นั้น (that, those) are used and should follow the word they qualify, e.g. *the house*=**baan nanh;** บ้านนั้น *this book*=**nangsue ni** หนังสือนี้ or **nangsue lem ni.** หนังสือเล่มนี้

(b) Nouns

The Thai noun undergoes no inflection to denote gender, number or case.

Gender is defined by placing the words **shaai** ชาย (*male*) and **ying** หญิง (*female*) after nouns denoting persons, e.g.: **dek-shaai** เด็กชาย (*boy*) and **dek-ying** เด็กหญิง (*girl*).

For animals the word **tua-phu** ตัวผู้ is used to denote the males and **tua-mia** ตัวเมีย to denote females after the nouns, e.g.:

woa tua-phu วัวตัวผู้ = *a bull*
woa tua-mia วัวตัวเมีย = *a cow*
maew แมว = *a cat*
maew tua-phu แมวตัวผู้ = *a male cat*
maew tua-mia แมวตัวเมีย = *a female cat*

Designatory Particles

One peculiarity of the Thai language is that there is no declension of nouns or objectives. This being so, it is essential that some other way be offered for indicating number. Therefore, a designatory particle follows the noun and the particle in turn is followed by a number. This list includes designatory particles in most common use:

anh อัน things (in general), especially small objects
bai ใบ round hollow objects
chaan จาน plates of food

shabap ฉบับ	letters and newspapers
shaw ช่อ	bunches of flowers
shin ชิ้น	slices of meat; also pieces of small arttices
shoud ชุด	suits of clothing; also sets of things
daam ด้าม	pens
dawk, dork ดอก	flowers
duang ดวง	stars, individuals lights; also postage stamps
fawng, fong ฟอง	eggs (of poultry)
haw ห่อ	bundles, parcels
kaew แก้ว	drinking glasses
kham คำ	words; also mouthfuls of food
khan คัน	vehicles, including bicycles; also umbrellas
khon คน	person or persons
khou คู่	pairs of articles or of animals
krabork กระบอก	tubes and cylinders, including firearms
la หลา	yards (when buying dry goods)
lam, lamh ลำ	airplanes; also boats and ships
lang หลัง	houses and other buildings;
lem เล่ม	books; also sharp-edged knives
louk ลูก	fruits (hard, one-seeded varieties)
maled, med เมล็ด, เม็ด	fruits, pills and gems
met เมตร	meters (when buying dry goods)
muan มวน	cigarettes and cigars
ong, onk องค์	statues of Buddha, kings, holy personages
phaen แผ่น	sheets of paper or galvanized iron
phanaek แผนก	divisions, departments
phuen ผืน	blankets, carpets
plaeng แปลง	lands, including rice paddies

reuan เรือน	clocks and watches
roup รูป	monks and novices
saai สาย	roads and waterways; also belts and bracelets
sawng, song ซอง	envelopes
senh เส้น	hair; also lines drawn in ink
si ซี่	teeth, ribs
thaeng แท่ง	pencils
thuai ถ้วย	cups
tonh ต้น	trees and plants; also posts
tua ตัว	animals, insects, fish; tables and chairs; shirts, pants and coats
wi, hwi หวี	bananas (by the bunch)
wong วง	circles; especially rings and bracelets

Plurals

The above-listed designatory particles are used in indicating plurals. For example:

ying sib khon หญิงสิบคน (literally, "women ten people") means ten women.
woa sib tua วัวสิบตัว (literally, "oxen ten animals") means ten oxen.
baan sib lang บ้านสิบหลัง (literally, "house ten buildings") means ten houses.

Plurals can also be made by duplication, as in this sentence: **Dek-dek rian nangsue thi rong-rian.** เด็ก ๆ เรียนหนังสือที่โรงเรียน (Children are attending the school.)

Comparatives

Words of comparison may also be used to indicate plurals. These include **maak** มาก or **laai** หลาย (*many);* **nid-noi** นิดหน่อย or **song-sarm** สองสาม (*a few);* **maak kwa** มากกว่า (*more than);* and **maak thisout** มากที่สุด (most). Examples:

Mi khon laai khon nai baan nanh. มีคนหลายคนในบ้านนั้น (There are many people in the house.)

(c) Adjectives

As attribute, the adjective follows the noun it qualifies. The demonstrative pronoun, if employed, comes behind it.

Khon phomm คนผอม	=	*Thin man* or *men*
Khon soung nanh คนสูงนั้น	=	*That tall man*
Ying ouan หญิงอ้วน	=	*Fat woman*
Reuan maai เรือนไม้	=	*Wooden house*
Baan yai lang ni บ้านใหญ่หลังนี้	=	*This large house*

When speaking Thai, there are a few basic rules. Adjectives always follow the noun. **Baan** บ้าน (house) and **yai** ใหญ่ *(large)* together as **baan** บ้านใหญ่ mean "a large house" and so on.

Among the more commonly employed adjectives are **riap-roy** เรียบร้อย (*polite), **sanuk** สนุก *(fun),* **chai-dee** ใจดี *(warm-hearted),* **chai-yen** ใจเย็น (*cold-hearted),* **chai-ron** ใจร้อน (*hot-tempered),* **chai-raai** ใจร้าย *(wicked),* **ngarm** งาม *(pretty),* **na-kliad** น่าเกลียด *(ugly),* **waan** หวาน *(sweet)* and **priao** เปรี้ยว *(sour).* See the vocabulary list at the back of this book for others.

(d) Verbs

When constructing a sentence the principle order is : *subject-verb-object.* The order of words in a simple sentence is as follows:

1.	**Shan** ฉัน I	**kin** กิน eat	**khao** ข้าว rice
2.	**Khow** เขา He	**pai** ไป goes	**Khrungthep** กรุงเทพฯ to Bangkok
3.	**Khow** เขา He	**chah ma** จะมา will come	**phrung-ni** พรุ่งนี้ tomorrow

Context determines the voice of the Thai verb, though the simple verb generally expresses the active. Examples:

1.**Proad dou phaen-thi nanh.** โปรดดูแผนที่นั่น (Please look at the map.)

2.**Khun tharn a-harn aroi mai?** คุณทานอาหารอร่อยไหม (Did you have a good dinner?)

There is no change in the form of the Thai verb to indicate person or number:

Shan duem narm ฉันดื่มน้ำ	= I drink water
Joe duem narm โจดื่มน้ำ	= Joe drinks water
Dek-dek duem narm เด็ก ๆ ดื่มน้ำ	= The children drink water

There is, however, a change in grammar according to the tense of verb employed:

(Present) **Shan kin khao.** ฉันกินข้าว (I eat rice.)

(Past) **Shan kin khao meu waan.** ฉันกินข้าวเมื่อวาน (I ate rice yesterday.)

(Future) **Sha kin.** จะกิน (I will eat.)

(Continuous present) **Kumlung kin.** กำลังกิน (I am eating.)

(Continuous future) **Kumlung chah kin.** กำลังจะกิน (I will be eating.)

(Action finished) **Kin laow**. กินแล้ว (I ate already.)
(Action not yet finished) **Yang mai kin**. ยังไม่กิน (I have not eaten yet.)
(Might) **Ard chah kin khao**. อาจจะกินข้าว (I might eat rice.)
(Should) **Khuan shah kin khao**. ควรจะกินข้าว (I should eat rice.)
(Must) **Tong kin khao**. ต้องกินข้าว (I must eat rice.)
(Desire) **Yak shah kin khao**. อยากกินข้าว (I would like [I want] to eat rice.)

The Thai verb for *to be* and *to have* is the same: mi มี *Examples:*

Mi khon-Thai maak nai Saharat Amerika. มีคนไทยมากในสหรัฐอเมริกา (There are many Thais in U.S.A.)
Khun mi pha-ched-na mai? คุณมีผ้าเช็ดหน้าไหม(Do you have a handkerchief?)
Bonh toh mi arai? บนโต๊ะมีอะไร (What is on the table?)
Mi ngoen baang mai? มีเงินบ้างไหม (Do you have some money?)
Mi vela mai? มีเวลาไหม (Do you have time?)
Phom mai mi leui. ผมไม่มีเลย (I don't have any.)

There is no copula, such as is, are, was or were, in the Thai language. The connecting word is understood. Examples:
Chan cheb. ฉันเจ็บ (I [am] sick.)
Khow taai. เขาตาย (He [is] dead.)
Yang mai thouk. ยังไม่ถูก (It [is] not yet right.)
Khun hiew mai? คุณหิวไหม (Are you hungry?)
Phom mai hiew. ผมไม่หิว (I [am] not hungry.)
Phom hiew. ผมหิว (I [am] hungry.)

In making requests, three different verbs may be employed: **tongkarn**, ต้องการ **aow** เอา or **yak-chah**. อยากจะ **Tongkarn** is a polite form of *to want,* while aow is an informal version of the same verb.

Yak-chah actually translates as *would like.* Examples:

Phom tongkarn phoud kap khun-phaw khong khun.
ผมต้องการพูดกับคุณพ่อของคุณ (I want to speak to your father.)
Phom khaw-yuem ngoen. ผมขอยืมเงิน (I want to borrow money from you.)
Phom mai tong-karn ik laew. ผมไม่ต้องการอีกแล้ว (I don't want any more.)
Phom yaak-chah pai thi-ni. ผมอยากจะไปที่นี่ (I would like to go to this address.)

The verb **tham** ทำ is used for *to do.* Examples:

Tham vi-thi ni. ทำวิธีนี้ (Do it this way.)
Tham eng sih. ทำเองซิ (Do it yourself.)
Ya tham yaang nanh. (Don't do it that way.)
Laew khun tham yaang-rai? (What did you do about it?)

(e) Personal Pronouns

The Thais are world-famous for their politeness and courtesy to other people, and this has resulted in the fact that there is no single word which is always safe for the English equivalent of *you.* The word khun is fairly safe in most contexts and is recommended for wider use in place of the English *Mr., Mrs.* or *Miss.* But although polite, it sometimes may not be polite enough. **Khun** is really more like in *Herr* in German or *Monsieur* in French. Normally it is singular in meaning, and is reduplicated **Khun-Khun** when more than one person is addressed.

Khun is generally used to address a Thai whose name is unknown. It is also used when addressing younger or older persons. The Thais are very sentimental people and get offended quickly when they are rudely addressed. On the other hand, they are ready and willing to help anyone who speak to them in a polite manner.

The following is a table of personal pronouns and their uses.

Person speaking	I	We	You	He, She, They
Foreigner to Thai	**Phom (m.)** **Di-Shan (f.)**	Raow	**Khun**	**Khow**
Thai to European or other foreigner	**Phom (m.)** **Di-Shan (f.)**	Raow	**Khun,** **Thanh**	**Khow (singular)** **Phuak Khow (plural)**
Intimate and close friends	**Shan**	Raow	**Phi,** **Theu**	**Khow**
Older person to younger (stangers)	**Shan**	Raow	**Khun,**	**Khow**
Older person to younger (Family)	**Shan**	Raow	**Theu**	**Khow**
Younger person to older (strangers)	**Phom, Kraphom** **Di-Shan (f.)**	Raow	**Khun**	**Khow**
Younger person to older (Family)	**Shan**	Raow	**Loung(uncle)** **Pâ, Nâ (auntie)**	**Khow**
Husband to wife	**Shan, Phom**	Raow	**Theu, Khun**	**Khow**
Wife to husband	**Di-Shan, Shan**	Raow	**Khun, Theu**	**Khow**
Man to married woman	**Shan, Phom**	Raow	**Khun-Nai, Khun**	**Khun-Nai,**
Man to unmarried woman	**Shan, Phom**	Raow	**Khun**	**Khow**
Commoner to nobility	**Kraphom(m.)** **Di-Shan (f.)**	Raow	**Tai-thao,** **Thanh**	**Thanh**
Peasants to one another	**Kha**	Raow	**Kae**	**Khow**
Formal discourse, official documents	**Kha-pha-chao**	Raow	**Thanh**	**Khow**

Than ท่าน is much more polite than Khun คุณ and should always be used when addressing a government official. It would normally be used by a junior employee to his boss, and is roughly equivalent in politeness to the English word Sir. It is also, by courtesy, frequently extended to foreign visitors to Thailand.

Khun-naai คุณนาย is the feminine equivalent of **Than** ท่าน and is used more and more as title with similar meaning to Mrs. or Madam in English.

Kae แก is a rude form of address, implying the inferiority of the person spoken to. It should not be used by visitors at all. Generally, use of the word Kae is avoided by substituting the name of the person addressed, his title, or the Thai equivalent of Mr. —**Khun** คุณ or **Thanh.** ท่าน

Khun คุณ is in polite use between husband and wife, while **Theu** is for brother and sister, friends and colleagues. But it is generally rude to use Theu with anyone except those very junior to you in age and status.

Tai-thao ใต้เท้า is used before the name of nobility of people of high rank, to serve as the pronoun you.

The word **Phi,** พี่ often used to connote brother or sister or close friend, is coming increasingly into use as a polite equivalent for you. To a person younger than oneself, it is common to use the word **Theu**.

There are various ways to address those with whom you are in contact on a regular basis, such as the cook, gardener, office boy or canteen girl. If the person is a lot older than you, address them as **Loung** ลุง (uncle) or **Pâ** ป้า (auntie). For a woman a little younger than your mother, call her **Nâ.** น้า

Unmarried Thai women are usually addressed as **Khun.** It is proper to address married Thai women as **Khun Naai** คุณนาย. And elderly woman is politely addressed as **Khun-Yaai** คุณยาย or Grandma.

You should always call a Thai policeman or private constable **Mou;**หมู่ a police officer **Phou Muad;** ผู้หมวด and a chief police officer **Phou Kamkab**. ผู้กำกับ

Chinese born in Thailand are commonly addressed as **Ah-check** อาเจ๊ก (men) or **Ah-sim** อาซิ้ม (women). Rich Chinese merchants, irrespective of place of birth, are generally called **Thow-kae** เถ้าแก่ or **Siâ,** เสี่ย the latter implying a very rich man. Thais speaking to Chinese will probably use the words **oua** อั๊ว (I) and **lue** ลื้อ (you) in conversation. It should be stressed, however, that none of these words is polite. These should not be used by foreigners in speaking to Chinese, as they might easily be construed as offensive.

When referring to one's own belongings, the following words of possession are used:

My or Mine	= **Khong-phom,** ของผม	**Khong-shan** ของฉัน
Your	= **Khong-thanh,** ของท่าน	**Khong-khun** ของคุณ
Our	= **Khong-raow** ของเรา	
Their	= **Khong-khow** ของเขา	

When Thais tell you they are **phi-nawngkan** พี่น้องกัน or **Khrob-khrua**, ครอบครัว it means they are somehow related. Following is a list of words commonly used in correctly addressed various family relations:

Spouse	**Sami**	สามี
Husband	**Phoua** (informal)	ผัว
Wife	**Phanraya (polite), Mia** (informal)	ภรรยา, เมีย
Parents	**Bida Marn-da**	บิดา มารดา
Father	**Bida, Phaw**	บิดา, พ่อ
Mother	**Mae, Marn-da**	แม่, มารดา
Stepmother	**Mae-liang**	แม่เลี้ยง
Brother, Sister	**Nong, Phi**	น้อง, พี่
Elder Sibling	**Phi** *(also applies to one older but unrelated)*	พี่
Elder Brother	**Phi-shaai**	พี่ชาย
Elder Sister	**Phi-sao**	พี่สาว
Younger Brother	**Nong-shaai**	น้องชาย
Younger Sister	**Nong-sao**	น้องสาว
Children	**Bout, Louk**	บุตร, ลูก
Stepson, Stepdaughter	**Louk-liang**	ลูกเลี้ยง
Eldest child	**Louk khon toh**	ลูกคนโต
Son	**Louk-shaai, Bout-shaai**	ลูกชาย, บุตรชาย
Daughter	**Louk-sao, Louk-ying, Bout-ying**	ลูกสาว, ลูกหญิง บุตรหญิง
Grandchild	**Laan**	หลาน
Great Grandchild	**Lenn**	เหลน
Ancestors	**Banpha-bourud**	บรรพบุรุษ

Grandfather	**Pou**	ปู่
Maternal Grandfather	**Ta**	ตา
Maternal Great Grandfather	**Ta-thuad**	ตาทวด
Grandmother	**Ya, Khun-yaai**	ย่า, คุณยาย
Great Grandmother	**Shouad**	ชวด
Maternal Great Grandmother	**Yaai-thuad**	ยายทวด
Uncle (older brother of either parent)	**Loung**	ลุง
Aunt (elder sister of either-parent)	**Pa**	ป้า
Father 's younger brother or sister	**Aa**	อา
Mother 's younger brother or sister	**Na**	น้า
Nephew	**Laan-shaai**	หลานชาย
Niece	**Laan-sao**	หลานสาว
Father-in-law	**Phaw-ta**	พ่อตา
Mother-in-law	**Mae-yaai**	แม่ยาย
Sister-in-law	**Phi-saphai**	พี่สะใภ้
Elder sister's husband	**Phi-kheui**	พี่เขย
Cousin	**Yart**	ญาติ
Distant relations	**Yart haang-haang**	ญาติห่าง ๆ

SOCIAL CUSTOMS AND HOME LIFE

Social customs differ in all parts of the world. Informality and general friendliness in personal relationships in all age, economic, and social groups characterize the Thai people. Thais will gladly tell you what they would do in certain situations. They also will be interested in knowing how you do things in your country. A few "Thai ways" may be of help to you in your visit to Thailand.

The Thai people do not say "good morning," "good afternoon," "good evening" or "good night." They greet one another with the word **Sawadi** and instead of shaking hands, they put their two palms together in front of their chests under the chins and bow slightly. It is customary for the younger or lower in social status, to begin the greeting. When taking leave, the same word and procedure is repeated.

In Thailand the head is a respected part of the body and normally should not be touched, except perhaps in a fatherly manner by one's parents. There appear to be many reasons for this peculiar Thai characteristic.

Since the head contains the most delicate and important substance in the human body, the brain, it should be carefully treated and jealously guarded. Thus, Thais consider it improper to stand above or near the head of another person of higher or equal rank or status. On the other hand, when in the presence of the sovereign head of state, all Thais would instinctively and spontaneously bow their heads, as if to pay obeisance.

A woman will **"wai"** first (to show respect to) by placing the hand palms and raising them to the chin or forehead during an introduction in which a man is presented. If the woman does not **"wai"** the man should not persume to **"wai"** first. The woman is not obliged to extend this courtesy, and when she does, it is because of sincere pleasure at the introduction.

When one greets a person with a "**wai,**" that person must reply with the same gesture. Not to do so, or to content oneself with merely nodding, would be a sign of low, breeding.

A polite man will never touch a woman.

Another sign of bad breeding is to point an object out with one's foot. It is with one's right hand that one must show things. Also, to receive something from a superior, a courteous Thai will rest his right hand—the one he is holding out—upon his left hand.

If you are invited into a Thai house it is usual to take off your shoes before entering. The host will probably tell you not to, but will respect you if you do.

Thai people are generally very kind and polite, but rural Thais are still extremely jealous of their privacy. They may be smiling, but do not stare at them. Do not look into their eyes too long. Young and old might react violently to such gesture, which they consider to be rude insult. They might consider it an invitation to fight, or a challenge to a duel to the finish.

Any time you pay a visit to a friend, you must go through a complicated ritual. To begin with, it is unseemly to knock at the door. A visitor who is well up in the ways of polite society will announce himself by a discreet cough. He will then come in on tiptoe, his hands clasped in the Thai manner.

Though the Thai temples are an irresistible magnet for tourists and well worth visiting, it should be remembered that they are primarily places of worship rather than tourist attractions. Remember to remove your shoes before entering a temple. While people pray, it is polite for those not participating to quietly stand aside. Ask politely for permission to take photographs; the request is seldom refused. Make it a point to wear proper attire and not brief skirts or shorts. Ladies must on no account enter within the boundary stones of a **bote** (pronounced boat)—the most important building in the **wat** or monastery. It is not necessarily the largest building. What sets it apart are the eight or more boundary stones which surround it. Only inside the limits of this specially consecrated section of the temple area may monks be ordained.

Ladies must never touch a monk or hand things directly to him. Remember always that a monk is looked up to and respected. He cannot ask you for anything, but he may accept things if they are offered. Woman should never be alone in the presence of a monk.

Finally, it is an unpardonable error of sacrilege to misuse any Buddha image. Icons should be kept at a place of worship, not used as a piece of furniture or for an ornament or commercial advertisement. Foreigners living in Thailand must be especially aware of this. Through history, the Thai people have witnessed many notorious instances of looting of relics in temples and pagodas, beheading and dismembering of Buddha images. These acts constitute the most heinous offences not only against the kingdom but against all the people of Thailand.

WORDS AND PHRASES IN COMMON USE

(a) Greetings and Farewells

Good morning, Good afternoon	**Sawadi**	สวัสดี
Good evening, Good night	**Sawadi**	สวัสดี
Hello (lit, "Where are you going?")	**Pai-nai**	ไปไหน
Hello (in response)	**Pai dern-lenh**	ไปเดินเล่น
How are you?	**Khun sabaai di rue?**	คุณสบายดีหรือ?
What is your name?	**Khun shue arai?**	คุณชื่ออะไร?
It 's nice to see you again.	**Yindi thi phob khun ik.**	ยินดีที่พบคุณอีก
How is your wife?	**Phanraya khong khun pen yaang-rai?**	ภรรยาของคุณเป็นอย่างไร?
I am going now.	**Phom pai lah.***	ผมไปละ

* ***Lah**, ละ or **Nah**, นะ is a sort of verbal exclamation underscoring a preceeding word of sentence, with no spoken English equivalent. It is pronounced softly, lending gentle emphasis.*

Must you go so soon?	**Tham-mai klab réow?**	ทำไมกลับเร็ว?
I will be back.	**Phom chah klab (ma).**	ผมจะกลับมา
See you later.	**Phob kan mai**	พบกันใหม่
Goodbye (lit. "I'm going before you.")	**Pai-konn**	ไปก่อน
Farewell	**La-konn, Sawadi**	ลาก่อน สวัสดี

(b) Yes/No Words

Yes (male)	**Cha, Khrap****	จ้ะ, ครับ
Yes (female)	**Cha, Khah****	จ้ะ, ค่ะ
Yes (affirmative reply: "Yes, it is.")	**Shai**	ใช่
No	**Mai**	ไม่
No (negative reply: "No, it isn't.")	**Mai-shai**	ไม่ใช่
Okay, All right, Agreed	**Tok-long**	ตกลง
I don't agree	**Mai henh duai**	ไม่เห็นด้วย
Certainly, I'm sure	**Nae-nonn**	แน่นอน
I'm not certain.	**Mai nae-nonn**	ไม่แน่นอน
I think so, too	**Henh duai**	เห็นด้วย
I don' t think so	**Phom mai khid yaang-nanh**	ผมไม่คิดอย่างนั้น
Do you understand?	**Khow-chai mai?**	เข้าใจไหม?
I understand you.	**Phom khow-chai khun**	ผมเข้าใจคุณ

** ***Khrap*** is a polite final particle used by men at the end of most sentences. By itself, it can be taken to mean "Yes." Women use ***Khah*** in the same manner, if spoken with a short low tone; if ***Khah*** is spoken with a short high tone, it makes the sentence into a question.

I don' t understand you.	**Phom mai khow-chai khun**	ผมไม่เข้าใจคุณ
I don' t know.	**Phom mai saab.**	ผมไม่ทราบ
You don' t understand me.	**Khun mai khow-chai phom.**	คุณไม่เข้าใจผม
You misunderstood me.	**Khun khow-chai phid.**	คุณเข้าใจผิด
It doesn't make sense.	**Mai dai khwaam.**	ไม่ได้ความ
I like it.	**Phom shobb.**	ผมชอบ
I don' t like it.	**Phom mai shobb.**	ผมไม่ชอบ
Is that true?	**Ching mai?**	จริงไหม
Yes, it's true.	**Ching si.**	จริงซิ
It's not true.	**Mai ching.**	ไม่จริง
That's all wrong.	**Phid thang-phé.**	ผิดทั้งเพ
Really?	**Ching rue?**	จริงหรือ
Not yet	**Yang**	ยัง
Perhaps	**Baang-thi**	บางที
Possibly	**Kaw penh dai**	ก็เป็นได้

(c) Polite Phrases

Thank you.	**Khob khun, Khob chai**	ขอบคุณ, ขอบใจ
Thank you very much.	**Khob khun maak**	ขอบคุณมาก
You are welcome.	**Mai pen rai‡**	ไม่เป็นไร
Please	**Karuna (formal)**	กรุณา,
Please (as in, "Give me, please")	**Proad Khaw**	โปรด ขอ

‡ ***Mai pen rai*** is a unique phrase. Not only does it mean "You're welcome," if can also mean "Don't worry about it,""That's all right."

Please (as an invitation)	**Shern**	เชิญ
Please come in.	**Shern khow ma.**	เชิญเข้ามา
Make yourself comfortable, please.	**Shern tarm sabaai.**	เชิญตามสบาย
I beg your pardon.	**Khaw aphai (formal), Khaw thod**	ขออภัย ขอโทษ
I ′ m sorry, please excuse me.	**Prathaan thod (formal) Khaw thod**	ประทานโทษ ขอโทษ
I am very sorry	**Phom sia-chai maak**	ผมเสียใจมาก.
That ′s too bad.	**Yae maak. Yae ching**	แย่มาก, แย่จริง
Take care!	**Rawang!**	ระวัง
Excuse me for troubling you	**Khaw thode thi rob-kuan.**	ขอโทษที่รบกวน
Can I help you?	**Phom shuai arai dai-mai?**	ผมช่วยอะไรได้ไหม?
I don't mind.	**Phom mai rang-kiat.**	ผมไม่รังเกียจ
What do you call this in Thai?	**Phasaa thai riak wâ yang-rai?**	ภาษาไทยเรียกว่าอย่างไร?
I don't speak Thai	**Phom phoud Thai mai-dai**	ผมพูดไทยไม่ได้
Best of luck!	**Shôke di nah!**	โชคดีนะ!

(d) Questions and Requests

Who?	**Khrai?**	ใคร?
What?	**Arai?**	อะไร?
When?	**Meuarai?**	เมื่อไร?
Where?	**Nai? Thi-nai?**	ไหน, ที่ไหน?

Why?	**Tham-mai?**	ทำไม?
Which?	**Anh nai?**	อันไหน?
How?	**Yangai? Yaang-rai?**	ยังไง, อย่างไร?
How far is it?	**Klai sak thao-rai?**	ไกลสักเท่าไร?
How long?	**Naan thao-rai?**	นานเท่าไร?
How much?	**Thao-rai?**	เท่าไร?
How many?	**Ki** *(plus noun or classifier)*	กี่?
How much does it cost?	**Ni rakhaa thao-rai?**	นี่ราคาเท่าไร?
How about you?	**Laew khun laow?**	แล้วคุณเล่า?
What's that?	**Arai nah?**	อะไรนะ?
What's the matter?	**Mi reuang arai?**	มีเรื่องอะไร?
What does it matter?	**Chah penh arai pai?**	จะเป็นอะไรไป?
What more do you want?	**Chah aow arai ik mai?**	จะเอาอะไรอีกไหม?
What do you say?	**Khun chah wa yaang-rai?**	เขาจะว่าอย่างไร?
What dose he say?	**Khao wa arai nah?**	คุณว่าอะไรนะ?
What did you do about it?	**Laew khun tham yaang-rai?**	แล้วคุณทำอย่างไร?
What time is it now?	**Ki-mong laew?**	กี่โมงแล้ว?
Where is the American embassy?	**Satharn-thout America you thi-nai?**	สถานทูตอเมริกาอยู่ที่ไหน?
Where is the bus stop?	**Thi chawd-rot pracham-thaang you nai?**	ที่จอดรถประจำทางอยู่ไหน?
Where is the lavatory?	**Hong naam you thi-nai?**	ห้องน้ำอยู่ที่ไหน?

Where can I get something to eat?	**Chah ha-arai tharn dai thi-nai?**	จะหาอะไรทานได้ที่ไหน?
Where will you meet me?	**Chah phob phom thi-nai?**	จะพบผมที่ไหน?
Which is mine?	**Anh nai khong phom?**	อันไหนของผม?
Which is better?	**Anh nai di-kwa?**	อันไหนดีกว่า?
Which do you like?	**Khun shobb anh nai?**	คุณชอบอันไหน?
Which will you take?	**Khun chah aow anh nai?**	คุณจะเอาอันไหน?
Who are you?	**Khun penh khrai?**	คุณเป็นใคร?
Who is there?	**Khrai you nanh?**	ใครอยู่นั่น?
Who are you looking for?	**Khun ha khrai?**	คุณหาใคร?
Who are you waiting for?	**Khun khoi khrai?**	คุณคอยใคร?
Who told you so?	**Khrai bawk khun?**	ใครบอกคุณ?
Whose is this?	**Ni khong khrai?**	นี่ของใคร?
Is this yours?	**Ni pen khong khun rue?**	นี่เป็นของคุณหรือ?

The particle **mai,** ไหมplaced after a word, has the function of question mark. It is a short form of **rue mai** หรือไม่(or not). In Thai, the same verb impression is used in all cases—first, second or third person, singular or plural.

In asking for something or seeking permission, the verb **dai** ได้(*can* or *may*) is used. Be sure to remember that when **mai** ไหมfollows **dai**ได้, **(dai-mai)**ได้ไหม, it constitutes a question *(Can you? May I?)* but if **mai**ไม่ precedes **dai**ได้ *(mai-dai)*, it makes the negative *cannot*. Examples:

Can I help you?	**Phom shuai arai dai-mai?**	ผมช่วยอะไรได้ไหม?
Can you come?	**Khun ma dai-mai?**	คุณมาได้ไหม?

Can you do me a favor?	**Karuna tham arai hai phom noi dai-mai?**	กรุณาทำอะไรให้ผมหน่อยได้ไหม?
Can you teach me to speak Thai?	**Sawn phom phoud Thai dai-mai?**	สอนผมพูดไทยได้ไหม?
Can you show me the way to......?	**Karuna shi thaang pai...hai phom dai-mai?**	กรุณาชี้ทางไป....ให้ผมได้ไหม?
May I know your name?	**phom khaw saap shue khun dai-mai?**	ผมขอทราบชื่อคุณได้ไหม?
May I take your picture?	**Phom khaw thaai-pharb khun dai-mai?**	ผมขอถ่ายภาพคุณได้ไหม?
May I visit at your home?	**Phom pai thiao thi baan khun dai-mai?**	ผมไปเที่ยวที่บ้านคุณได้ไหม?
May I smoke?	**Phom soup buri dai-mai?**	ผมสูบบุหรี่ได้ไหม?
May I dance with you?	**Phom khaw tenh ram kap khun dai-mai?**	ผมขอเต้นรำกับคุณได้ไหม?
May I have this?	**Phom khaw ni dai-mai?**	ผมขอนี่ได้ไหม?
May I use your phone?	**Phom khaw shai thorasap dai-mai?**	ผมขอใช้โทรศัพท์ได้ไหม?
May I see the room?	**Khaw shom hong dai-mai?**	ขอชมห้องได้ไหม?

There are a few cases in which dai-mai is not used in asking permission. Examples:

May I borrow your pen?	**Phom khaw yuem pak-ka?**	ผมขอยืมปากกา?
May I introduce my friend, Mr. Kim?	**Khaw naeh-namm phuen Phom, Mr. Kim?**	ขอแนะนำเพื่อนผม? คุณคิม?

May I offer you a drink?	**Khun duem arai mai?**	คุณดื่มอะไรไหม?
May I go now?	**Phom pai dai rue yung?**	ผมไปได้หรือยัง?

(e) Commands and Exclamations

Wake up.	**Louk! Louk-khuen.**	ลุก, ลุกขึ้น
Be on time.	**Hai trong-véla.**	ให้ตรงเวลา
Don' t be late.	**Ya shâ nah.**	อย่าช้านะ
Don' t forget.	**Ya Luem.**	อย่าลืม
Be good.	**Chong tham di.**	จงทำดี
Come in!	**Khow ma si!**	เข้ามาสิ
Come this way.	**Ma thaang ni.**	มาทางนี้
Do not enter.	**Ya khow ma.**	อย่าเข้ามา
Get out from here	**Awk-pai chaak thi-ni!**	ออกไปจากที่นี่
Go! Go away!	**Pai!**	ไป
Go back!	**Klab pai!**	กลับไป
Go ahead, talk!	**Phoud pai!**	พูดไป
Keep quiet!	**Ngiap noi!**	เงียบหน่อย
Speak slowly.	**Phoud shâ-shâ.**	พูดช้า ๆ
Go slow.	**Pai shâ-shâ.**	ไปช้า ๆ
Don' t drive so fast	**Ya khap reow nak**	อย่าขับเร็วนัก
Hurry up!	**Réow-réow!**	เร็ว ๆ
Watch out!	**Rawang!**	ระวัง
Stop! Stop here.	**Yout! Yout thi-ni.**	หยุด, หยุดที่นี่
Give me...	**Khaw....**	ขอ
Do this for me.	**Tham hai shanh noi.**	ทำให้ฉันหน่อย
Put it right here (right there)	**Waang thi-ni (thi-nanh).**	วางที่นี่ (ที่นั่น)

Keep it.	**Aow-wai.**	เอาไว้
Look! Look here!	**Ni! Dou-ni!**	นี่! ดูนี่!
See who is at the door.	**Dou-si, khrai ma thi pratou.**	ดูซิ, ใครมาที่ประตู
Shut the door.	**Pit pratou.**	ปิดประตู
Lock it.	**Lok kunchae sia.**	ล็อคกุญแจเสีย
Help!	**Shuai-duai!**	ช่วยด้วย!
I've been robbed!	**Phom thouk khamoai!**	ผมถูกขโมย!
Beautiful! (aesthetics)	**Ngarm thae!**	งามแท้!
Beautiful! (women or object)	**Suai di!**	สวยดี!
Handsome!	**Law maak!**	หล่อมาก!
Delicious!	**Aroi!**	อร่อย!
How comfortable!	**Sabaai!**	สบาย!
This is fun!	**Sanuk!**	สนุก!
That's funny!	**Na Kham! Talok-di!**	น่าขำ! ตลกดี!
How strange!	**Plaek ching!**	แปลกจริง!
Crazy!	**Bâ-chang!**	บ้าจัง!
Don't be crazy.	**Ya ba noi leui.**	อย่าบ้าหน่อยเลย
Disgusting!	**Khaya Khayaeng!**	ขยะแขยง!
Sickening!	**Nâ beu-a!**	น่าเบื่อ!
What a horrible smell!	**Menh chang!**	เหม็นจัง!
What a nuisance!	**Ram kharn chang!**	รำคาญจัง!
You are so stupid!	**Khun ngo chang leui!**	คุณโง่จังเลย!
You 're talking nonsense!	**Phoud arai mai dai khwaam!**	พูดอะไรไม่ได้ความ!
You shut up!	**Yud phoud!**	หยุดพูด!
You 're a liar!	**Khun ko hok!**	คุณโกหก!

Shame on you!	**Nâ mai-aye!**	หน้าไม่อาย!
I'm full. (I've had enough to eat.)	**Im**	อิ่ม!
That 's enough	**Phaw thi. Phaw-laew.**	พอที, พอแล้ว
Happy New Year!	**Sawadi pi mai!**	สวัสดีปีใหม่!

(f) Numbers

Cardinal

1	**Nueng**	หนึ่ง
2	**Sawng or Song**	สอง
3	**Sarm or Saam**	สาม
4	**Si**	สี่
5	**Ha**	ห้า
6	**Hok**	หก
7	**Ched**	เจ็ด
8	**Paed**	แปด
9	**Kow**	เก้า
10	**Sib**	สิบ
11	**Sib-ed**	สิบเอ็ด
12	**Sib-sawng**	สิบสอง
13	**Sib-sarm**	สิบสาม
14	**Sib-si**	สิบสี่
15	**Sib-ha**	สิบห้า
16	**Sib-hok**	สิบหก
17	**Sib-ched**	สิบเจ็ด
18	**Sib-paed**	สิบแปด
19	**Sib-kow**	สิบเก้า
20	**Yi-sib**	ยี่สิบ
21	**Yi-sib-ed**	ยี่สิบเอ็ด
22	**Yi-sib-sawng**	ยี่สิบสอง
23	**Yi-sib-sarm**	ยี่สิบสาม
24	**Yi-sib-si**	ยี่สิบสี่
25	**Yi-sib-ha**	ยี่สิบห้า
26	**Yi-sib-hok**	ยี่สิบหก
27	**Yi-sib-ched**	ยี่สิบเจ็ด
28	**Yi-sib-paed**	ยี่สิบแปด
29	**Yi-sib-kow**	ยี่สิบเก้า
30	**Sarm-sib**	สามสิบ
31	**Sarm-sib-ed**	สามสิบเอ็ด
32	**Sarm-sib-sawng**	สามสิบสอง
33	**Sarm-sib-sarm**	สามสิบสาม
34	**Sarm-sib-si**	สามสิบสี่
35	**Sarm-sib-ha**	สามสิบห้า
36	**Sarm-sib-hok**	สามสิบหก
37	**Sarm-sib-ched**	สามสิบเจ็ด
38	**Sarm-sib-paed**	สามสิบแปด
39	**Sarm-sib-kow**	สามสิบเก้า
40	**Si-sib**	สี่สิบ
41	**Si-sib-ed**	สี่สิบเอ็ด
42	**Si-sib-sawng**	สี่สิบสอง

43	**Si-sib-sarm**	สี่สิบสาม
44	**Si-sib-si**	สี่สิบสี่
45	**Si-sib-ha**	สี่สิบห้า
46	**Si-sib-hok**	สี่สิบหก
47	**Si-sib-ched**	สี่สิบเจ็ด
48	**Si-sib-paed**	สี่สิบแปด
49	**Si-sib-kow**	สี่สิบสี่
50	**Ha-sib**	ห้าสิบ
55	**Ha-sib-ha**	ห้าสิบห้า
60	**Hok-sib**	หกสิบ
65	**Hok-sib-ha**	หกสิบห้า
70	**Ched-sib**	เจ็ดสิบ
75	**Ched-sib-ha**	เจ็ดสิบห้า
80	**Paed-sib**	แปดสิบ
85	**Paed-sibha**	แปดสิบห้า
90	**Kow-sib**	เก้าสิบ
95	**Kow-sib-ha**	เก้าสิบห้า
100	**Nueng-roi**	หนึ่งร้อย
101	**Nueng-roi-nueng**	หนึ่งร้อยหนึ่ง
102	**Nueng-roi-sawng**	หนึ่งร้อยสอง
103	**Nueng-roi-sarm**	หนึ่งร้อยสาม
104	**Nueng-roi-si**	หนึ่งรอ้ยสี่
105	**Nueng-roi-ha**	หนึ่งร้อยห้า
106	**Nueng-roi-hok**	หนึ่งร้อยหก
107	**Nueng-roi-ched**	หนึ่งร้อยเจ็ด
108	**Nueng-roi-paed**	หนึ่งร้อยแปด
109	**Nueng-roi-kow**	หนึ่งร้อยเก้า
110	**Roi-sib**	ร้อยสิบ
111	**Roi-sib-ed**	ร้อยสิบเอ็ด
112	**Roi-sib-sawng**	ร้อยสิบสอง
113	**Roi-sib-sarm**	ร้อยสิบสาม
114	**Roi-sib-si**	ร้อยสิบสี่
115	**Roi-sib-ha**	ร้อยสิบห้า
116	**Roi-sib-hok**	ร้อยสิบหก
117	**Roi-sib-ched**	ร้อยสิบเจ็ด
118	**Roi-sib-paed**	ร้อยสิบแปด
119	**Roi-sib-kow**	ร้อยสิบเก้า
120	**Roi-yi-sib**	ร้อยยี่สิบ
130	**Roi-sarm-sib**	ร้อยสามสิบ
140	**Roi-si-sib**	ร้อยสี่สิบ
150	**Roi-ha-sib**	ร้อยห้าสิบ
200	**Sawng-roi**	สองร้อย
300	**Sarm-roi**	สามร้อย
400	**Si-roi**	สี่ร้อย
500	**Ha-roi**	ห้าร้อย
1,000	**Nueng-phan**	หนึ่งพัน
5,000	**Ha-phan**	ห้าพัน
10,000	**Nueng-muen**	หนึ่งหมื่น
100,000	**Nueng-saen**	หนึ่งแสน
1,000,000	**Nueng-laan**	หนึ่งล้าน
1,500,000	**Nueng-laan-ha-saen**	หนึ่งล้านห้าแสน

2,000,000	**Sawng-laan**	สองล้าน
5,000,000	**Ha-laan**	ห้าล้าน
100,000,000	**Roi-laan**	ร้อยล้าน
1,000,000,000	**Phan-laan**	พันล้าน

Ordinal

First	**Thi-nueng**	ที่หนึ่ง
Second	**Thi-sawng**	ที่สอง
Third	**Thi-sarm**	ที่สาม
Fourth	**Thi-si**	ที่สี่
Fifth	**Thi-ha**	ที่ห้า
Sixth	**Thi-hok**	ที่หก
Seventh	**Thi-ched**	ที่เจ็ด
Eighth	**Thi-paed**	ที่แปด
Ninth	**Thi-kow**	ที่เก้า
Tenth	**Thi-sib**	ที่สิบ
Eleventh	**Thi-sib-ed**	ที่สิบเอ็ด
Twelfth	**Thi-sib-sawng**	ที่สิบสอง
Thirteenth	**Thi-sib-sarm**	ที่สิบสาม
Fourteenth	**Thi-sib-si**	ที่สิบสี่
Fifteenth	**Thi-sib-ha**	ที่สิบห้า
Sixteenth	**Thi-sib-hok**	ที่สิบหก
Seventeenth	**Thi-sib-ched**	ที่สิบเจ็ด
Eighteenth	**Thi-sib-paed**	ที่สิบแปด
Nineteenth	**Thi-sib-kow**	ที่สิบเก้า
Twentieth	**Thi-yi-sib**	ที่ยี่สิบ
Twenty-first	**Thi-yi-sib-ed**	ที่ยี่สิบเอ็ด
Twenty-second	**Thi-yi-sib-sawng**	ที่ยี่สิบสอง
Twenty-third	**Thi-yi-sib-sarm**	ที่ยี่สิบสาม

Twenty-fourth	**Thi-yi-sib-si**	ที่ยี่สิบสี่
Twenty-fifth	**Thi-yi-sib-ha**	ที่ยี่สิบห้า
Thirtieth	**Thi-sarm-sib**	ที่สามสิบ

(g) Time

Clock Time

12:00 (noon)	**Sib-sawng nalika (Thiang)**	สิบสองนาฬิกา (เที่ยง)
1:00 p.m.	**Sib-sarm nalika (Baai Mong)**	สิบสามนาฬิกา (บ่ายโมง)
3:00 p.m.	**Sib-ha nalika (Baai Sarm Mong)**	สิบห้านาฬิกา (บ่ายสามโมง)
6:00 p.m.	**Sib-paed nalika (Hok Mong Yenh)**	สิบแปดนาฬิกา (หกโมงเย็น)
9:00 p.m.	**Yi-sib-ed nalika (Sarm Thoum)**	ยี่สิบเอ็ดนาฬิกา (สามทุ่ม)
12:00 (midnight)	**Yi-sib-si nalika (Sawng Yaam, Thiang Khuen)**	ยี่สิบสี่นาฬิกา (สองยาม, เที่ยงคืน)
3:00 a.m.	**Sarm nalika (Ti Sarm)**	สามนาฬิกา (ตีสาม)

* Although official time is based on the 24-hour clock, the 12-hour system is used in conversation.

6:00 a.m.	**Hok nalika (Hok Mong Shao)**	หกนาฬิกา (หกโมงเช้า)
9:00 a.m.	**Kao nalika (Kao Mong Shao)**	เก้านาฬิกา (เก้าโมงเช้า)

One minute	**Nueng nathi**	หนึ่งนาที
15 seconds	**Sib-ha vinathi**	สิบห้าวินาที
One hour	**Nueng shua mong**	หนึ่งชั่วโมง
Time	**Véla**	เวลา
What time is it now?	**Diao-ni véla ki-mong laew?**	เดี๋ยวนี้เวลากี่โมงแล้ว
Please tell me the correct time	**Karuna bawk véla thi thouk-tong**	กรุณาบอกเวลาที่ถูกต้อง
How many hours?	**Ki shua-mong?**	กี่ชั่วโมง?
How many minutes?	**Ki nathi?**	กี่นาที?
How many seconds?	**Ki vinathi?**	กี่วินาที?
It is still early.	**Yang wanh you; Yang shao you.**	ยังวันอยู่, ยังเช้าอยู่
It is late.	**Saai-pai-laew; sha-pai**	สายไปแล้ว, ช้าไป
My watch is fast	**Nalika khong phom réow**	นาฬิกาของผมเร็ว
Your watch is slow.	**Nalika khong khun sha**	นาฬิกาของคุณช้า

Time

This morning	**Meua chao ni; Chao ni**	เมื่อเช้านี้, เช้านี้
This afternoon	**Meua baai ni; Baai ni**	เมื่อบ่ายนี้, บ่ายนี้
This evening	**Yenh ni**	เย็นนี้
Today	**Wan-ni**	วันนี้
Tonight	**Khuen-ni**	คืนนี้
Tomorrow	**Phroung-ni**	พรุ่งนี้
Tomorrow morning	**Phroung-ni shao**	พรุ่งนี้เช้า
Tomorrow evening	**Phroung-ni yenh**	พรุ่งนี้เย็น
Tomorrow night	**Khuen phroung-ni**	คืนพรุ่งนี้
Last night	**Meua-khuen ni**	เมื่อคืนนี้

A day	**Wanh**	วัน
Yesterday	**Waan; Meua waan**	วาน, เมื่อวาน
Day before yesterday	**Waan-suen**	วานซืน
Day after tomorrow	**Maruen**	มะรืน
Three days ago	**Sarm wan laew**	สามวันแล้ว
A week	**Sap-da, Athit**	สัปดาห์, อาทิตย์
Last Monday	**Chand thi laew**	จันทร์ที่แล้ว
Last week	**Sapda konn**	สัปดาห์ก่อน
Last month	**Deuan thi laew**	เดือนที่แล้ว
Last year	**Pi thi-laew**	ปีที่แล้ว
Next Monday	**Chand na**	จันทร์หน้า
Next Week	**Sap-da na**	สัปดาห์หน้า
A fortnight	**Nueng pak**	หนึ่งปักษ์
Next month	**Deuan na**	เดือนหน้า
Next year	**Pee na**	ปีหน้า
Every morning	**Thouk-thouk shao**	ทุก ๆ เช้า
Every day	**Thouk-thouk wan**	ทุก ๆ วัน
Every week	**Thouk-thouk sap-da**	ทุก ๆ สัปดาห์
Every year	**Thouk-thouk pi**	ทุก ๆ ปี
This year/That year	**Pi-ni/Pi-nanh**	ปีนี้, ปีนั้น
The whole day	**Talawd wan**	ตลอดวัน
The whole year	**Talawd pi**	ตลอดปี
Now	**Diao-ni**	เดี๋ยวนี้
Always	**Sameu**	เสมอ
Sometimes	**Baang-thi**	บางที
A while	**Khrou nueng**	ครู่หนึ่ง
When	**Meua**	เมื่อ
Then (at that time)	**Laew:Laew-kaw: Dang-nanh**	แล้ว, แล้วก็ ดังนั้น
Another time	**Ik-khrang**	อีกครั้ง

Anytime	**Véla-dai kaw-dai**	เวลาใดก็ได้
How long?	**Naan thao-rai?**	นานเท่าไร
A long time ago	**Naan-ma-laew**	นานมาแล้ว
Just now	**Meua-ki-ni**	เมื่อกี้นี้
Just recently	**Meua-réow-réow-ni**	เมื่อเร็ว ๆ นี้
A century	**Nueng sattawat**	หนึ่งศตวรรษ

The Days of Week

Sunday	**Wan Athit**	วันอาทิตย์
Monday	**Wan chand**	วันจันทร์
Tuesday	**Wan Angkharn**	วันอังคาร
Wednesday	**Wan Phud**	วันพุธ
Thursday	**Wan Pharuehat**	วันพฤหัส
Friday	**Wan Souk**	วันศุกร์
Saturday	**Wan Sao**	วันเสาร์

The Months

January	**Makara-khom**	มกราคม
February	**Kumpha-phan**	กุมภาพันธ์
March	**Mina-khom**	มีนาคม
April	**Mésa-yon**	เมษายน
May	**Phruesapha-khom**	พฤษภาคม
June	**Mithuna-yon**	มิถุนายน
July	**Karakada-khom**	กรกฎาคม
August	**Singha-khom**	สิงหาคม
September	**Kanya-yon**	กันยายน
October	**Toula-khom**	ตุลาคม
November	**Phruesachika-yon**	พฤศจิกายน
December	**Thanwakhom**	ธันวาคม

The Seasons

Hot Season	**Ruedou Ronn or Na-ronn**	ฤดูร้อน, หน้าร้อน
Cold Season	**Ruedou Nao or Na-nao**	ฤดูหนาว, หน้าหนาว
Rainy Season	**Ruedou Fonh or Na-fonh**	ฤดูฝน, หน้าฝน

(h) Weather

What is the weather like today?	**Wan-ni akas pen yaang-rai?**	วันนี้อากาศเป็นอย่างไร?
The Meteorological Department said we can expect warmer weather today and tomorrow.	**Krom Ou-tu wa akas chah ronn wan-ni lae phroung-ni.**	กรมอุตุฯ ว่าอากาศจะร้อน วันนี้และพรุ่งนี้
Today is a beautiful day.	**Wan-ni akas chaem-sai.**	วันนี้อากาศแจ่มใส
It's a sunny day today	**Wan-ni daed di.**	วันนี้แดดดี
Do you think it'll rain tomorrow?	**Khun khid-wa phroung-ni fonh chah-tok mai?**	คุณคิดว่าพรุ่งนี้ฝนจะตกไหม?
I think we're going to have bad weather.	**Phom khid-wa akas chah-léow long.**	ผมคิดว่าอากาศจะเลวลง
It may rain. It looks like rain.	**Fonh ach-tok. Dou-meuan fonh tok.**	ฝนอาจตก ดูเหมือนฝนตก

Should I take an umbrella with me?	**Phom aow rom pai-duai di mai?**	ผมเอาร่มไปด้วยดีไหม?
You should, it is raining now.	**Aow-pai si, fonh kamlang tok.**	เอาไปซิ ฝนกำลังตก
It 's raining heavily	**Fonh tok nak.**	ฝนตกหนัก
It rained all day	**Fonh tok talawd-wan**	ฝนตกตลอดวัน
Now is the rainy season.	**Diao-ni pen rue-dou fonh.**	เดี๋ยวนี้เป็นฤดูฝน
The wind is blowing pretty hard.	**Lom kamlang phad raeng.**	ลมกำลังพัดแรง
It is drizzling.	**Fonh-tok phram-phram.**	ฝนตกพรำ ๆ
It is hailing	**Louk-hep tok.**	ลูกเห็บตก
It 's thundering	**Fâ rong.**	ฟ้าร้อง
It 's raining, but it looks like it' ll clear up soon.	**Fonh kamlang tok, tae dou-meuan mai sha kaw haai.**	ฝนกำลังตก แต่ดูเหมือนไม่ช้าก็หาย
It has stopped raining.	**Fonh yout laew.**	ฝนหยุดแล้ว
It 's warm. Very hot weather.	**Ronn. Aka ronn maak.**	ร้อน อากาศร้อนมาก
It 's cold. Extremely cold weather.	**Nao. Aka yen (or nao) maak.**	หนาว อากาศเย็น (หรือหนาว) มาก
The storm. It is stormy.	**Lom-phayu. Phayu chad.**	ลมพายุ, พายุจัด
Lightning	**Fa-laep; Fa-phâ**	ฟ้าแลบ, ฟ้าผ่า
Overcast	**Akas mued-mua**	อากาศมืดมัว
Rainstorm	**Phayu-fonh**	พายุฝน
Drought	**Fonh-laeng**	ฝนแล้ง

(i) Asking Directions

Can you tell me which way is ......?	**Thaang nai pai ....?**	ทางไหนไป.........?
- the airport	**- sanarm-bin**	- สนามบิน?
- the business centre	**- soun karn-kha**	- ศูนย์การค้า?
Where is ....?	- **.......you thi nai?**	.........อยู่ที่ไหน?
- the railway station	**- Sathani Rot-fai**	- สถานีรถไฟ
- the Malaysian embassy	**- Satharn-thout Malaysia**	- (สถานทูตมาเลเซีย)
How far is it?	**Klai sak thao dai?**	ไกลสักเท่าใด?
How far is it from here to ....?	**Chaak-ni pai ......klai thaorai?**	จากนี่ไป.....ไกลเท่าไร?
- the Market	**- Talad-sod**	- ตลาดสด
- the Government Provincial Office	**- Sala Klaang Changwad**	- ศาลากลางจังหวัด
- the Community Hall	**- Sala Pracha-khom**	- ศาลาประชาคม
- the Bus Terminal	**- Sathani Khon Song**	- สถานีขนส่ง
- the Municipal Office	**- Samnak-Ngarn Thesabarn**	- สำนักงานเทศบาล
- the Immigration Office	**- Samnak-Ngarn Khon Khow-Meuang**	- สำนักงานคนเข้าเมือง
- the Police Station	**- Sathani Tamruad**	- สถานีตำรวจ
- the Hospital	**- Rong Phaya-barn**	- โรงพยาบาล

Should I ....?	**- Phom tong....rue?**	- ผมต้อง.........หรือ?
- go straight on	**- dern trong-pai**	- เดินตรงไป
- turn to the right	**- liao-khwaa**	- เลี้ยวขวา
- turn to the left	**- liao-saai**	- เลี้ยวซ้าย
- turn back	**- dern klap-pai**	- เดินกลับไป
I wish to take the shortest route to ...	**Phom tongkarn dern-latt pai ....**	ผมต้องการเดินลัดไป...
Can I walk there?	**Phom dern thaang-nanh dai mai?**	ผมเดินทางนั้นได้ไหม?
Is this the right direction?	**Dern thaang-ni thouk mai?**	เดินทางนี้ถูกไหม?
Is it within walking distance?	**Rayah-thaang chaak-ni khong mai klai?**	ระยะทางจากนี้คงไม่ไกล?
Go farther on.	**Pai ik.**	ไปอีก
Which way shall I go?	**Phom khuan dern-pai thaang nai?**	ผมควรเดินไปทางไหน?
Is this the road to the airport?	**Thaang-ni pai Sanarm-bin dai mai?**	ทางนี้ไปสนามบินได้ไหม?
Would you please direct me to........?	**Karuna shi thaang hai phom pai thi ....?**	กรุณาชี้ทางให้ผมไปที่.....?
- the Governor's residence	**- Baan phu wâ**	- บ้านผู้ว่าฯ
- the American Consulate	**- Kong xun American**	- กงสุลอเมริกัน
- the Community Development Office	**- Samnak-ngarn Phathana Shoum-shon**	- สำนักงานพัฒนาชุมชน
- the Teachers' Training School	**- Rongrian Fuek-hat Khru**	- โรงเรียนฝึกหัดครู

Anywhere	**Thi-nai kaw-dai**	ที่ไหนก็ได้
I don't know the city.	**Phom mai rou-chak baan-meuang ni di.**	ผมไม่รู้จักบ้านเมืองนี้ดี
I believe you know the city very well	**Phom sheua wa khun rouchak baan-meuang ni di.**	ผมเชื่อว่าคุณรู้จักบ้านเมืองนี้ดี
Can you show me where I am on this map?	**Proad shi bonh phaen-thi wa diao-ni phom you thi-nai?**	โปรดชี้บนแผนที่ว่า เดี๋ยวนี้ผมอยู่ที่ไหน?
What street is this?	**Ni thanon arai?**	นี่ถนนอะไร?
Is this not Phya Thai Road?	**Ni mai shai thanon Phya-Thai rue?**	นี่ไม่ใช่ถนนพญาไทหรือ?
Do you know where the American embassy is?	**Satharn-thout American you thi nai?**	สถานทูตอเมริกันอยู่ที่ไหน?
How long does it take to walk there?	**Dern pai dai mai?**	เดินไปได้ไหม?
Where is the bus stop?	**Thi chawd-rot pracham-thaang you nai?**	ที่จอดรถประจำทางอยู่ไหน?
Does a bus that will take me to the Ramathibodi Hospital stop here?	**Rot pracham-thaang thi chawd ni pai Rong-phaya-barn Rama Thibodi mai?**	รถประจำทางที่จอดนี้ไป โรงพยาบาลรามาธิบดีไหม?

Please inform me if there is a person named Joe E. Brown in this office.	**Mi khon shue Joe E. Brown you thi ni mai.**	มีคนชื่อ โจ อี. บราวน์ อยู่ที่นี่ไหม
I want to go to this address.	**Phom tongkarn pai thi ni.**	ผมต้องการไปที่นี่
Isn't there a young lady living in this neighbor-hood called Rita Michael?	**Thi ni mi maem shue Rita Micheal mai?**	ที่นี่มีแหม่มชื่อริต้า มิเชล ไหม?
She is an English teacher from England.	**Pen khru, ma chaak Prathed Angkrit.**	เป็นครู, มาจากประเทศอังกฤษ
Where dose she live?	**Theu you thi nai?**	เธออยู่ที่ไหน?
Could you please direct me to her house?	**Karuna pha phom pai thi bann theu dai mai?**	กรุณาพาผมไปที่บ้านเธอได้ไหม?
Is it very near here?	**Khong cah mai klai?**	คงจะไม่ไกล?
Thank you very much.	**Khob khun maak.**	ขอบคุณมาก

Directions

North	**Thit Neua (Udorn)**	ทิศเหนือ (อุดร)
Northeast	**Thit Tawan-awk Shiang Neua (Isarn)**	ทิศตะวันออกเฉียงเหนือ (อีสาน)
South	**Thit Taai (Taksin)**	ทิศใต้ (ทักษิน)
Southeast	**Thit Tawan-awk Shiang Taai (Akhané)**	ทิศตะวันออกเฉียงใต้ (อาคเนย์)

East	**Thit Tawan-awk (Burapha)**	ทิศตะวันออก (บูรพา)
West	**Thit Tawan -Tok (Pakjim)**	ทิศตะวันตก (ประจิม)
Northwest	**Thit Tawan-tok Shiang Neua (Phayab)**	ทิศตะวันตกเฉียงเหนือ (พายัพ)
Southwest	**Thit Tawan-Tok Shiang Taai (Hawradi)**	ทิศตะวันตกเฉียงใต้ (หรดี)

Dimensions

Length	**Khwaam Yao**	ความยาว
Breadth	**Khwaam Kwaang**	ความกว้าง
Height	**Khwaam Soung**	ความสูง
Thickness	**Khwaam Na**	ความหนา
Depth	**Khwaam Luek**	ความลึก

YOUR ARRIVAL IN THAILAND

All foreign nationals entering Thailand must be in possession of a valid passport, as well as a visa, obtained before your arrival from a Thai embassy or consulate abroad. Tourist visas are good for 60 days(although citizens of the United States, West Germany, Denmark, Sweden and Norway can stay up to 15 days without a visa). Check with a Thai embassy or your travel agent for other specific requirements.

Your airline or steamship will give you a Thai Customs Declaration Form to fill out. Upon arrival, you will be questioned by health inspectors, immigration authorities and customs officials. The following few phrases may be helpful at immigration checkpoints.

(a) At Immigration

Passport please.	**Nangsue dern-thaang**	หนังสือเดินทาง
Here is my passport.	**Ni nangsue dern-thaang phom.**	นี่หนังสือเดินทางผม
- border pass	**- bai pharn-daen**	- ใบผ่านแดน
- identity card	**- bat prashâ-shon**	- บัตรประชาชน

How long are you planning to stay?	**Khun chah you thi-ni narn thao-rai?**	คุณจะอยู่ที่นี่นานเท่าไร?
-a few days	**- song-sarm wan**	- สองสามวัน
-a week	**- nueng sapda**	- หนึ่งสัปดาห์
-a couple of weeks	**- song-sarm sapda**	- สองสามสัปดาห์
-a month	**-nueng deuan**	- หนึ่งเดือน
It depends upon circumstances.	**Thang-ni laew tae kaw-rani.**	ทั้งนี้แล้วแต่กรณี
I'm just passing through.	**Phom dern-thaang pharn thao-nanh.**	ผมเดินทางผ่านเท่านั้น
Is a visa necessary?	**Visa champenh duai rue?**	วีซ่าจำเป็นด้วยหรือ?
I am	**Phom ....**	ผม........
married	**mi pharaya laew**	- มีภรรยาแล้ว
-still single	**-yang pen sode**	- ยังเป็นโสด
-divorced	**-yâ laew**	- หย่าแล้ว
-widowed	**-pen maai**	- เป็นหม้าย
-a Christian	**-nab-thue sasana Christ**	- นับถือศาสนาคริสต์
-a Buddhist	**- nab-thue Phut**	- นับถือพุทธ
What will be your address?	**Khun chah phak thi-nai?**	คุณจะพักที่ไหน?
I will be at the President Hotel.	**Phom chah phak thi rongraem President.**	ผมจะพักที่โรงแรม เพรสิเดนท์
I will be with	**Phom chah phak**	ผมจะพัก
a friend	**- you-kab pheuan.**	- อยู่กับเพื่อน
-a relative	**-you kab yart**	- อยู่กับญาติ

Do you have any friend or relative in Thailand?	**Khun mi yart-phi-nong nai prathed Thai mai?**	คุณมีญาติพี่น้องในประเทศไทยไหม?
None at all.	**Mai mi.**	ไม่มี
What is the reason for your visit?	**Chud-prasong a-rai khun chueng ma thi-ni?**	จุดประสงค์อะไรคุณจึงมาที่นี่?
I am on	**Phom mâ ....**	- ผมมา............
- a business trip	**-thamh kid-thurah**	- ทำกิจธุระ
- a holiday	**-thiao**	- เที่ยว
- a field and observation trip	**- dou ngarn**	- ดูงาน
- an official mission	**-rajakarn**	- ราชการ
My local sponsor is ...	**Phu rap-rawng khong phom khue ....**	ผู้รับรองของผมคือ........
What is your nationality?	**Khun thue san-shart a-rai?**	คุณถือสัญชาติอะไร?
I am an	**Phom penh ....**	ผมเป็น........
- American	**- khon American**	- คนอเมริกัน
- Australian	**- shao Australia**	- ชาวออสเตรเลีย
- Austrian	**- shao Austria**	- ชาวออสเตรีย
- Belgian	**- shao Belgium**	- ชาวเบลเยี่ยม
- Brazilian	**- shao Brasil**	- ชาวบราซิล
- British	**- shao Angkrit**	- ชาวอังกฤษ
- Canadian	**- shao Canada**	- ชาวแคนาดา
- Chinese	**- khon Chine**	- คนจีน
- Danish	**- shao Denmark**	- ชาวเดนมาร์ก
- Dutch	**- shao Holanda**	- ชาวฮอลันดา

- Egyptian	**- shao Egypt**	- ชาวอียิปต์
- Filipino	**- shao Filipine**	- ชาวฟิลิปปินส์
- French	**- shao Farangset**	- ชาวฝรั่งเศส
- German	**- shao Jerman**	- ชาวเยอรมัน
- Indian	**- khon India**	- คนอินเดีย
- Indonesian	**- shao Indonesia**	- ชาวอินโดนีเซีย
- Iranian	**- shao Iran**	- ชาวอิหร่าน
- Iraqui	**- shao Iraq**	- ชาวอิรัก
- Israeli	**- shao Israel, khon Yew**	- ชาวอิสราเอล, คนยิว
- Italian	**- shao Italy**	- ชาวอิตาลี
- Japanese	**- shao Yipun**	- ชาวญี่ปุ่น
- Jordanian	**- shao Jordan**	- ชาวจอร์แดน
- Korean	**- khon Kaoli**	- คนเกาหลี
- Lebanese	**- shao Lebanon**	- ชาวเลบานอน
- Malaysian	**- khon Malaysia**	- คนมาเลเซีย
- Mexican	**- shao Mexico**	- ชาวเม็กซิโก
- Nepalese	**- shao Nepal**	- ชาวเนปาล
- New Zealander	**- shao New Zealand**	- ชาวนิวซีแลนด์
- Norwegian	**- shao Norway**	- ชาวนอรเวย์
- Pakistani	**- shao Pakistan**	- ชาวปากีสถาน
- Palestinian	**- shao Palestai**	- ชาวปาเลสไตน์
- Panamanian	**- shao Panama**	- ชาวปานามา
- Polish	**- shao Poland**	- ชาวโปแลนด์
- Portuguese	**- khon Portuked**	- คนโปรตุเกส
- Russian	**- khon Russia**	- คนรัสเซีย
- Romanian	**- khon Romania**	- คนโรมาเนีย
-Scandinavian	**-shao Scandinavia**	- ชาวสแกนดิเนเวีย
-Singaporean	**-khon Sinkhapo**	- คนสิงคโปร์

- Singhalese	**- shao Singhol, khon Lanka**	- ชาวสิงหล, คนลังกา
- Spanish	**- shao Spain**	- ชาวสเปน
- Swedish	**- shao Sweden**	- ชาวสวีเดน
- Swiss	**- shao Swisserland**	- ชาวสวิสเซอร์แลนด์
- Taiwanese	**- khon Taiwan**	- คนไต้หวัน
- Turkish	**- shao Turaki**	- ชาวตุรกี
- Yugoslav	**- shao Yugoslav**	- ชาวยูโกสลาฟ
What is your occupation?	**Khun mi ar-sheep a-rai?**	คุณมีอาชีพอะไร?
I am	**Phom penh ....**	ผมเป็น...
- an actor (actress)	**- nak sadaeng**	- นักแสดง
- an architect	**- shaang awk-baep kaw-saang**	- ช่างออกแบบก่อสร้าง
- an auto mechanic	**- shaang kae rot-yont**	- ช่างแก้รถยนต์
- a businessman	**- nak thurakit**	- นักธุรกิจ
- a church worker	**- khon tham-ngarn karn sasana**	- คนทำงานการศาสนา
- a clothes designer	**- nak awk-baep seua-phâ**	- นักออกแบบเสื้อผ้า
- a doctor	**- phaed**	- แพทย์
- an economist	**- nak setha-sart**	- นักเศรษฐศาสตร์
- an engineer	**- visavakorn**	- วิศวกร
- a hair stylist	**- shaang tham-phom**	- ช่างทำผม
- a hotel manager	**- phu chat-karn rongraem**	- ผู้จัดการโรงแรม
- an insurance agent	**- tua-thaen prakan phai**	- ตัวแทนประกันภัย

-a journalist	**-nak nangsue-phim**	- นักหนังสือพิมพ์
-a lawyer	**-thanaai-khwaam**	- ทนายความ
-a model	**-narng-baep**	- นางแบบ
-a musician	**-nak don-tri**	- นักดนตรี
- a public health expert	**-phu shiao-sharn karn ana-mai**	- ผู้เชี่ยวชาญการอนามัย
-a purchasing agent	**-tua-thaen sue sinkhâ**	- ตัวแทนซื้อสินค้า
-a real-estate agent	**-tua-thaen sue-khaai thi-din**	- ตัวแทนซื้อขายที่ดิน
-a schoolteacher	**-khru rongrian**	- ครูโรงเรียน
- a scientist	**-nak vithaya-saat**	- นักวิทยาศาสตร์
-a social worker	**-chao-nathi prashâ song-khraw**	-เจ้าหน้าที่ประชาสงเคราะห์
-a travel agent	**-tua-thaen chat borikarn karn thong-thiao**	- ตัวแทนจัดบริการ - การท่องเที่ยว
-a university lecturer	**-acharn mahâ vithayalai**	- อาจารย์มหาวิทยาลัย
I can afford a security deposit	**Phom samart chaai ngoen prakanh tuaeng dai.**	ผมสามารถจ่ายเงินประกันตัวเองได้

(b) At Customs

Porter, please take my luggage.	**Khun, shuai yok khong thi.**	คุณช่วยยกของที
There is one suitcase missing.	**Krapaow haai-pai nueng bai.**	กระเป๋าหายไปหนึ่งใบ

Open this suitcase, please.	**Proad perd-krapaow ni.**	โปรดเปิดกระเป๋านี้
I cannot open my case. I have lost my keys.	**Phom thamh kun-chae haai, perd mai-dai.**	ผมทำกุญแจหาย, เปิดไม่ได้
These two suitcases are mine.	**Krapaow song-bai ni penh khong phom.**	กระเป๋าสองใบนี้ เป็นของผม
That trunk is mine.	**Bai nanh penh khong phom.**	ใบนั้นเป็นของผม
This is not my suitcase.	**Krapaow bai-ni mai-shai khong phom.**	กระเป๋าใบนี้ไม่ใช่ของผม
Have you anything to declare?	**Khun mi a-rai tong chaeng mai?**	คุณมีอะไรต้องแจ้งไหม?
Not that I know of.	**Phom mai-mi a-rai tong chaeng.**	ผมไม่มีอะไรต้องแจ้ง
These things are all gifts.	**Khong laow-ni khao hai pen thi-ra-luek.**	ของเหล่านี้เขาให้เป็นที่ระลึก
These things are for my own private use.	**Khong laow-ni phom shai suan-tua.**	ของเหล่านี้ผมใช้ ส่วนตัว
What is in that suitcase?	**Mi a-rai nai krapaow nan?**	มีอะไรใน กระเป๋านั่น?
Nothing but clothing.	**Mee tae seua pha**	มีแต่เสื้อผ้า
The jewelery is not new.	**Khreuang-pradab laow-ni shai laew.**	เครื่องประดับเหล่านี้ ใช้แล้ว
I have	**Phom mi ....**	ผมมี..........
- a carton of cigarettes	- **buri nueng hor**	บุหรี่หนึ่งห่อ

- a movie camera	- **klong thaai nang**	- กล้องถ่ายหนัง
- a still camera	- **klong thaai roop**	- กล้องถ่ายรูป
- three rolls of movies-camera film	- **film thaai nang sarm muan**	- ฟิล์มถ่ายหนัง - สามม้วน
- five rolls of still-camera film	- **film thammadâ ha muan**	- ฟิล์มธรรมดา - ห้าม้วน
- a radio cassette recorder	- **vithayu cassette**	- วิทยุคาสเซ็ท
- a bottle of whisky	- **whisky nueng khuad**	- วิสกี้หนึ่งขวด
- no firearms/ no narcotics	- **mai-mi avudh/ mai-mi yâ-sep-tit**	- ไม่มีอาวุธ, - ไม่มียา เสพติด
- a typewriter	- **phim-deed**	- พิมพ์ดีด
I will take these things back with me when I leave Thailand.	**Phom chah aow khong laow-ni klab-pai meua dern-thaang klab**	ผมจะเอาของเหล่านี้กลับไป เมื่อเดินทางกลับ
Do I have to pay a duty on this?	**Phom tong-sia phâsi mai?**	ผมต้องเสียภาษีไหม?
How much is it?	**Kha phâ-si thaorai?**	ค่าภาษีเท่าไร?
I have not enough money with me.	**Phom mi ngoen mai-phaw.**	ผมมีเงินไม่พอ
Here is my passport.	**Ni— nangsue dern-thaang khong phom.**	นี่....หนังสือเดินทางของ ผม
Can I go now?	**Phom pai-dai rue yang?**	ผมไปได้หรือยัง?
My luggage has been examined.	**Krapaow phom dai rab karn-truad laew.**	กระเป๋าผมได้รับการ ตรวจแล้ว

(c) Leaving the Airport

Is there a Tourist Information Bureau here?	**Samnak-ngarn Karn Thong Thiao you thi nai?**	สำนักงานการท่องเที่ยว อยู่ที่ไหน?
Which way to the city, please?	**Thaang nai khao meuang?**	ทางไหนเข้าเมือง?
Where is the bus stop?	**Thi chawd-rot pracham thaang you nai?**	ที่จอดรถประจำทาง อยู่ไหน?
Which buses go to the office of Thai Airways International?	**Rot khanh nai pharn Karn Bin Thai thanon Vibhavadi?**	รถคันไหนผ่านการบินไทย ถนนวิภาวดี?
Show me please which bus do I have to take.	**Phom tong khuen rot beur a-rai?**	ผมต้องขึ้นรถเบอร์อะไร?
I need a porter.	**Phom tongkarn khon yok khong.**	ผมต้องการคนยกของ
Please help me, I cannot speak Thai.	**Karuna therd khrap, phom phoud Thai mai-dai.**	กรุณาเถิดครับ ผมพูด ไทยไม่ได้
Help me with my luggage, please	**Karuna shuai phom yok khong.**	กรุณาช่วยผมยกของ
Will you take these bags?	**Aow krapaow laow-ni pai**	เอากระเป๋าเหล่านี้ไป
Put them in the taxi.	**Waang nai rot-taxi.**	วางในรถแท็กซี่
Don't take that bag, I'll carry it myself.	**Yâ aow krapaow nanh pai, phom chah thue pai-eng.**	อย่าเอากระเป๋านั่นไป ผมจะถือไปเอง

)on't take that suitcase. It's not mine.	**Yâ aow krapaow nanh pai. Mai-shai khong phom.**	อย่าเอากระเป๋านั่นไป ไม่ใช่ของผม
'here is another bag over there.	**Mi krapaow you nône ik bai nueng.**	มีกระเป๋าอยู่โน่น อีกใบหนึ่ง
'axi, I want to go to the Ambassdor Hotel	**Taxi, phom tongkarn pai rongraem Ambassador.**	แท็กซี่ ผมต้องการไป โรงแรมแอมบาสเดอร์
want to go to the German Embassy	**Phom tongkarn pai Satharn-thout Jerman.**	ผมต้องการไปสถานทูต เยอรมัน
)o you know where it is?	**Khun saab mai wâ you thi nai?**	คุณทราบไหมว่าอยู่ ที่ไหน?
łow much do you want for taking me there?	**Phâ phom pai song thi-nanh aow thaorai?**	พาผมไปส่งที่นั่นเอา เท่าไร?
)on't you think it is too much?	**Mai phaeng pai rue?**	ไม่แพงไปหรือ?
3e careful, don't drive too fast.	**Rawang, yâ khab réow.**	ระวัง อย่าขับเร็ว
5top here. Please wait for me here.	**Yout! Proad khoi phom thi-ni.**	หยุด โปรดคอยผมที่นี่
łow much do I owe you?	**Phom tong hai khun thaorai?**	ผมต้องให้คุณเท่าไร?
⟨eep the change.	**Keb thi-leua wai. Mai tong thawn**	เก็บที่เหลือไว้ ไม่ต้องทอน

(d) Currency Regulations and Exchange

The unit of Thai currency is the **baht** (or **tical**), which is divided into 100 **satangs**. There are coins of 25 and 50 **satangs** and 1, 5 and 10 baht. Bank notes are issued in denominations of 10, 20, 50, 100, 500 and 1000 **baht**.

As a traveler entering Thailand, you may bring in any amount of foreign currency for personal use, but you must fill in currency declaration form. A false declaration can lead to heavy penalties. As a non-resident traveler leaving Thailand, you are not allowed to take out foreign currency in excess of the amount shown on your customs declaration. No one is permitted to bring in or take out of Thailand more than 50,000 **baht**, there is no limit on traveler's checks or bank drafts.

Tourists can change money or travelers' checks at hotels, banks and other authorized money changer. Large stores also generally accept travelers' checks, and some take letters of credit as well.

Money should never be carried or left in suitcases or trunks. In public lodgings, money and valuables should be checked for safekeeping with the manager of the hotel, instead of being left in the room.

Can I change money here?	**Thi-ni rab laek ngoen mai?**	ที่นี่รับแลกเงินไหม?
I want to change some dollars (pounds)	**Phom tongkarn laek ngoen dollar (pound) pen ngoen Thai.**	ผมต้องการแลกเงิน ดอลลาร์ (ปอนด์) เป็นเงินไทย
What's the rate of	**Attrâ laek-plian**	อัตราแลกเปลี่ยน

exchange today?	**wan-ni thaorai?**	วันนี้เท่าไร?
Do you accept travelers' checks?	**Khun rab shek dern thaang**	คุณรับเช็คเดินทางไหม?
would like to cash this check.	**Phom tongkarn laek check bai ni.**	ผมต้องการแลกเช็คใบนี้
Give me 100 baht notes and some small change.	**Khaw thanabat bai-lah roi baht hai phom lae ngoen pleek baang.**	ขอธนบัตรใบละร้อยบาท ให้ผม และเงินปลีกบ้าง
May I have some small change for this note?	**Phom khaw thanabat ni pen ngoen pleek?**	ผมขอธนบัตรนี้เป็น เงินปลีก?
have	**Phom mi ....**	ผมมี...........
- a banker's draft	**- draft thanakharn**	- ดราฟท์ธนาคาร
- a letter of credit	**- letter of credit**	- เล็ตเตอร์ออฟเครดิต
m expecting some money from New York.	**Phom raw ngoen chaak New York.**	ผมรอเงินจากนิวยอร์ค
Has it arrived yet?	**Khun saab mai wa ma thueng laew rue yang?**	คุณทราบไหมว่า มาถึงแล้วหรือยัง?

TRAVELING AROUND

If you want to see Thailand in style, travel by motor coach i armchair comfort, watching the beautiful countryside roll past you window. Thailand's highways are good, expecially the extensiv Asian highway network. Regular express coach services cover th country every day, and you can plan an interesting itinerary makin use of these services from point to point. Vehicles are driven on th left side of the road.

Around Bangkok, transport varies greatly in style and price. Ther are more than 100,000 taxis, recognizable either by the sign "TAX on the roof or by their number plates. Taxis with "TAXI METER" sig on tops use meters. Few taxi drivers understand English even if the do try to speak it. Before you start your journey try to find someon to interpret for you to be sure the driver really understands wher you are going. It may help to have the name of your destination, an the name of your hotel, written out in Thai. Hotel staff will oblige and may also advise on how much you should pay (for those with out meter).

More than 10,000 city buses ply regular routes between mo

ɔints in Bangkok. The buses are usually crowded and a ride may ɛ quite an adventure to the visitor unfamiliar with the city. But for ıe individual equipped with a good road map and a sense of hu- ıor, riding the Bangkok buses may be an inexpensive and interest- ıg way to get to know the city and its people.

The microtaxi called ***tuk-tuks*** and ***rot song-thaew*** are also avail- ɔle for short journeys in many towns. A leisurely ride in one of ıese vehicles is a good way of getting in touch with Thailand and ; people. You should determine the fare before entering the ve- cle. In cities, samlor (pedicab) are the most common means of ıily transportation.

ı) *Local Events and Points of Interest*

For detailed information on places of interest and travel arrange- ents, please consult your local travel agent.

ɔINTS OF INTEREST	*THAI INTERPRETATION*	*LOCALITY*
ncient City	**Meuang Boran**	Samut Prakarn
quarium	**Suan-liang-pla, Sawaangkha-niward**	Samut Prakarn
yuthaya National Museum	**Piphitphand Chao Sarm-phraya**	Ayuthaya
ıng Pa-In Summer Palace	**Phra Rajawang Baang Pa-In**	Ayuthaya
ıngsaen Seaside Resort	**Shaai-Thale Bangsaen**	Chon Buri
ıumibol Dam	**Kheuan Yan Hi**	Taak
idge on the River Kwai	**Saphaan Tha Makharm**	Kanchanaburi

Buddha Sanctuary	**Buddha Monthon**	Nakhon Pathom
Bull Fighting	**Shon Woa**	Songkhla
Celebration of the King's Birthday	**Chalerm Phrashon Phansa**	Whole Country
Ceremony of the First Tilling of the Soil	**Raek-na**	Bangkok
Cha-Am Beach	**Shai-haad Cha-Am**	Petchaburi
Chainaad Dam	**Kheuan Chao Phya**	Chainaad
Chiang Dao Caves	**Thamh Chiang Dao**	Chiang Mai
Chiangmai National Museum	**Piphitphand Satharn**	Chiang Mai
China Town	**Yaowaraad**	Bangkok
Chinese Buddhist Monastery	**Wat Leng Neui-yi**	Bangkok
Crocodile Farm	**Farm Chawrakhe**	Samut Prakarn
Doi Inthanon National Park	**Doi Inthanon**	Chiang Mai
Dusit Zoological Gardens	**Suan-Sat Dusit**	Bangkok
Elephant Roundup	**Ngarn Shaang Surind**	Surin
Emerald Buddha	**Phra Kaew Mawrakot**	Bangkok
Erawan Falls	**Narm Tok Erawan**	Kanchanaburi
Floating Market	**Talaad Narm Damnern Saduak**	Rajburi,
Thonburi		
Flower Carnival	**Ngârn Prakuat Rot Buphashart**	Chiang Mai
Giant Stupa	**Phra Pathom Chedi**	Nakhon Patho
Giant Swing	**Sao Shingsha, Wat Suthat**	Bangkok

olden Buddha	**Wat Traimit**	Bangkok
olden Mount	**Phukhao Thong**	Bangkok
rand Palace	**Phra Boromaha Rajawang**	Bangkok
indu Temple	**Wat Khaek Silom**	Bangkok
orse Racing	**Sanarm Raja-trinnamai**	Bangkok
ua Hin On Sea	**Shaai Thale Hua Hin**	Prachuap
m Thompson 's Thai House	**Baan Jim Thompson, Soi Kasem**	Bangkok
aeng Kracharn Water Catchment	**Aang Keb-narm Kaeng Kracharn**	Petchaburi
oh Larn Vac	**Koh Larn. off Pattaya**	Chon Buri
oconut Island	**Koh Samui**	Surat Thani
adda Land	**Ladda Land**	Chiang Mai
argest Sitting Buddha	**Phra Buddha Khodom**	Suphanburi
ae Klaang Water Fall	**Narm Tok Mae Klaang**	Chiang Mai
arble Temple	**Wat Benchama Bophit**	Bangkok
asked Play	**Khone Silpakorn**	Bangkok
onkey Show	**Lakhorn Ling**	Bangkok
ational Assembly Hall	**Sabha Phu-thaen**	Bangkok
ational Library	**Haw Samud Haeng Shart**	Bangkok
ational Museum	**Piphitphand Satharn**	Bangkok
ational Park & Wildlife Reserve	**Uthayarn Khao Yai**	Nakhon Rajsima
ational Sports Stadium	**Sanarm Kila Haeng Shart**	Bangkok

Orchid & Flower Gardens	**Suan Luang Raw Kao**	Bangkok
Palace of King Mongkut	**Khao Wang**	Petchaburi
Pattaya Seaside Resort	**Haad Pattaya**	Chon Buri
Phimai Stone Palace	**Prasaad Phanom Rung**	Buriram
Phu Kradueng National Park	**Vana Uthayarn Phu Kradueng**	Loei
Phu Thai Village	**Renu Nakhorn**	Nakhon Phnom
Phra Buddha Shinaraj	**Phra Buddha Shinaraad**	Phitsanulok
Public Park	**Suan Chatuchak**	Bangkok
Ramkhamhaeng Museum	**Piphitphand Satharn**	Sukhothai
Reclining Buddha	**Phra Nonn Wat Pho**	Bangkok
Rose Garden	**Suan Sarm-phraan**	Nakhon Pathom
Royal Phuphing Palace	**Phra Tamnak Phuphing**	Chiang Mai
Sacred Three-spired Pagodas	**Phra-naang Sarm Yawd**	Lop Buri
Saiyoke Water Fall	**Narm Tok Saiyoke**	Kanchanaburi
Shrine of Holy Footprint	**Phra Phuthabart**	Saraburi
Snake Farm	**Satharn Saowapha**	Bangkok
Shell Museum	**Piphitphand Pleuak Hoi**	Samut Prakarn
Sirikit Hydroelectric Dam	**Kheuan Sirikit**	Uttaradit

Songkhla Beach Resort	**Shaai-haad Songkhla**	Songkhla
Spirit House of the City	**Sarn Lak Meuang**	Bangkok
Suan Pakkard Palace	**Wang Suan Pakkard**	Bangkok
Temple of the Dawn	**Phra-praang Wat Arun**	Bangkok
Temple of the Emerald Buddha	**Wat Phra Kaew**	Bangkok
Thai Boxing	**Muai Thai**	Bangkok
Thai Classical Dancing	**Ram Thai**	Bangkok
Thung Salaeng Luang	**Thung Salaeng Luang**	Phitsanulok
Throne Hall	**Phra Thinang Anan**	Bangkok
Umbrella Village	**Baan Baw Saang**	Chiang Mai
Viking Cave	**Tham Phya Naak**	Krabi
Wat Indra Standing Buddha	**Wat Indra**	Bangkok
Wang Kaew Beach Resort	**Wang Kaew**	Rayong
Wat Phra Sri Ratana Maha Thart	**Phra Thart Doi Suthep**	Chiang Mai

(b) Rail Travel

The Thai State Railway is inexpensive, safe, punctual, comfortable, and by far the most relaxing way of getting from place to place. First class offers accommodation for two people with upper and lower berths. You will be wise to travel first class for long trips and second class for shorter distances.

Classification of Trains

Trains in Thailand are classified as follows:

Rot-duan Phaan Khet: รถด่วนผ่านเขต International express trains running between Bangkok and Butterworth (for Penang): roomette or twinette cabin on first class air-conditioned coaches and sleeperette on second class; supplementary fare required. Dinner and breakfast are available in the dining car attached. No third class.

Rot-duan: รถด่วน Internal express trains stopping only at main stations; roomette or twinette cabin on first class; air-conditioned coaches and sleeperette on second class; supplementary fare required. Dinner and breakfast are available in the dining car attached. No third class.

Rot-réow: รถเร็ว Long distance rapid trains stopping only at main stations: first, second and third class; sleeperettes are available on first and second class coaches; supplementary fare required. Food, drinks and light refreshments are available to passengers of all classes on the day and night rapid trains.

-Rot-thammada: รถธรรมดา Local passenger trains stopping at all stations.

-Rot-ruam : รถร่วม Mixed trains stopping at all stations.

-Rot-sinkha : รถสินค้า Local goods trains.

-Rot-diesel raang : รถดีเซลราง Diesel rail car used only on short runs.

You may also travel by some goods trains, subject to certain conditions. Inquire at station offices.

First, second and third class seats can be reserved on rapid trains, while first and second class reservations are available on express trains. For bookings and detailed information contact the station master or your travel agent.

At the Station

Where is the Inquiry Office?	**Phanaek sobb-tharm you thi-nai?**	แผนกสอบถามอยู่ที่ไหน?
At what time will the rapid train leave for Haadyai?	**Rot-réow chah awk pai Haadyai ki mong?**	รถเร็วจะออกไปหาดใหญ่กี่โมง?
Can I break the trip at Hua Hin?	**Phom chah long phak Hua Hin dai mai?**	ผมจะลงพักหัวหินได้ไหม?
Does the train stop at Thap Sakae?	**Rot yout thi sathani Thap Sakae mai?**	รถหยุดที่สถานีทับสะแกไหม?
At what time does the train for Pitsanuloke leave?	**Rot-thammada chah awk pai Phitsanuloke ki mong?**	รถธรรมดาจะออกไปพิษณุโลกกี่โมง?
From what platform does the train leave?	**Rot chah awk-chaak shan-shâlâ nai?**	รถจะออกจากชานชาลาไหน?
At what time will the express arrive at Chiang Mai?	**Ki mong rot-duan chah thueng Sathani Chiang Mai?**	กี่โมงรถด่วนจะถึงสถานีเชียงใหม่?
Where is ....?	**............. you thi nai?**	.............อยู่ที่ไหน?
- the information office	**- Prasha samphand**	- ประชาสัมพันธ์
- the reservation office	**- Hong chawng tua**	- ห้องจองตั๋ว
- the ticket offices	**- Hong chamnaai tua**	- ห้องจำหน่ายตั๋ว

- the waiting room	**- Hong-phak Phu-doai-sarn**	- ห้องพักผู้โดยสาร
- the cloak room	**- Hong faak khong**	- ห้องฝากของ
- the rest room	**- Hong-phak shua-khrao**	- ห้องพักชั่วคราว
- the station master	**- Naai sathani**	- นายสถานี
- the lavatory	**- Hong-narm, Hong-suam**	- ห้องน้ำ, ห้องส้วม
- the guard's van-	**- Rot chao-na-thi**	- รถเจ้าหน้าที่
- the luggage van	**- Rot banthouk-Khong**	- รถบรรทุกของ
- the dining car	**- Rot sabiang**	- รถเสบียง
- the sleeping car	**- Rot nonn**	- รถนอน
- the air-pressurized coach	**- Rot prab-akaad**	- รถปรับอากาศ
- the railway police	**- Tamruat rot-fai**	- ตำรวจรถไฟ
- Platform No. 2	**- Shan-shâlâ song**	- ชานชาลาสอง

Booking Seats and Berths

I want to reserve seats on	**Phom khaw samrong thi bonh.......**	- ผมขอสำรองที่บน......
- the International Express to Butterworth	**- Rot-duan Butterworth**	- รถด่วนบัตเตอร์เวิร์ธ
- the Southern Express Bangkok-Sungei Golok	**- Rot-duan Krungthep-Sungei Golok**	- รถด่วนกรุงเทพฯ-สุไหงโกลก
- the Rapid Train, Bangkok-Haadyai	**- Rot-réow Krungthep-Haadyai**	- รถเร็วกรุงเทพ - หาดใหญ่

- the Chiang Mai Express	**- Rot duan Chiang Mai**	- รถด่วนเชียงใหม่
- the Nongkhai Express	**- Rot-duan Nongkhaai**	- รถด่วนหนองคาย
- the Ubol Express	**- Rot-duan Ubol**	- รถด่วนอุบลฯ
would like to have...	**Phom khaw........**	ผมขอ......
- an upper berth	**- thi-nonn khaang-bonh**	- ที่นอนข้างบน
- a lower berth	**- thi-nonn khaang-laang**	- ที่นอนข้างล่าง
- a seat near the window	**- thi-nang shid na-taang**	- ที่นั่งชิดหน้าต่าง
- a seat facing the engine	**- thi-nang hanh-na pai thaang rot-chak**	- ที่นั่งหันหน้าไปทางรถจักร
- a seat with my back to the engine	**- thi-nang hanh-lang pai thaang rot-chak**	- ที่นั่งหันหลังไปทางรถจักร
- a seat on the left	**- thi-nang darn saai**	- ที่นั่งด้านซ้าย
- a seat on the right	**- thi-nang darn khwâ**	- ที่นั่งด้านขวา
wish to obtain a seat in	**Phom khaw samrong thi-nang bonh......**	ผมขอสำรองที่นั่งบน......
- the first class air-conditioned coach	**- Rot-nang Shan Nueng prab-akaak**	- รถนั่งชั้นหนึ่งปรับอากาศ
- the first class non air-conditioned coach	**- Rot-nang Shan Nueng thammada**	- รถนั่งชั้นหนึ่งธรรมดา

Tickets

I want to buy a.........	**Phom khaw sue ....**	ผมขอซื้อ......
- first class ticket	**- tua Shanh-nueng**	- ตั๋วชั้นหนึ่ง
- second class ticket	**- tua Shanh-song**	- ตั๋วชั้นสอง
- third class ticket	**- tua Shanh-sarm**	- ตั๋วชั้นสาม
- One-way ticket	**- tua thiao-diao**	- ตั๋วเที่ยวเดียว
- Round-trip ticket	**- tua pai-klab**	- ตั๋วไปกลับ
- Platform ticket	**- tua Shaan-shâlâ**	- ตั๋วชานชาลา
For how long is the round-trip ticket valid?	**Tua pai-klab shai dai naan thao-rai?**	ตั๋วไปกลับใช้ได้นานเท่าไร?
How much is the fare to Lampang?	**Kha-doai-sarn pai Lampang thao-rai?**	ค่าโดยสารไปลำปางเท่าไร?
Is it half-price for a child?	**Dek khrueng-rakha shai mai?**	เด็กครึ่งราคาใช่ไหม?
How old is the child?	**Dek a-you thao-rai?**	เด็กอายุเท่าไร?
Thirteen	**Sib-sarm**	สิบสาม
No, it's half-price up to the age of 12.	**Mai, a-you tam-kwâ sib-song khid khrueng rakha.**	ไม่ อายุต่ำกว่าสิบสอง คิดครึ่งราคา
You'll have to pay full fare.	**Khun tong sia tem rakha.**	คุณต้องเสียเต็มราคา

In the Train With Other Passengers

Is this seat taken?	**Mi khon nang thi-ni laew rue yang?**	มีคนนั่งที่นี่แล้วหรือยัง?
Yes, it is taken.	**Mi laew.**	มีแล้ว

No, it's free.	**Yang mai-mi.**	ยังไม่มี
Do you smoke?	**Khun soub buri mai?**	คุณสูบบุหรี่ไหม?
Thanks, I don' t smoke.	**Khob-khun, Phom mai soub.**	ขอบคุณ ผมไม่สูบ
I do smoke, but I don't have any match.	**Phom soub, tae mai-mi mai khide-fai.**	ผมสูบ แต่ไม่มีไม้ขีดไฟ
Do you mind if I smoke?	**Khun rangkiat phom soub buri mai?**	คุณรังเกียจผมสูบบุหรี่ไหม?
What station is this?	**Thi-ni sathani arai?**	ที่นี่สถานีอะไร?
This is Hua Hin, Thailand's oldest and most popular seaside resort.	**Thi-ni sathani Hua Hin, shaai-thale mi shue khong Thai.**	ที่นี่สถานีหัวหิน ชายทะเล มีชื่อของไทย
Where will you get off?	**Khun chah long thi-nai?**	คุณจะลงที่ไหน?
I am going to Butterworth.	**Phom pai Butterworth.**	ผมไปบัตเตอร์เวิร์ธ
Where do you live in Thailand?	**Khun you thi-nai nai Prathed Thai?**	คุณอยู่ที่ไหนใน ประเทศไทย?
I live in Bangkok.	**Phom you nai Krungthep.**	ผมอยู่ในกรุงเทพฯ
Would you like to look at my newspaper?	**Khun yaak ann nangsue-phim mai?**	คุณอยากอ่านหนังสือ พิมพ์ไหม?
Do you mean a Thai newspaper?	**Nangsue-phim phasa Thai shai-mai?**	หนังสือพิมพ์ภาษาไทย ใช่ไหม?
That's right, the Daily News.	**Shai, nangsue-phim Daily News.**	ใช่ หนังสือพิมพ์เดลินิวส์

I am sorry, I am not very fluent in Thai.	**Phasa Thai phom mai khlong.**	ภาษาไทยผมไม่คล่อง
I want to go to.......	**Phom tongkarn pai ....**	ผมต้องการไป......
- the lavatory	**- hong-narm, hong-suam**	- ห้องน้ำ ห้องส้วม
- eat in the dining car	**- tharn a harn thi rot-sabiang**	- ทานอาหารที่รถเสบียง
May I ask you to look after my seat for a while?	**Karuna shuai dou thi-nang phom khrou nueng dai mai?**	กรุณาช่วยดูที่นั่งผมครู่หนึ่งได้ไหม?
I'd like to have your name and address.	**Phom yaak dai shue lae thi-you khong khun.**	ผมอยากได้ชื่อและที่อยู่ของคุณ
What is the name of your friend?	**Pheuan khun shue arai?**	เพื่อนคุณชื่ออะไร?
Here is my name card.	**Ni narm-bat phom.**	นี่นามบัตรผม
What's your telephone number?	**Thorasab khun beur a-rai?**	โทรศัพท์คุณเบอร์อะไร?
I'd like to visit you in Bangkok.	**Phom yaak pai-yiam khun thi krungthep.**	ผมอยากไปเยี่ยมคุณที่กรุงเทพฯ

In the Train With Railway Officials

Please help me get two seats.	**Proad hâ thi-nang hai phom song thi.**	โปรดหาที่นั่งให้ผมสองที่
Where are these berths?	**Thi-nonn you nai?**	ที่นอนอยู่ไหน?
I'm afraid I've gotten on the wrong train.	**Phom khid wâ phom khuen rot phid khabuan.**	ผมคิดว่าผมขึ้นรถผิดขบวน

May I get off at the next station?	**Phom khaw long thi sathani khaang nâ?**	ผมขอลงที่สถานีข้างหน้า?

In the Dining car

Do you have cold water?	**Khun mi narm-yen duem mai?**	คุณมีน้ำเย็นดื่มไหม?
Please let me have....	**Phom khaw ....**	ผมขอ.......,
- a plate of fried rice	**- khao-phad nueng chaan**	- ข้าวผัดหนึ่งจาน
- sausage and eggs	**- khai-dao sai-krawk**	- ไข่ดาวไส้กรอก
- two slices of buttered toast	**- khanom-pang ping thâ neui song phaen**	- ขนมปังปิ้งทาเนย สองแผ่น
- Singha Beer	**- Beer Singh**	- เบียร์สิงห์
- a glass of lemon drink	**- narm manao nueng kaew**	- น้ำมะนาวหนึ่งแก้ว
- white coffee, cold	**- kafae yenh sai nom**	- กาแฟเย็นใส่นม
- black coffee, cold	**- kafae damh yenh**	- กาแฟดำเย็น
Your bill, please.	**Proad khid ngoen.**	โปรดคิดเงิน

Arriving by Train and Going to Your Hotel

Porter, take all this luggage.	**Khon yok khong, shuai-phom yok khong laow-ni.**	คนยกของ ช่วยผมยก ของเหล่านี้
There are two suitcases and six plastic bags.	**Mi krapaow dern-thaang song bai, krapaow plastic hok bai.**	มีกระเป๋าเดินทางสอง ใบ กระเป๋าพลาสติกหกใบ
Three small parcels	**Haw-lek sarm haw.**	ห่อเล็กสามห่อ

Call a taxi for me, please.	**Karuna riak rot-taxi hai phom.**	กรุณาเรียกรถแท็กซี่ให้ผม
Put this luggage in the taxi.	**Aow khong laow-ni waang nai rot.**	เอาของเหล่านี้วางในรถ
I want to go to the Imperial Hotel.	**Phom tongkarn pai thi rongraem Imperial.**	ผมต้องการไปที่โรงแรมอิมพีเรียล
Here's something for you.	**Ni penh sommanâ-khun.**	นี่เป็นสมนาคุณ

(c) Renting a Private Car

Hire cars, some air-conditioned, or self-drive rentals are available in Bangkok. Almosts any travel agent or hotel clerk can arrange to get one for you. A valid U.S. driver's licence is accepted; however, an International Driver's Permit will be accepted by the rental transaction. Many visitors find driving to be a pleasant way to see Thailand, although roads can be dangerous in some parts of the country, particularly the south.

I would like to go sightseeing.	**Phom tongkarn pai thasanachorn.**	ผมต้องการไปทัศนาจร
I'm only here for......	**Phom mi véla you thi-ni ....**	ผมมีเวลาอยู่ที่นี่........
- a few hours	**- song-sarm chua mong**	- สองสามชั่วโมง
- a day	**- wanh diao**	- วันเดียว
- three days	**- sarm wanh**	- สามวัน
- a week	**- sapda diao**	- สัปดาห์เดียว
I would like to hire a car.	**Phom tongkarn shao rot.**	ผมต้องการเช่ารถ

What is the charge per day?	**Khun khid wanh-lah thao-rai?**	คุณคิดวันละเท่าไร?
Can I rent a car by the week?	**Shao pen sapda dai mai?**	เช่าเป็นสัปดาห์ได้ไหม?
I have a driver's licence.	**Phom mi bai khab-khi.**	ผมมีใบขับขี่
I have an International Driver's Permit.	**Phom mi bai anuyart khab-khi sakon.**	ผมมีใบอนุญาตขับขี่สากล
How much deposit do you require?	**Tongkarn mat-chamh thao-rai?**	ต้องการมัดจำเท่าไร?
Will you accept my credit card for payment?	**Hai credit card thaen ngoen-sod dai mai?**	ให้เครดิตการ์ดแทนเงินสดได้ไหม?
Can you supply me with a good map of Thailand?	**Mi phaen-thi thanonh di-di mai?**	มีแผนที่ถนนดี ๆ ไหม?
What is the best road to Rayong?	**Thanonh saai-nai di samrap pai Rayong?**	ถนนสายไหนดีสำหรับไประยอง?
Is the road good or bad?	**Thanonh di rue mai-di?**	ถนนดีหรือไม่ดี?
Is it very hilly?	**Mi nern-khao maak mai?**	มีเนินเขามากไหม?
How many kilometers to Phra Buddhabat?	**Ki kilometre thueng Phra Phuthabart?**	กี่กิโลเมตรถึงพระพุทธบาท?
Where dose (this road) go?	**(Thanonh ni) pai thueng nai?**	(ถนนนี้) ไปถึงไหน?

(d) At a Gas Station

Where is there a gas (petrol) station?	**Pump-narm-manh you thi nai?**	ปั๊มน้ำมันอยู่ที่ไหน?

Please give me thirty liters.	**Term narm-manh hai sarm-sib lit.**	เติมน้ำมันให้สามสิบลิตร
The tank is.....	**Thang ....**	ถัง........
- empty	**- mai-mi narm manh**	- ไม่มีน้ำมัน
- full	**- yang-mi narm-manh you-tem**	- ยังมีน้ำมันอยู่เต็ม
Fill her up, please.	**Proad term hai tem.**	โปรดเติมให้เต็ม
The engine overheats.	**Khreuang-yont rawn chad.**	เครื่องยนต์ร้อนจัด
The radiator has boiled over.	**Maw-narm rawn chad.**	หม้อน้ำร้อนจัด
Please put water in the radiator.	**Proad term narm nai maw-narm.**	โปรดเติมน้ำในหม้อน้ำ
Please wash the car and change the oil.	**Proad laang-rot lae plian narm-manh khrueuang.**	โปรดล้างรถและเปลี่ยนน้ำมันเครื่อง
Lubricate the car please.	**Term narm-manh law-luen.**	เติมน้ำมันหล่อลื่น
Please check the engine's oil level.	**Proad truad narm-manh khreuang.**	โปรดตรวจน้ำมันเครื่อง
The tire is punctured.	**Yaang rua; Yaang-faeb; Yaang-taek.**	ยางรั่ว ยางแฟบ ยางแตก
Do you have spare tires?	**Khun mi yaang-alai mai?**	คุณมียางอะไหล่ไหม?
Can you repair flat tires?	**Khun pah-yaang hai dai mai?**	คุณปะยางให้ได้ไหม?
How long will it take?	**Naan-thaorai chah set?**	นานเท่าไรจะเสร็จ?
Please check the tires.	**Proad truad yaang duai.**	โปรดตรวจยางด้วย

Add some air if necessary.	**Tha champenh, soup yaang hai duai.**	ถ้าจำเป็น, สูบยางให้ด้วย
The shock absorbers aren't working.	**Choke-up mai tham-ngarn.**	โช้คอัพ ไม่ทำงาน
The battery is still discharging.	**Battery yang chaai-fai**	แบตเตอรี่ยังจ่ายไฟ
The fan belt is broken.	**Saai-pharn khaad**	สายพานขาด
The brakes don' t work.	**Brakes shai-karn mai-dai**	เบรคใช้การไม่ได้
The motor stalls.	**Khreuang-yont yout-yout dern-dern.**	เครื่องยนต์หยุด ๆ เดิน ๆ
I don' t know what the matter is.	**Phom mai saab arai pen hed.**	ผมไม่ทราบอะไรเป็นเหตุ?
Please check the battery electrolyte level.	**Proad truad battery lae term narm-klanh.**	โปรดตรวจแบตเตอรี่และเติมน้ำกลั่น
Can you charge the battery for me?	**Khun charge-fai khow battery dai mai?**	คุณชาร์จไฟเข้าแบตเตอรี่ได้ไหม?
The right front headlight is out.	**Fai-na mai tit.**	ไฟหน้าไม่ติด
Please check the operation of all lights.	**Proad truad rabop-fai thang mod.**	โปรดตรวจระบบไฟทั้งหมด
Please inspect the fan and check the fan belt.	**Proad truad phad-lom lae saai-pharn.**	โปรดตรวจพัดลมและสายพาน
Please check the brake fluid and pedal action.	**Proad truad narm-manh brake lae khan-réng**	โปรดตรวจน้ำมันเบรคและคันเร่ง

Check the brake linings and adjust the brakes.	**Truad pha-break lae kae-khai brake sia mai.**	ตรวจผ้าเบรคและแก้ไขเบรคเสียใหม่
Please examine the steering and wheel alignment.	**Truad phuang-malai lae tang soun-law.**	ตรวจพวงมาลัยและตั้งศูนย์ล้อ
Please check the operation of the windshield wipers.	**Truad khreuang shed-krachok na rot.**	ตรวจเครื่องเช็ดกระจกหน้ารถ
What do you charge for a grease job?	**Term narm-manh law-luen, add-charabi khid thaorai?**	เติมน้ำมันหล่อลื่น - อัดจารบีคิดเท่าไร?

(e) Traveling by Bus or Coach

Where can I get a bus to.....?	**Phom tongkarn pai ....?**	ผมต้องการไป.....?
- Klong Teui Wharf	**- Tha-reua Klong Teui**	- ท่าเรือคลองเตย
- Pattaya	**- Pattaya**	- พัทยา
- Sadao immigration Deport	**- Darn truad-khon khow meuang Sadao**	- ด่านตรวจคนเข้าเมืองสะเดา
- Nongkhai Immigration Deport	**- Darn truad-khon khow meuang Nong-khaai**	- ด่านตรวจคนเข้าเมืองหนองคาย
- Padang Basar Customs Checkpoint	**- Darn Sulkakorn Padang Besar**	- ด่านศุลกากรปาดังเบซาร์

Does this bus go to Sadao?	**Rot-bus ni pai Sadao mai?**	รถบัสนี้ไปสะเดาไหม?
Where is the bus stop?	**Thi chawd-rot pracham-thaang you thi nai?**	ที่จอดรถประจำทางอยู่ที่ไหน?
What's the fare to Phuket?	**kha doai-sarn pai Phuket thao-rai?**	ค่าโดยสารไปภูเก็ตเท่าไร?
How long must I wait?	**Tong khoi naan mai?**	ต้องคอยนานไหม?
- 15 minutes	**- sib-ha nathi**	- สิบห้านาที
- 30 minutes	**- sarm-sib nathi**	- สามสิบนาที
- one hour	**- nueng shua-mong**	- หนึ่งชั่วโมง
How many buses are there daily to Yala?	**Mi rot pai Yala wan-lah ki-thiao?**	มีรถไปยะลาวันละกี่เที่ยว?
Please reserve a seat for me.	**Samrong thi-nang hai phom nueng thi.**	สำรองที่นั่งให้ผมหนึ่งที่
I would like to have...	**Phom tongkarn .....**	ผมต้องการ..........
- a seat in front	**- thi-nang khang nâ**	- ที่นั่งข้างหน้า
- a seat near the window	**- thi-nang chid na-taang**	- ที่นั่งชิดหน้าต่าง
- a seat on the left/right	**- thi-nang saai-mue/ khwa mue**	- ที่นั่งซ้ายมือ / ขวามือ
I want to get off at Na Thavi.	**Phom long thi Na Thawi.**	ผมลงที่นาทวี
Is Na Thavi far from here?	**Na Thawi klai mai?**	นาทวีไกลไหม?
Please tell me when to get off.	**Meua thueng Na Thawi karuna bawk duai.**	เมื่อถึงนาทวีกรุณาบอกด้วย

Please let me get off at the next stop.	**Phom chah long thi paai khang-na.**	ผมจะลงที่ป้ายข้างหน้า
I want to get out here.	**Phom long thi-ni.**	ผมลงที่นี่

(f) Traveling by Taxi (without meter)

Please call.......for me	**Karuna riak ....hai thi.**	กรุณาเรียก......ให้ที
- a taxi	**- rot taxi**	- รถแท็กซี่
- a mini bus.	**- rot tuk-tuk**	- รถตุ๊ก ๆ
I wish to go to......	**Phom tongkarn pai ......**	ผมต้องการไป......
I plan to remain there some hours,.	**Chah you thi-nanh sawng-sarm shua mong**	จะอยู่ที่นั่นสองสามชั่วโมง
Do you know where this place is?	**Khun pai thi-nanh thouk mai?**	คุณไปที่นั่นถูกไหม?
Is it far from here?	**Klai maak mai?**	ไกลมากไหม?
What do you charge..	**Chah aow ....?**	จะเอา......?
- per hour	**- shua-mong lah thao-rai**	- ชั่วโมงละเท่าไร?
- per trip	**- thiao-lah thao-rai**	- เที่ยวละเท่าไร?
Don' t drive so fast.	**Ya khap réow.**	อย่าขับเร็ว?
Go slowly, please.	**Proad khap shâ-shaâ.**	โปรดขับช้า ๆ
Look out!	**Rawang!**	ระวัง!
Stop here.	**Yout thi-ni.**	หยุดที่นี่
Let me get out here.	**Phom long thi-ni.**	ผมลงที่นี่
Stop here a moment.	**Yout thi-ni khrou nueng.**	หยุดที่นี่ครู่หนึ่ง
I want to buy something	**Phom tong-karn sue khong**	ผมต้องการซื้อของ......

- Wait a minute.	**- Khoi sak-khrou nueng.**	- คอยสักครู่หนึ่ง
Take me back to.......	**Khap pai song thi ....**	กลับไปส่งท**........**
Here is the fare.	**Ni kha-doai sarn.**	นี่ค่าโดยสาร
Give me the change.	**Thawn-ma hai phom.**	ทอนมาให้ผม
Keep the change.	**Kep aow wai.**	เก็บเอาไว้

(G) At the Seaside

Is there a good ocean beach around here?	**Boriven-ni mi shaai-haad di-di mai?**	บริเวณนี้มีชายหาด ดี ๆ ไหม?
Yes, there is one at Songkhla	**Mi thi Songkhla.**	มีที่สงขลา
How far is it from here?	**Chaak-ni klai thaorai?**	จากนี่ไกลเท่าไร?
It will take about 40 minutes by taxi from Haadyai.	**Si-sib nathi doai rot-taxi chaak Haadyai.**	สี่สิบนาทีด้วยรถแท็กซี่ จากหาดใหญ่
You can go to Songkhla by bus.	**Chah pai rot-pracham thaang kaw-dai.**	จะไปรถประจำทางก็ได้
I like swimming.	**Phom shob waai-narm.**	ผมชอบว่ายน้ำ
Let's go for a swim.	**Pai waai-narm kanh.**	ไปว่ายน้ำกัน
Where can I buy a bathing suit?	**Chah sue shoud waai-narm dai thi-nai?**	จะซื้อชุดว่ายน้ำได้ที่ไหน?
From one of the fancy goods stores.	**Thi raan khai sinkha bet-ta-let.**	ที่ร้านขายสินค้าเบ็ดเตล็ด
I like to walk along the beach at low tide.	**Phom shob dern tarm shaai-haad, meua narm long.**	ผมชอบเดินตามชายหาด เมื่อน้ำลง

What a lovely beach!	**Shaai-haad suai leua-kern!**	ชายหาดสวยเหลือเกิน
We'll stay half an hour in the water.	**Raow chah len narm khrueng shua-mong.**	เราจะเล่นน้ำครึ่งชั่วโมง
After that we'll dry in the sun.	**Laew chah tak daed.**	แล้วจะตากแดด
You swim very well.	**Khun waai-narm keng maak.**	คุณว่ายน้ำเก่งมาก
It's almost one o'clock now.	**Keuab baai laew.**	เกือบบ่ายแล้ว
The tide has gone down.	**Narm-long laew.**	น้ำลงแล้ว
We'd better get dressed for lunch.	**Reep taeng-tua pai ha arai tharn di-kwa.**	รีบแต่งตัวไปหาอะไรทานดีกว่า
Let's go to an eating shop.	**Pai thi raan a-harn.**	ไปที่ร้านอาหาร
You're not hungry., Are you?	**Khun mai-hiew rue?**	คุณไม่หิวหรือ?
Here we are. The "Good Food" Restaurant.	**Ni raan a-harn "Good Food."**	นี่ร้านอาหาร กูดฟู้ด
The food is marvelous.	**A-harn a-roi ching.**	อาหารอร่อยจริง
Thank you for bringing me here.	**Khob-khun maak thi phâ phom ma thi-ni.**	ขอบคุณมากที่พาผมมาที่นี่

AT YOUR HOTEL

Hotel accommodation leaves itself wide open to personal preference. There are several international class hotels in Bangkok which would hold their own anywhere. Most small Thai towns do not offer the cosmopolitan facilities of a worldwide hotel chain, but they do provide the personal touch, offering convenient accommodations to visitors traveling through rural Thailand. A typical street is dotted with little budget hotels renting simply furnished rooms. If there is no air-conditioning, there will probably be an electric fan; and if there is no screening, the bed should have a mosquito net. Such hotels rarely have their own restaurants, but the staff will bring in food and drinks from nearby stalls or restaurants at all hours of the day and night.

When checking into your room, ask to see it first, and select one that seems to be located in the quietest corner, away from staircases, bathrooms, the water closet, etc. Always lock your hotel rooms when going out, and deposit your valuables with the manager. Your accomodations in Thailand may be a delux hotel, a modest hotest, a boarding house, or whatever, but it is important to be able to ex-

press your needs to be sure you get what you want. Outside o
Bangkok, few people are likely to be able to help you if you do nc
speak Thai, so we have given expressions to cover most situations

(a) Inquiries

Is there a hotel somewhere here?	**Thi klai-klai ni mi rongraem mai?**	ที่ใกล้ ๆ นี้มีโรงแรมไหม?
Can you recommend a small hotel?	**Khun rou-chak rongraem thi phaw you dai mai?**	คุณรู้จักโรงแรมที่พออยู่ได้ไหม?
Have you any rooms vacant?	**Khun mi hong-waang mai?**	คุณมีห้องว่างไหม?
I want a room.......	**Phom tongkarn hong.....**	ผมต้องการห้อง.....
- on the ground floor	**- thi pen shan-laang**	-ที่เป็นชั้นล่าง
- upstairs	**- Shan-bonh**	-ชั้นบน
I want a quiet but airy room.	**Phom tongkarn hong ngiap-ngiap akaad-di.**	ผมต้องการห้องเงียบ ๆ อากาศดี
I want a room with two beds.	**Phom tongkarn hong mi song tiang.**	ผมต้องการห้องมีสองเตียง
I want a single-bed room.	**Phom tongkarn hong tiang diao.**	ผมต้องการห้องเตียงเดียว
I want a room with bathroom inside.	**Phom tongkarn hong. Thi mi hongnarm**	ผมต้องการห้องที่มีห้องน้ำ
I want an air-conditioned room.	**Phom tongkarn hong mi khreuang prab-akaad.**	ผมต้องการห้องมีเครื่องปรับอากาศ

I want a cheaper room.	**Phom tongkarn hong ra-kha thouk-kwa nid-noi.**	ผมต้องการห้องราคาถูกกว่านิดหน่อย
Let me see the room, please.	**Phom khaw dou hong.**	ผมขอดูห้อง
This room is small.	**Hong ni lek pai.**	ห้องนี้เล็กไป
I want a larger room.	**Phom tongkarn hong yai kwâ ni.**	ผมต้องการห้องใหญ่กว่านี้
Could you show me any other room?	**Khaw dou mai ik hong nueng?**	ขอดูใหม่อีกห้องหนึ่ง?
What about the opposite room?	**Khaw dou hong trong kharm?**	ขอดูห้องตรงข้าม?
What is the charge for this room?	**Hong ni khid ra-kha yang-rai?**	ห้องนี้คิดราคาอย่างไร?
For one night only.	**Samrab khuen diao.**	สำหรับคืนเดียว
I want to stay here a day or two.	**Phom tongkarn you wan rue song wan.**	ผมต้องการอยู่วันหรือสองวัน
For a week, perhaps longer.	**You nueng sap-da rue maak-kwâ ni.**	อยู่หนึ่งสัปดาห์หรือมากกว่านี้
Is that the lowest price for a longer stay?	**Phak narn-narn kaw khid ra-khâ meuan-kanh rue?**	พักนาน ๆ ก็คิดราคาเหมือนกันหรือ?
Can you make it cheaper?	**Lod rakhâ ik dai mai?**	ลดราคาอีกได้ไหม?
I'll take this room.	**Phom aow hong ni.**	ผมเอาห้องนี้
Do you serve meals in the hotel?	**Rongraem mi a-harn khaai mai?**	โรงแรมมีอาหารขายไหม?

Have you a garage or some place where I can put my car?	**Mi thi chawd-rot mai?**	มีที่จอดรถไหม?
Where is the bathroom? (toilet)?	**Hong-narm you nai?**	ห้องน้ำอยู่ไหน?
Where is the telephone?	**Mi thorasab mai?**	มีโทรศัพท์ไหม?
Do you have overnight laundry service?	**Mi borikarn sak-reed wan-diao set mai?**	มีบริการซักรีด วันเดียวเสร็จไหม?
What is your telephone number?	**Thorasab khong rongraem beur arai?**	โทรศัพท์ของโรงแรม เบอร์อะไร?
What is the number of my room?	**Hong phom beur arai?**	ห้องผมเบอร์อะไร?
PLease bring up my luggage.	**Proad yok krapaow khong-phom khuen ma**	โปรดยกกระเป๋า ของผมขึ้นมา

(b) With Hotel Attendants

Please let me have......	**Khaw ....**	ขอ...............
- an extra blanket	**- phâ hom- ik phuen**	- ผ้าห่มอีกผืน
- extra pillows	**- monn song-sarm bai**	- หมอนสองสามใบ
- a bloster (pillow)	**- monn-khâng**	- หมอนข้าง
- another bath towel	**- pha-shed-tua**	- ผ้าเช็ดตัว

- an ashtray	**- thi khia-bouri**	- ที่เขี่ยบุหรี่
- some toilet tissue	**- kradaad shamrah**	- กระดาษชำระ
- a pair of slippers	**- rong-thao fong-narm**	- รองเท้าฟองน้ำ
- some coat-hangers	**- thi khwaen seua**	- ที่แขวนเสื้อ
- chilled towels	**- phâ yenh**	- ผ้าเย็น
- a cake of soap	**- sabou**	- สบู่
- a pot of Chinese tea	**- shâ-chine nueng ka**	- ชาจีนหนึ่งกา
- an English newspaper	**- nangsue-phim phasa Angkrit**	- หนังสือพิมพ์ภาษาอังกฤษ
- some writing papers	**- kradaad khian chodmaai song-sarm phaen**	- กระดาษเขียนจดหมายสองสามแผ่น
- a few envelopes	**- sawng song-sarm sawng**	- ซองสองสามซอง
- a ballpoint pen	**- pakka louk-luen**	- ปากกาลูกลื่น
The sheets are not clean. They must be changed.	**Phâ pou thi nonn mai sa-ard, plian hai noi.**	ผ้าปูที่นอนไม่สะอาด - เปลี่ยนให้หน่อย
The air-conditioner doesn' t work.	**Khreuang tham-khwaam- yen mai tham ngarn.**	เครื่องทำความเย็นไม่ทำงาน
I want to have........	**Phom khaw ....**	ผมขอ............
- breakfast in this room	**- tharn a-harn shao nai hong ni.**	- ทานอาหารเช้าในห้องนี้

- dinner in the reception hall	**- a-harn yenh thi hong rab-khaek**	- อาหารเย็นที่ห้องรับแขก
Can you buy imported cigarettes for me?	**Sue bouri taang-prathed hai noi dai mai?**	ซื้อบุหรี่ต่างประเทศให้หน่อยได้ไหม?
Please wake me up at	**Karuna plouk phom hai tuen véla.......**	กรุณาปลุกผมให้ตื่นเวลา............
- five o ' clock (morning)	**- ti ha**	- ตีห้า
- five o ' clock (evening)	**- hâ mong yenh (sib-ched nalikâ)**	- ห้าโมงเย็น (สิบเจ็ดนาฬิกา)
I shall be out for about two hours.	**Phom chah pai khang-nawk sak song-sarm shua-mong.**	ผมจะไปข้างนอกสักสองสามชั่วโมง
Arrange my room comfortably.	**Shuai chad hong hai riap-roi.**	ช่วยจัดห้องให้เรียบร้อย

(c) Washing and Mending

Do you do any washing in the hotel?	**Nai rongraem mi borikarn sak-reed mai?**	ในโรงแรมมีบริการซักรีดไหม?
I want these clothes to be.....	**Shan tongkarn seua-pha laow ni.......**	ฉันต้องการเสื้อผ้าเหล่านี้.....
- dry-cleaned	**- sak haeng**	- ซักแห้ง
- washed	**- sak**	- ซัก
- ironed	**- reed hai riap**	- รีดให้เรียบ
I need them........	**Shan tongkarn ....**	ฉันต้องการ............
- today	**- wan-ni**	- วันนี้

- tonight, this evening	- **khuen ni, yenh ni**	- คืนนี้, เย็นนี้
- tomorrow	- **phroung ni**	- พรุ่งนี้
- before Saturday	- **konn Wan Saow**	- ก่อนวันเสาร์
:an you take out these stains?	**Aow roi-peuan ni awk dai mai?**	เอารอยเปื้อนนี้ออกได้ไหม?

'he laundry list

;athrobe	**Seua khlowm ab-narm**	เสื้อคลุม
;ath towel	**Phâ shed tua**	ผ้าเช็ดตัว
;louse(Short sleeves)	**Seua khaen sanh**	เสื้อแขนสั้น
;oy's shirt	**Shirt dek**	เชิ้ตเด็ก
)ressing gowns	**Seua gown phuying**	เสื้อกาวน์ผู้หญิง
ʌen's shirts	**Shirt phu-shaai**	เชิ้ตผู้ชาย
ɨandkerchiefs	**Phâ shed nâ**	ผ้าเช็ดหน้า
eans	**Jeans**	ยีนส์
ɹight gowns	**Seua-nonn phuying**	เสื้อนอนผู้หญิง
'ajamas	**Kangkeng nonn**	กางเกงนอน
'etticoats	**Kraprong shan nai**	กางโปรงชั้นใน
;horts	**Kangkeng khâ sanh**	กางเกงขาสั้น
;kirts	**Kraprong**	กระโปรง
;ocks, Stockings	**Thoung-thao sanh, Thoung-nong**	ถุงเท้าสั้น ถุงน่อง
'rousers	**Kangkeng khâ-yao**	กางเกงขายาว

(d) Checking Out

I am leaving tomorrow morning after breakfast.	**Phom chah pai meua tharn a-harn shao laew.**	ผมจะไปเมื่อทานอาหารเช้าแล้ว
May I see the manager?	**Phom khaw phob phu chad karn?**	ผมขอพบผู้จัดการ?
This bill is not correct.	**Bill ni yang mai thouk tong.**	บิลนี้ยังไม่ถูกต้อง
I want to have time to check this.	**Phom khaw véla truad sak noi.**	ผมขอเวลาตรวจสักหน่อย
I want to pay now.	**Phom chah shamrah bill diao-ni.**	ผมจะชำระบิลเดี๋ยวนี้
Do you accept traveler's checks?	**Khun rab shek dern-thaang (traveler's checks) mai?**	คุณรับเช็คเดินทางไหม?
Get my luggage down from my room.	**Karuna yok krapaow seua-phâ phom long ma chaak hong.**	กรุณายกกระเป๋าเสื้อผ้าผมลงมาจากห้อง
Have you got everything?	**Khun yok khawng awk ma mod laew rue?**	คุณยกของออกมาหมดแล้วหรือ?
Please call a taxi for me.	**Karuna riak taxi hai phom duai.**	กรุณาเรียกแท็กซี่ให้ผมด้วย
What is the taxi fare to the railway station?	**Kha rot taxi pai Sathani rot-fai thao-rai?**	ค่ารถแท็กซี่ไปสถานีรถไฟเท่าไร?
Here is the key for my room.	**Ni — kunchae hong phom.**	นี่---กุญแจห้องผม

EATING AND DRINKING

There are many types of eating and drinking places in Thailand. hai people take a critical interest in food—in its preparation as ell as its consumption. So it is not surprising that Bangkok has an normous number of restaurants and foodshops. Bangkok's restau-ants are not all Thai, Chinese or Indian. As a matter of fact you can aste scores of other foods like German, Hungarian, Japanese, Ko-ean, Mexican, Vietnamese, Indonesian and Italian. Other places pecialize in French cuisine and, of course, there are English restau-ants where the roast beef is thick and rare. Indeed the wide range f food available in Bangkok could delight the most sophisticated picure or gourmet.

a) Cooking and Restaurant Terms

ppetizers; hors d'oeuvres	**Kap-klaem**	กับแกล้ม
aked	**Ob**	อบ
arbecued	**Yaang**	ย่าง
eef(roast)	**Neua ob**	เนื้ออบ

Boiled	**Tomh**	ต้ม
Bone stock	**Narm tom kradouk**	น้ำต้มกระดูก
Breadcrumbs	**Khanompang ponh**	ขนมปังป่น
Broiled	**Yang, Ping,**	ย่าง, ปิ้ง
Brown sauce	**Narm-daeng**	น้ำแดง
Bouillon or consomme	**Soup sai**	ซุปใส
Buttered	**Tha-neui, sai-neui**	ทาเนย, ใส่เนย
Cafe au lait	**Kafae sai nom**	กาแฟใส่นม
Cafe noir	**Kafae damh**	กาแฟดำ
Chicken	**Kai**	ไก่
Chicken broth	**Narm-soup kai**	น้ำซุปไก่
Chilled or iced tea	**Shae-yenh**	แช่เย็น
Chili sauce	**Sauce phrik**	ซอสพริก
Chili vinegar	**Phrik narm-somh**	พริกน้ำส้ม
Chop	**Sab**	สับ
Chopped or finely ground	**Sab la-iat**	สับละเอียด
Chopped meat	**Neua-sab**	เนื้อสับ
Crispy fried	**Thawd kropp-kropp**	ทอดกรอบ ๆ
Cold towel	**Pha yenh**	ผ้าเย็น
Cordials	**Narm phola-mai**	น้ำผลไม้
Crab	**Pou**	ปู
Curry stuffs	**Khreuang kaeng**	เครื่องแกง
Coconut milk	**Kathih**	กะทิ
Dark beer	**Beer damh**	เบียร์ดำ
Deep fried	**Thawd narm-manh maak-maak**	ทอดน้ำมันมาก ๆ
Desserts	**Khawng-waan**	ของหวาน

arthenware casseroles	**Maw-din**	หม้อดิน
gg	**Khai**	ไข่
ggs (hard-cooked)	**Khai tom-souk**	ไข่ต้มสุก
ggs (half-boiled)	**Khai luak**	ไข่ลวก
ggs (fried)	**Khai thawd**	ไข่ทอด
ggs (steamed)	**Khai toun**	ไข่ตุ๋น
ggs (stuffed)	**Khai yat sai**	ไข่ยัดไส้
ishballs	**Louk-shin pla**	ลูกชิ้นปลา
ish cakes	**Thawd-manh pla**	ทอดมันปลา
ruit compote	**Phola-mai loi-kaew**	ผลไม้ลอยแก้ว
rench dressing	**Narm-salad sai**	น้ำสลัดใส
rench toast	**Khanompang shoup khai thawd**	ขนมปังชุบไข่ทอด
ish sauce	**Narm pla**	น้ำปลา
ritter	**Shoup-paeng thawd**	ชุบแป้งทอด
ry	**Phad; Thawd**	ผัด, ทอด
Glutinous rice balls	**Khao-niao panh**	ข้าวเหนียวปั้น
Glutinous rice toast	**Khao-niao ping**	ข้าวเหนียวปิ้ง
Gravy	**Narm sauce; Narm daeng**	น้ำซอส, น้ำแดง
Grill	**Yaang**	ย่าง
Ground beef	**Neua-bod; Sab**	เนื้อบด, สับ
Heating the fat	**Khiao narm-manh**	เคี่ยวน้ำมัน
Home-style cooked food (refers to any country-style dish)	**A-harn baep phuen-baan**	อาหารแบบพื้นบ้าน
Hot food	**A-harn proung mai-mai**	อาหารปรุงใหม่ ๆ

Instant egg noodles (precooked noodles)	**Bah-mi samret roop**	บะหมี่สำเร็จรูป
Lobster	**Koung**	กุ้ง
Mayonnaise dressing	**Narm-salad khon**	น้ำสลัดข้น
Margarine	**Margarine; Neui-thiam**	มาร์การีน, เนยเทียม
Meat balls	**Neua konn; Louk-shin neua**	เนื้อก้อน, ลูกชิ้นเนื้อ
Meat stock	**Narm soup neua**	น้ำซุปเนื้อ
Medium done (meats)	**Souk phaw-di phaw-di**	สุกพอดี ๆ
Minced finely	**Sab; Bod la-iat**	สับ, บดละเอียด
Mixed vegetable prickles	**Si-sek shaai**	ซีเซ็กฉ่าย
Milk	**Nomh**	นม
Monosodium glutamate	**Phong shu-rot**	ผงชูรส
Mulligatawny	**Soup khaek**	ซุปแขก
Mustard sauce	**Mustart**	มัสตาร์ด
Narrow rice-noodles	**Kwaitiao senh-lek**	ก๋วยเตี๋ยวเส้นเล็ก
Noodles	**Sen-mi**	เส้นหมี่
Rice noodles	**Sen-mi mai-fan**	เส้นหมี่ไหมฝัน
Egg noodles	**Sen bah-mi**	เส้นบะหมี่
Transparent noodles	**Voun-senh**	วุ้นเส้น
Oyster fritters	**Hoi thawd**	หอยทอด
Oyster sauce	**Narm-manh hoi**	น้ำมันหอย
Paratas(Indian)	**Roti**	โรตี
Pilau	**Khao-mok**	ข้าวหมก
Pork balls	**Louk-shin mou**	ลูกชิ้นหมู
Pork bone soup	**Narm tom kradouk mou**	น้ำต้มกระดูกหมู

Pork skin	**Nang mou**	หนังหมู
Potato chips	**Manh-thawd**	มันทอด
Potatoes(mashed)	**Manh-bod**	มันบด
Reheated	**Oun hai ronn**	อุ่นให้ร้อน
Rice	**Khao**	ข้าว
Cooked rice	**Khao souk**	ข้าวสุก
Rice soup	**Khao tomh**	ข้าวต้ม
Rice water	**Narm-khao**	น้ำข้าว
Rice vermicelli	**Sen-khanom chine**	เส้นขนมจีน
Roast	**Ob**	อบ
Roasted on a skewer	**Ping bonh takraeng**	ปิ้งบนตะแกรง
Roast crispy pork	**Mou yaang**	หมูย่าง
Salad dressing	**Narm salad**	น้ำสลัด
Salted	**Mak kleua; Shae kleua**	หมักเกลือ, แช่เกลือ
Saute	**Thawd narm-manh noi-noi**	ทอดน้ำมันน้อย ๆ
Scrambled	**Kuan**	กวน
Seasoning	**Khluk-khlow hai dai rot**	คลุกเคล้าให้ได้รส
Shrimp	**Koung-lek**	กุ้ง (เล็ก)
Smoked	**Romh-kwan**	รมควัน
Soup meats	**Narm-soup neua**	น้ำซุปเนื้อ
Spirits	**Sura, lao**	สุรา, เหล้า
Strainers	**Kra-shonn**	กระชอน
Stuffing	**Yat-sai**	ยัดไส้
Slightly undercooked	**Dip pai-noi**	ดิบไปหน่อย
Slice of bread and butter	**Khanompang kap neui**	ขนมปังกับเนย
Spattering	**Prah or Phrom**	ประหรือพรม
Steaming	**Toun**	ตุ๋น

Thai curry	**Kaeng-phed Thai**	แกงเผ็ดไทย
Thai food	**A-harn Thai**	อาหารไทย
Tomato juice	**Narm makheua thed**	น้ำมะเขือเทศ
Tomato sauce	**Sauce Makheua thed**	ซอสมะเขือเทศ
Underdone	**Yang mai souk**	ยังไม่สุก
Vegetable stock	**Narm tom phak**	น้ำต้มผัก
Worcestershire sauce	**Sauce farang**	ซอสฝรั่ง
Well-done	**Souk di; Kamlang di**	สุกดี, กำลังดี
White of eggs	**Khai khao**	ไข่ขาว
White sauce	**Sauce khao**	ซอสขาว
Yolk of eggs	**Khai daeng**	ไข่แดง
Yellow egg noodles	**Senh-mi leuang**	เส้นหมี่เหลือง

(b) At a Restaurant

Can you recommend a good restaurant, not too expensive?	**Rouchak raan-aharn di-di rakha mai phaeng thi-nai baang?**	รู้จักร้านอาหารดี ๆ ราคาไม่แพงที่ไหนบ้าง?
I am hungry.	**Phom hiew.**	ผมหิว
I am thirsty.	**Phom hiew-narm.**	ผมหิวน้ำ
I want to eat	**Phom tongkarn tharn....**	ผมต้องการทาน....
- Thai food	**- a-harn Thai**	- อาหารไทย
- Chinese food	**- a-harn Chine**	- อาหารจีน
Can you take me to a - restaurant serving - Muslim food?	**Pha phom pai raan - aharn Muslim dai-mai?**	พาผมไปร้านอาหาร - มุสลิมได้ไหม?
Do you have a menu in English?	**Mi menu aharn phasa Angkrit mai?**	มีเมนูอาหารภาษาอังกฤษไหม

Vhat is today's special?	**Wan-ni mi arai phised?**	วันนี้มีอะไรพิเศษ?
)o you have a private dining room?	**Mi hong tharn-aharn samrab khrop-khrua mai?**	มีห้องทานอาหารสำหรับครอบครัวไหม?
am expecting some friends.	**Phom kamlang raw pheuan.**	ผมกำลังรอเพื่อน
Can we dine in this room?	**Raow tharn kan nai hong-ni dai-mai?**	เราทานกันในห้องนี้ได้ไหม?
want a large table to seat six persons.	**Phom khaw toh-yai nang-dai hok khon.**	ผมขอโต๊ะใหญ่นั่งได้หกคน
\ table for two, please.	**Toh samrab song khon.**	โต๊ะสำหรับสองคน
That table will be fine.	**Toh nanh khaw-di.**	โต๊ะนั้นก็ดี
Vill you reserve this table for me?	**Khun sam-rong toh-ni wai hai phom dai-mai?**	คุณสำรองโต๊ะนี้ไว้ให้ผมได้ไหม?
Ve shall arrive at about 7:30 p.m.	**Raow chah-ma thueng thi-ni pramarn thoum-khrueng.**	เราจะมาถึงที่นี่ประมาณทุ่มครึ่ง
don't know what to order.	**Phom mai-saab chah sang arai-di.**	ผมไม่ทราบจะสั่งอะไรดี
What would you suggest?	**Khun wa chah sang arai di?**	คุณว่าจะสั่งอะไรดี?
The food must not be too sweet.	**A-harn tong mai waan-chad.**	อาหารต้องไม่หวานจัด
The food must not be very hot.	**A-harn tong mai phed maak.**	อาหารต้องไม่เผ็ดมาก

Please serve us quickly, we are in hurry.	**Karuna reep-reep noi, phom mi thurah tong klab reow.**	กรุณารีบ ๆ หน่อย ผมมีธุระต้องกลับเร็ว
Please bring me	**Karuna aow ....**	กรุณาเอา.........
- a large bottle of beer	**- beer-yai nueng khouad**	- เบียร์ใหญ่หนึ่งขวด
- whisky and soda	**- Whiskey lae soda**	- วิกี้และโซดา
- a small bottle of stout	**- beer-damh lek**	- เบียร์ดำเล็ก
- a peg of brandy	**- brandy sak nueng peg**	- บรั่นดีสักหนึ่งเป๊ก
- a plate of French-fried potatoes	**- manh-farang thawd nueng chaan**	- มันฝรั่งทอดหนึ่งจาน
- a jug of crushed ice	**- narm-khaeng thoup nueng yeuak**	- น้ำแข็งทุบหนึ่งเหยือก
Can we have ....?	**Khaw ....?**	ขอ...........?
- crab salad	**- salad pou thale**	- สลัดปูทะเล
- stuffed cabbage	**- kalampli sawd-sai**	- กะหล่ำปลีสอดไส้
- fried rice	**- khao-phad**	- ข้าวผัด
- chicken with bean sprouts	**- kai phad thua-ngork**	- ไก่ผัดถั่วงอก
- fried pork with ginger	**- mou-phad khing**	- หมูผัดขิง
- stuffed omelet	**- khai sawd-sai**	- ไข่สอดไส้
- fried beef with oyster sauce	**- neua-phad narm-manh hoi**	- เนื้อผัดน้ำมันหอย
- steamed sole	**- pla nueng**	- ปลานึ่ง
- fish in tomato sauce	**- pla raad sauce makheua-thed**	- ปลาราดซอสมะเขือเทศ

- chicken cashew nuts	- **kai-phad mamuang himapharn**	- ไก่ผัดมะม่วงหิมพานต์
- sweet and sour pork	- **mou-phad priao-waan**	- หมูผัดเปรี้ยวหวาน
- Chinese barbecued pork(char-siew)	- **mou-daeng**	- หมูแดง
- beef curry	- **phanaeng neua**	- พะแนงเนื้อ
- mixed Chinese vegetable soup	- **kaeng-chued phak**	- แกงจืดผัก
- minced pork omelet	- **khai-chiao mou-sab**	- ไข่เจียวหมูสับ
'd like to change my order.	**Phom khaw plian a-harn thi sang.**	ผมขอเปลี่ยนอาหารที่สั่ง
Vhat vegetables do you have?	**Khun mi phak a-rai bang?**	คุณมีผักอะไรบ้าง?
ried chicken is my favorite.	**Phom shobb kai-thawd maak.**	ผมชอบไก่ทอดมาก
3ring me	**Aow ....**	เอา...............
- a plate of plain rice	- **khao-plao nueng chaan**	- ข้าวเปล่าหนึ่งจาน
- another pair of fork & spoon	- **shonn-somm ik nueng khou**	- ช้อนส้อมอีกหนึ่งคู่
- another large plate	- **chaan-yai ik bai**	- จานใหญ่อีกใบ
- salt and pepper	- **phrik-thai kleua**	- พริกไทยเกลือ
- tomato ketchup	- **sauce makheua thed**	- ซอสมะเขือเทศ

- Sriraja chili sauce	**- sauce-phrik srirasha**	- ซอสพริกศรีราชา
- cold drinking water	**- narm-yen**	- น้ำเย็น
- a pot of Chinese tea	**- sha-chine nueng ka**	- ชาจีนหนึ่งกา
- an ash tray	**- thi khia-bouri**	- ที่เขี่ยบุหรี่
- paper napkins	**- kradaad shed-paak**	- กระดาษเช็ดปาก
- some toothpicks	**- mai chim-fanh**	- ไม้จิ้มฟัน
- chilled face towel	**- pha-yenh**	- ผ้าเย็น
- Chinese lychees in syrup	**- linchi krapong**	- ลิ้นจี่กระป๋อง
- some imported cigarettes	**- bouri taang prathed**	- บุหรี่ต่างประเทศ
I don't want to eat anything more.	**Phom mai tharn a-rai ik laew.**	ผมไม่ทานอะไรอีกแล้ว
May I have the bill, please?	**Proad khid ngoen duai?**	โปรดคิดเงินด้วย?
Is service included?	**Ruam kha borikarn duai rue-plao?**	รวมค่าบริการด้วยหรือเปล่า?
Please give me a receipt.	**Khaw bai-set.**	ขอใบเสร็จ
That was a very good meal, we enjoyed that.	**A-harn aroi di.**	อาหารอร่อยดี
We'll come again some time.	**Mi o-kaad raow chah-ma ik.**	มีโอกาสเราจะมาอีก

c) Breakfast at the Hotel

Most of the larger hotels in Bangkok provide a breakfast of the nglish or American type. However, the smaller upcountry hotels nay provide you with any of the following:

ea/Coffee	**Nam-sha/Kafae**	น้ำชา, กาแฟ
resh milk	**Nom sod**	นมสด
Half-boiled eggs	**Khai luak**	ไข่ลวก
Hard-boiled eggs	**Khai tom souk**	ไข่ต้มสุก
ried eggs/Fried bacon	**Khai dao/Mou bacon**	ไข่ดาว, หมูเบคอน
ried eggs and sausages	**Khai-dao sai-krawk**	ไข่ดาวไส้กรอก
Ham and eggs	**Mou haem khai-dao**	หมูแฮมไข่ดาว
ried pork and eggs	**Khai-dao mou thawd**	ไข่ดาวหมูทอด
lain omelet	**Khai chiao**	ไข่เจียว
tuffed omelet	**Khai sawd-sai**	ไข่สอดไส้
uttered toast	**Khanompang tha neui**	ขนมปังทาเนย
read and jam	**Khanompang tha jam**	ขนมปังทาแยม
ried rice	**Khao-phad**	ข้าวผัด
hinese vegetable soup	**Kaeng-chued phak**	แกงจืดผัก
hinese porridge	**Choke**	โจ๊ก
hinese doughnuts	**Pa-thong-ko**	ปาท่องโก๋
hai curry and rice	**Khao raad-kaeng**	ข้าวราดแกง
lease let me have	**Khaw........**	ขอ...............
- hot tea with milk	**- Sha ronn sai nom**	- ชาร้อนใส่นม
- hot coffee with milk	**- Kafae ronn sai nom**	- กาแฟร้อนใส่นม

- hot tea without milk or sugar	**- Sha ronn mai-sai nom, namtarn**	- ชาร้อนไม่ใส่นม, น้ำตาล
- strong hot coffee without milk or sugar	**- Kafae ronn kae-kae mai-sai nom lae namtarn**	- กาแฟร้อนแก่ ๆ ไม่ใส่นม และน้ำตาล
- iced coffee with milk	**- Kafae yen sai nom**	- กาแฟเย็นใส่นม
- iced tea with milk	**- Sha yen sai nom**	- ชาเย็นใส่นม
- black coffee with crushed ice	**- Owe-liang, kafae dam-yen.**	- โอเลี้ยง, กาแฟดำเย็น
- black tea with crushed ice	**- Sha dam yen**	- ชาดำเย็น
- a glass of water	**- Narm nueng-kaew**	- น้ำหนึ่งแก้ว
- a glass of hot water	**- Narm ronn**	- น้ำร้อน
- a glass of crushed ice	**- Narm-khaeng plao, narm-khaeng haeng mai-sai narm**	- น้ำแข็งเปล่า, - น้ำแข็งแห้งไม่ใส่น้ำ
- a pot of Chinese tea	**- Sha chine nueng ka**	- ชาจีนหนึ่งกา
- a glass of Chinese tea with some crushed ice	**- Narm-khaeng sai narm-sha**	- น้ำแข็งใส่น้ำชา
- another cup, please	**- Ik thuai nueng**	- อีกถ้วยหนึ่ง
- another glass, please	**- Ik kaew nueng**	- อีกแก้วหนึ่ง
- another bottle, please	**- Ik khouad nueng**	- อีกขวดหนึ่ง

don't want to eat anything more.	**Phom tharn a- rai mai dai ik laew.**	ผมทานอะไรไม่ได้อีกแล้ว
enjoy the food very much.	**Kap-khao a-roi di.**	กับข้าวอร่อยดี

'd) Common Thai Dishes

Thai food has a reputation for being hot and spicy, and while ıis is true of a number of dishes, Thai cuisine has something to suit veryone's taste. Visitors in Thailand should try to get to know Thai ɔod. It's good and is worthy of greater recognition among Asian uisines.

Rice, of course, is the main food of the nation. Thailand's rice vill spoil your taste for all other types of rice. It is more fragrant, of better consistency, tastier, and each grain is long and pure white.

Beef or chicken curry, fried crispy noodles, roast or barbecued hicken, fried prawns, and barbecued beef—Thai style—are among ıe many popular dishes for Thai and Europeans alike. A Thai meal ; usually rounded off with either **khanom** ขนม (sweetmeats) or some f the delicious Thai fruit. The taste of Thai **khanom** may range from ıaple syrup to mixed cream; some look like jelly, cake, pudding or ustard. The outstanding feature of all Thai khanom is that coconut r rice in one form or another is almost always an ingredient.

Although the leading hotels and restaurants in Bangkok offer osmopolitan menus, printed in English as well as in Thai, but with ıe following handy list of common Thai foods, you can go into any 'hai restaurant or roadside shops and order exactly the food you vant. More list of Thai food could be found in the book "*Thai Hawker 'ood.*"

Main dishes

Chinese Chicken Rice	**Khao mun kai**	ข้าวมันไก่
Red Roast Pork	**Moo daeng**	หมูแดง
Duck in Red Soy Sauce	**Ped paloh**	เป็ดพะโล้
Giblet Soup	**Tue huan**	ตือฮวน
Thick Rice Soup (Congee)	**Joak**	โจ๊ก
Crispy Fish in Chillies	**Yum pla duk foo**	ยำปลาดุกฟู
Spicy Ground Beef	**Larb nua**	ลาบเนื้อ
Spicy Roast Beef Slices	**Nam tok**	น้ำตก
Thai Style Sukiyaki	**Sukiyaki**	ส้มตำ
Fried Rice	**Khao phad**	ข้าวผัด
Noodles on the boat	**Kuay tiao rua**	ก๋วยเตี๋ยวเรือ
Barbecued Chicken/ Pork	**Kai yang/moo yang**	ไก่ย่าง - หมูย่าง
Red-stewed Pork Legs	**Kha moo paloh**	ขาหมูพะโล้
Chinese leaf-wrapped Glutinous Rice	**Bah jang**	บ๊ะจ่าง
Shark's Fin Soup	**Hoo pla chalam**	หูปลาฉลาม
Fried Mussels in Batter	**Hoy thod**	หอยทอด
Fried Crab in Curry Sauce	**Pu phad pong kari**	ปูผัดผงกะหรี่

Fish Curry Cake in Banana Cup	**Hoh mok pla**	ห่อหมกปลา
Coconut Chicken Curry	**Kaeng kai**	แกงไก่
Beef/Chicken Curry with Peanuts	**Masaman nua/kai**	มัสมั่น เนื้อ/ไก่
Pork Rind Soup	**Kapoh pla**	กระเพาะปลา
Fried Rice with Shrimp Paste	**Khao kluk kapi**	ข้าวคลุกกะปิ
Boiled Cockles	**Hoy kraeng luak**	หอยแครงลวก
Boiled Rice with Delicacies	**Khaotom kui**	ข้าวต้มกุ๊ย
Fried Crab	**Pu ja**	ปูจ๋า
Fried Stuffed Chicken Wings	**Pik kai sod sai thot**	ปีกไก่สอดไส้ทอด
Fried Pork Meatballs	**Mu pan kon thot**	หมูปั้นก้อนทอด
Fried Sun-Dried Beef	**Neua daet diao**	เนื้อแดดเดียว
Stir-Fried Sweet and Sour Pork	**Phat mu priao wan**	ผัดหมูเปรี้ยวหวาน
Stir-Fried Stuffed Squid	**Phat pla meuk yat sai**	ผัดปลาหมึกยัดไส้
Stir-Fried Beef in Oyster Sauce	**Phat neua namman hoi**	ผัดเนื้อน้ำมันหอย
Stir-Fried Prawns in Tamarind Sauce	**Khung phat som makham piak**	กุ้งผัดส้มมะขามเปียก
Garlic Prawn	**Kung kra thiam**	กุ้งกระเทียม
Stir-Fried Chicken with Cashew Nut	**Phat kai kap met mamuang himaphan**	ผัดไก่กับเม็ดมะม่วงหินพานต์

Stir-Fried Kale in Oyster Sauce	**Phat kha-na namman hoi**	ผัดเนื้อน้ำมันหอย
Stir-Fried Crab in Curry Sauce	**Pu phat phong kari**	ปูผัดผงกะหรี่
Spicy Stir-Fried Chicken	**Phat khi mao kai**	ผัดขี้เมาไก่
Baked Stuffed Duck	**Pet thot sot sai**	เป็ดทอดสอดไส้
Braised Chicken	**Kai op nam daeng**	ไก่อบน้ำแดง
Crispy Baked Duck	**Pet op krop**	เป็ดอบกรอบ
Thai-Style Barbecued Chicken	**Kai yang**	ไก่ย่าง
Broiled Lobster in Tamarind Sauce	**Khung yang sot makham piak**	กุ้งย่างซอสมะขามเปียก
Barbecued Spareribs	**Si-khrong mu yang**	ซี่โครงหมูย่าง
Boiled Fresh Ham with the Five Spices	**Kha mu tom phalo**	ขาหมูต้มพะโล้
Baked Rock Cod in Tomato Sauce	**Pla kao op sot ma-kheua thet**	ปลาเก๋าอบซอสมะเขือเทศ
Broiled Tunny with Soy Sauce	**Pha o yang si iu**	ปลาโอย่างซีอิ๊ว
Stir- Fried Pork with Red Curry Paste	**Phat phet mu**	ผัดเผ็ดหมู
Savory Stir-Fried Chicken	**Phat phrik khing kai**	ผัดพริกขิงไก่
Savory Stir-Fried Pork with Yard-long Beans	**Phat phrik khing mu kap thua fak yao**	ผัดพริกขิงหมูกับถั่วฝักยาว

Sour and Spicy Prawn Soup	**Tom yam kung**	ต้มยำกุ้ง
Sour and Spicy Chicken Soup	**Tom yam kai**	ต้มยำไก่
Fish-Flavored Vegetable Soup	**Kaeng liang**	แกงเลียง
Prawns Steamed with Soy Sauce	**Kung neung si iu**	กุ้งนึ่งซีอิ๊ว
Sea Perch Steamed in Lime Sauce	**Pla kaphong khao neung manao**	ปลากะพงขาวนึ่งมะนาว
Beaten Egg Steamed with Pork	**Khai tun**	ไข่ตุ๋น
Thai Beef Green Curry	**Kaeng khiao wan neua**	แกงเขียวหวานเนื้อ
Beef Curried in Sweet Peanut Suace	**Pha-naeng neua**	พะแนงเนื้อ
Stuffed Chicken Wings in Pha-naeng Suace	**Pik kai sot sai pha-naeng**	ปีกไก่สอดไส้พะแนง
Fish Curry	**Chuchi pla thu sot**	ฉู่ฉี่ปลาทูสด
Red Curry of Duck	**Kaeng phet pet yang**	แกงเผ็ดเป็ดย่าง
Chicken in Red Curry with Bamboo Shoots	**Kaeng phet kai sai no mai**	แกงเขียวหวานเนื้อ
Curried Prawns	**Kaeng ka-ri kung**	พะแนงเนื้อ
Steamed Curried Fish, Chicken, or Pork	**Ho mok pla rue kai reu mu**	ห่อหมกปลาหรือไก่ หรือหมู
Red Curry of Mushrooms	**Khang phet het**	แกงเผ็ดเห็ด

Vermicell and Fish Sauce	**Khanom jin nam ya**	ขนมจีนน้ำยา
Vermicell and Prawn Sauce	**Khanom jin nam phrik**	ขนมจีนน้ำพริก
Fried Rice with Pork, Shrimp and Egg	**Khao phat mu kung sai khai**	ข้าวผัดหมู กุ้ง ใส่ไข่
Fried Rice and Shrimp paste	**Khao kluk kapi**	ข้าวคลุกกะปิ
Chinese Sausage Steamed in Rice	**Khao op kun chiang**	ข้าวอบกุนเชียง
Chicken in Sauce on Rice	**Khao rat na kai**	ข้าวราดหน้าไก่

Noodles

Fried Noodles Thai Style	**Phat thai sai khai**	ผัดไทยใส่ไข่
Stir-Fried Rice Noodles and Prawns	**Sen jan phat kung**	เส้นจันทร์ผัดกุ้ง
Fishball Noodles	**Kuay-tiao luk-chin pla**	ก๋วยเตี๋ยวลูกชิ้นปลา
Chicken Noodles	**Kuay-tiao kai**	ก๋วยเตี๋ยวไก่
Meatball Noodles	**Kuay-tiao luk-chin nua**	ก๋วยเตี๋ยวลูกชิ้นเนื้อ
Duck Noodles	**Kuay-tiao ped**	ก๋วยเตี๋ยวเป็ด
Noodles in Red Soup	**Yen tao fo**	เย็นตาโฟ
Noodles with Thick Vegetable Gravy	**Kuay-tiao rad na**	ก๋วยเตี๋ยวราดหน้า
Pan-Fried Noodles in Red Soy Sauce	**Kyua-tiao phad si iew**	ก๋วยเตี๋ยวผัดซีอิ๊ว

Noodle Soup with Boiled Giblets	**Kuay jub**	ก๋วยจั๊บ
Egg Noodle Soup	**Bah mee nam**	บะหมี่น้ำ
Steamed Noodle Rolls	**Kuay-tiao rod**	ก๋วยเตี๋ยวหลอด
Thai Fried Noodles	**Phad thai**	ผัดไทย
Crispy Noodles	**Mee krob**	หมี่กรอบ
Red Noodles soaked in Coconut Milk	**Mee kati**	หมี่กระทิ

Snack

Flour Pancake Rolls	**Poh piah sod**	ปอเปี๊ยะสด
Papaya Salad	**Som tam**	ส้มตำ
Bamboo Shoot Salad	**Sup nor mai**	ซุปหน่อไม้
Satay	**Sateh**	สเต๊ก
Roast Eggs	**Khai ping**	ไข่ปิ้ง
Thai Sausages	**Sai krok**	ไส้กรอก
Grilled Dry Squid	**Pla muk ping**	ปลาหมึกปิ้ง
Grilled Meat Balls	**Luk chin ping**	ลูกชิ้นปิ้ง
Roasted Sweet Potatoes	**Mun ping**	มันปิ้ง
Shredded Coconut Pudding	**Khanom paeng jee**	ขนมแป้งจี่
Pork Tapioca Balls	**Sakoo sai moo**	สาคูไส้หมู
Pork wrapped in Rice Pancakes	**Khao kriab pak moh**	ข้าวเกรียบปากหม้อ
Stuffed Vegetable in	**Khanom kui chai**	ขนมกุ้ยช่าย

Pudding		
Chinese dumpling	**Khanom jeeb**	ขนมจีบ
Chinese Steamed Buns	**Salapao**	ซาลาเปา
Steamed Nuts	**Tua tom**	ถั่วต้ม
Fried Vegetable Pudding	**Khanom kui chai thod**	ขนมกุ้ยช่ายทอด
Spring Rolls	**Poh piah thod**	ปอเปี๊ยะทอด
Fried Wonton	**Kiew thod**	เกี๊ยวทอด
Fried Fish Cakes	**Thod mun pla**	ทอดมันปลา
Curry Puffs	**Kari pud**	กะหรี่ปั๊ป
Fried Toast with Ground Pork/ Shrimp	**Khanom pung na mou/kung**	ขนมปังหน้าหมู/กุ้ง
Deep-fried Dough Sticks	**Pa thong koh**	ปลาท่องโก๋
Fried Nut	**Tua thod**	ถั่วทอด
Hot and Spicy Salad	**Yum**	ยำ
Crispy Coconut and Tidbits	**Miang khum**	เมี่ยงคำ
Fresh Fruits	**Pol-mai sod**	ผลไม้สด
Preserved Fruits	**Pol-mai dong**	ผมไม้ดอง
Thai Cookies	**Khanom ping**	ขนมผิง
Chinese Cakes with Filling	**Khanom piah**	ขนมเปี๊ยะ
Fried Potcrust and Dip	**Khao tang na tang**	ข้าวตังหน้าตั้ง
Fried Canapes with	**Khanom pang na kung**	ขนมปังหน้ากุ้งโรยงา

Prawn Spread	**rio nga**	
Fried Canapes with Pork Spread	**Khanom pang na mu**	ขนมปังหน้าหมู
Egg Rolls	**Po-pia thot**	ปอเปี๊ยะทอด
Crispy Fried Noodles	**Mi krop**	หมี่กรอบ
Fried Sweet Corn Patties	**Thot man khao poht**	ปอเปี๊ยะทอด

Dessert

Crispy Pancakes with Fillings	**Khanom buang**	ขนมเบื้อง
Indian Fried Pasta	**Roti**	โรตี
Tiny Pancakes with Fillings	**Khanom tokyo**	ขนมโตเกียว
Grilled Bananas	**Kluay ping**	กล้วยปิ้ง
Coconut Pudding	**Khanom krok**	ขนมครก
Roasted Sticky Rice in Banana Leaves	**Khao niew ping**	ข้าวเหนียวปิ้ง
Chinese Waffles & Poorman's Pancakes	**Khanom rang pung & khanom tang taek**	ขนมรังผึ้ง ขนมถังแตก
Pumpkin Custard	**Sangkaya fuk thong**	สังขยาฟักทอง
Steamed banana Cakes in Leaves	**Khanom kluay**	ขนมกล้วย
Steamed Sticky Rice in Banana Leaves	**Khao tom mud**	ข้าวต้มมัด
Fried Dough Balls	**Khanom khai hong**	ขนมไข่หงส์

Fried Bananas	**Kluay kaek**	กล้วยแขก
Fried Potato Balls	**Khai nok kratha**	ไข่นกกระทา
Gloden Threads/Egg Cakes	**Foi thong, thong yip, thong yod**	ฝอยทอง, ทองหยิบ, ทองหยอด
Tapioca Strings in Coconut Syrup	**Khanom pakrim kai tao**	ขนมปลากิมไข่เต่า
Sticky Rice with Different Toppings	**Khao niew moon**	ข้าวเหนียวมูล
Boiled Bananas in Coconut Syrup	**Kluay buad chee**	กล้วยบวชชี
Flower-shaped Cookies	**Khanom dok lamduan**	ขนมดอกลำดวน
Desserts on the Wheel	**Rod khen/khanom wann**	รถเข็นขนมหวาน
Flour-dipped Chestnuts in Syrup	**Tub tim krob**	ทับทิมกรอบ
Crushed-iced Sweets	**Nam kaeng sai**	น้ำแข็งใส
Black jelly	**Chao kuay**	เฉาก๊วย
Singapore Green Strings	**Lod chong Singapore**	ลอดช่องสิงคโปร์
Gingko Nut Soup	**Pae kuay**	แปะก๊วย
Sweet Silk Threads with Flour Pancakes	**Roti sai mai**	โรตีสายไหม
Banana in Syrup	**Kluay chuam**	กล้วยเชื่อม
Tapioca Balls in Coconut Syrup	**Bua loy**	บัวลอย
Mock Miniature Fruit	**Luk chub**	ลูกชุบ
Bean-Filled Crescents	**Khanom tua paeb**	ขนมถั่วแปบ

Chewy Strings	**Khanom niew**	ขนมเหนียว
Crispy Rolls	**Thong muan**	ทองม้วน
Coconut Pudding in Banana Leaf Cups	**Tako**	ตะโก้
Layer Cake	**Khanom chan**	ขนมชั้น
Mungbeans in Syrup	**Thua khiao tom nam tan**	ถั่วเขียวต้มน้ำตาล
Pumpkin in Coconut Cream	**Fak thong kaeng buat**	ฟักทองแกงบวด
Corn Pudding with Coconut Cream	**Khao phot piak**	ข้าวโพดเปียก
Bananas in Coconut Cream	**Kluai buat chi**	กล้วยบวชชี
Black Beans in Coconut Cream	**Thua dam kaeng buat**	ถั่วดำแกงบวด
Mungbean Balls in Coconut Cream	**Khanom bua loi thua khiao**	ขนมบัวลอยถั่วเขียว
Mungbean Strands in Coconut Syrup	**Lot chong sinkhapo**	ลอดช่องสิงคโปร์
Mock Pomegranate Seeds	**Thabthim grob**	ทับทิมกรอบ
Sweet Tapica with Coconut Custard	**Ta-ko sa-khu**	ตะโก้สาคู
Taro Coconut Custard	**Khanom mo kaeng pheuak**	ขนมหม้อแกงเผือก
Sweet Potatoes in Syrup	**Man cheuam**	มันเชื่อม
Sweet Potatoes in Syrup	**Man tom nam tan**	มันต้มน้ำตาล
Coconut Milk Ice Cream	**Aisa-khrim ka-thi -sod**	ไอศกรีมกะทิสด

Beverage

Sugar-cane Water	**Nam oy**	น้ำอ้อย
Longan Juice	**Nam lamyai**	น้ำลำไย
Fruit Juice	**Nam pol-mai**	น้ำผลไม้
Lotus Root Water	**Nam rak bua**	น้ำรากบัว
Green Leaf Water	**Nam bai buabok**	น้ำใบบัวบก
Chinese Herbal Water	**Nam jub liang**	น้ำจับเลี้ยง
Bean Crud Milk	**Nam tao hoo**	น้ำเต้าฮู้
Bird's Nest Soup	**Rung nok**	รังนก
Thai-Style Iced Coffee or Tea	**Kafae yen or cha yen**	กาแฟเย็น หรือ ชาเย็น

Salad

Southern Thai Salad	**Salat khaek**	สลัดแขก
Spicy Mungbean Noodle Salad	**Yam wun sen**	ยำวุ้นเส้น
Spicy Sardine Salad	**Yam pla krapong**	ยำปลากระป๋อง
Spicy Egg Salad	**Yam khai tom**	ยำไข่ต้ม
Spicy Frankfurter-and Ham Salad	**Yam saikrok kap haem**	ยำไส้กรอกกับแฮม
Spicy Barbecued Chicken Salad	**Yam kai yang**	ยำไก่ย่าง
Savory Chopped-Chicken Salad	**Lap kai**	ลาบไก่
Savory Pork Chopped Salad	**Lap mou**	ลาบหมู

Savory Baked Pork Salad	**Phla mou op**	พล่าหมูอบ
Spicy Squid Salad	**Yam pla muek**	ยำปลาหมึก
Savory Prawn Salad	**Phla koung**	พล่ากุ้ง
Savory Beef Salad	**Neua narm tok**	เนื้อน้ำตก

When you are eating Thai food, keep these simple rules of etiquette in mind:

— Food is served "family style," from a common dish or dishes. Take a little with the serving utensil to start. Put it on your plate and eat it with some rice. Then, having sampled the food, help yourself to more. Unless you are among good friends (in which case you can use your own spoon), always use the serving utensil.

— Eat with a spoon and fork. You shouldn't use a knife if you have one.

— Do not pass the serving dishes. Reach for the food, which is set in the middle of the table.

— Always put the food on your plate before eating it. Don't take it directly from the serving dish and put it in your mouth; this is considered rude.

— Eat from all of the serving dishes. Don't hog one kind of food alone. If there are a number of people at your table, shift the dishes' positions occasionally so that everyone may try all kinds.

— Try not to be offended if someone puts food on your plate for you. They are being friendly. Sometimes they will serve you food that is beyond your own reach. If you're getting too full to eat much more, eat slowly and leave food on your plate to discourage well-meaning servers.

— If you pick your teeth (which is not impolite), cover you mouth with one hand so it cannot be seen.

(e) Backstreet Foodstalls

In Thailand, good food appears in the most unexpected places along the edge of a canal or river, in a car park, by the side of a bus road or in a narrow soi (lane). A one-man mobile kitchen is all that' needed to produce cheap and astonishingly good food.

If you should suddenly feel hungry in the middle of the nigh you can find food here anytime. A list of a few common dishes ha been prepared so that you can at least order something and surviv until your next meal. The list may also be of use to those who wis to try some local food anyway.

Language is sometime a difficulty. If you are hesitant about th Thai pronunciation, you should repeat those words or phrases an make sure the stall-keeper or waiter understands. If you are stayin for a few days, it's good to cultivate the friendship of someone wh knows how to order the foods.

Bah-mi haeng บะหมี่แห้ง— Egg noodles laced with crab meat, ba becued pork and spring onions.

Bah-mi narm บะหมี่น้ำ— Broth and egg-noodles served in a bow garnished with sliced roast pork.

Bah-mi raad-na บะหมี่ราดหน้า— Fried egg-noodles topped with thick stew of shredded chicken or pork, mushrooms, bamboo shoot and vegetables.

Choke Kai; Choke Mou โจ๊กไก่, โจ๊กหมู— Soft porridge cooked in chicken stock with chunks of chicken or minced pork and sprin onions, topped with Chinese croissants (*iew-cha-kwai*).

Dim Sum ดิมซัม— **Chinese appetizers** — a delicious assortme f pastas and buns stuffed with meats or seafood, popular for lunch r tea-time snacking.

Hae-Kuen แฮ่กึ๊น— Chinese deep-fried rolls stuffed with minced ork, prawns and crab meat; traditionally served with sliced cu-umber and sweet Chinese plum sauce.

Haw Mok Pla or Koung ห่อหมกปลาหรือกุ้ง— Spicy fish or prawns in a anana-leaf cup with coconut cream, egg and vegetables, steamed ı a large aluminum steamer.

Hoi Luak หอยลวก— Shellfish scalded in hot water and served for ıe diner to pluck each one from its shell and dip it in a chili sauce.

Hoi-thawd หอยทอด— Sea mussels or oysters fried in egg batter easoned with chili sauce and spring onions.

Soup Hou Shalarm ซุปหูฉลาม— Boiled Chinese shark's fins made ıto a rich soup with shredded chicken, crab or crab roe.

Kai Laow-daeng ไก่เหล้าแดง— Chicken boiled in soy sauce, flavored vith brown sugar and a little Chinese wine.

Kai or Neua Phad-khing ไก่หรือเนื้อผัดขิง— Chicken or beef fried with hredded ginger.

Kai-phad Hed ไก่ผัดเห็ด— Chicken fried with muchrooms.

Kai phad Ka-phrao ไก่ผัดกะเพรา— Chicken fried with basil leaves nd fresh chilies.

Kai-phad Naw-mai ไก่ผัดหน่อไม้— Chicken fried with bamboo hoots.

Kai-phad Narm Man Hoi ไก่ผัดน้ำมันหอย— Fried chicken with oys-er sauce.

Kai-yaang ไก่ย่าง— Chicken heavily spiced and grilled over a char-oal fire.

Kai-toun ไก่ตุ๋น— Steamed chicken with mushrooms and ginger, avored with soy sauce.

Kaeng-chued Nang-mou แกงจืดหนังหมู— Pork-skin soup with prawn or fishballs, flavored with fish or any sauce.

Kaeng-chued Mou Ba-shaw แกงจืดหมูบะช่อ— Minced pork soup with egg, flavored with fish sauce, pickled cabbage and spring onions.

Kaeng-chued Pao-hue แกงจืดเป๋าฮื้อ— Abalone soup.

Kaeng-chued Phak แกงจืดผัก— Chinese green vegetable soup.

Kaeng-chued Tao-hou Khao แกงจืดเต้าหู้ขาว— Stuffed bean-curd soup with minced pork, flavored with fish or any sauce.

Kaeng—chued Voun-senh Mou-Sab Louk-shin แกงจืดวุ้นเส้นหมูสับลูกชิ้น— Transparent noodle soup with minced pork and prawn balls, flavored with fish or any sauce.

Kaeng Som; Kaeng Leuang แกงส้ม, แกงเหลือง— A sour curry soup made with vegetables and fish, in the southern fashion.

Kaeng Khiao-waan Kai แกงเขียวหวานไก่— Very hot chicken curry fresh green chilies are the main ingredient.

Kaeng-phed (Neua or Kai) แกงเผ็ด (เนื้อหรือไก่)— Thai curry (beef or chicken).

Kaeng Massaman (Neua or Kai) แกงมัสหมั่น (เนื้อหรือไก่)— Another type of spicy beef or chicken in southern fashion, slightly sweetened.

Kai Ob Bai-teui ไก่อบใบเตย— Cicken baked in screwpine leaves

Karm Pou Phad ก้ามปูผัด— Crab's claws fried with Chinese celery and fermented soya beans.

Khai-chiao Fou ไข่เจียวฟู— Fluffy omelet.

Khai Louk-kheui ไข่ลูกเขย— Hard boiled eggs in sweet-and-sour sauce.

Khai Toun ไข่ตุ๋น— Steamed egg custard.

Khai Sawd-Sai ไข่สอดไส้— Cooked minced meat, diced tomato and vegetables wrapped egg pancake.

Kha-mou Yat-Sai ขาหมูยัดไส้— Pig's feet stuffed with pork and ani-
ed.

Kaolaow Maw Fai เกาเหลาหม้อไฟ— The Chinese version of Swiss
ndue. This dish comprises chicken stock, an assortment of meats,
afood and vegetables. The diner serves himself from the charcoal-
eated cooking vessel.

Kaeng Kurma แกงกุรหม่า— Indian beef or chicken curry cooked in
ghurt, mixed with spices, coconut and poppy seeds.

Khao Buri ข้าวบุหรี่— Steaming mounds of saffron rice, drenched
spicy curries and crowned with burnt onions and raisins. A favor-
e Islamic dish.

Khao Laam ข้าวหลาม— Glutinous rice with coconut milk roasted
bamboo.

Khao Manh Kai (Hainanese Style) ข้าวมันไก่— White rice delicately
oked with chicken stock, onions and garlic, to be served with
eserved ginger, soy sauce, chili vinegar and slices of chicken.

Khao Mok (Kai or Neua) ข้าวหมก (ไก่หรือเนื้อ)— Persian-style pilau or
ffron rice cooked in ghee and coconut milk, served with chicken
beef.

Khao-niao raad-na kari ข้าวเหนียวราดหน้ากระหรี่— Islamic plates fa-
red in the four southern provinces of Thailand.

Khao Mou-daeng ข้าวหมูแดง— Rice with barbecued pork and a
sty sauce.

Khao Na-kai ข้าวหน้าไก่— Rice topped with fried chicken and bam-
oo shoots or mushrooms in gravy.

Khao-phad (Kai, Mou, Neua or Khai) ข้าวผัด (ไก่ หมู เนื้อหรือไข่)— Rice
ied with chicken, pork, beef or egg (according to order), sprinkled
ith tomato ketchup or fish sauce, served with cucumber, spring
nions and sliced lemon.

Khao-phad (Pou or Koung) ข้าวผัด (ปูหรือกุ้ง)— Rice fried with crab meat or prawns, sprinkled with tomato ketchup or fish sauce.

Khao-khluk Kapi ข้าวคลุกกะปิ— Rice mixed with fish or prawn paste and fried with pork or lobster, served with cucumber, spring onions and sliced lemon.

Khao-plao ข้าวเปล่า— Plain cooked rice.

Khao-tom ข้าวต้ม— Plain boiled rice.

Khanom-cheep ขนมจีบ— Steamed meat paties, a sort of dim sum, or more elegantly, bonne bouches.

Khanom-cheep khao ขนมจีบขาว— Translucent pasta circlets enclosing delicately pink shrimp, or ravioli-like crescents stuffed with black mushrooms and minced pork.

Khanom-chine Narm-ya ขนมจีนน้ำยา— Spicy fish gravy served with soft rice vermicelli, pea sprouts, basil leaves and chilies.

Kiao-krop เกี๊ยวกรอบ— Fried minced pork wrapped in flour batter.

Kiao-narm เกี๊ยวน้ำ— Wonton Broth, a sort of Chinese ravioli.

Koung shoup-paeng thawd กุ้งชุบแป้งทอด— Jumbo shrimp fried in egg batter and served with prepared mustard or ketchup.

Koung-thawd Phrik-thai Krathiem กุ้งทอดพริกไทยกระเทียม—Fried king prawns seasoned with coriander roots, garlic, salt and pepper.

Koung Ob Maw-din กุ้งอบหม้อดิน—Lobster steamed in earthenware casseroles.

Koung-phad Naw-mai กุ้งผัดหน่อไม้—Shrimp fried with bamboo shoots or asparagus.

Koung-phad Priao-waan กุ้งผัดเปรี้ยวหวาน—Sweet-and-sour fried shrimp.

Koung Phaow กุ้งเผา— Charcoal-grilled freshwater lobster.

Koung Phla กุ้งพล่า— Hot prawn salad with chilies and mint leaves.

Koung Tenh กุ้งเต้น— A whole freshwater lobster soaked in lemon ice with garlic and chili, garnished with mint leaves.

Koung Tom กุ้งต้ม—Lightly salted boiled shrimp in the shell.

Tom yam koung ต้มยำกุ้ง—Prawn soup flavored with lemon grass, ne leaves, garlic, chili paste and lemon.

Kwai-tiao Neua-woa ก๋วยเตี๋ยวเนื้อวัว—A clear beef soup with cenoodles and boiled meat.

Kwai-tiao Ped ก๋วยเตี๋ยวเป็ด—Boiled duck with flat rice-noodles rved in soup.

Kwai-tiao phad Si-iew ก๋วยเตี๋ยวผัดซีอิ๊ว—Fried flat rice-noodles with ack bean sauce, pork and some vegetables.

Kwai-tiao phad Thai ก๋วยเตี๋ยวผัดไทย—Fried narrow rice-noodles with g, pea sprouts and chili.

Kwai-tiao raad-na Neua-sap ก๋วยเตี๋ยวราดหน้าเนื้อสับ—Fried flat rice-odles laced with minced beef and vegetables in gravy.

Laab (Neua, Kai or Mou) ลาบ (เนื้อ, ไก่ หรือ หมู)—A condiment made chopped semi-cooked beef, chicken or pork, garnished with asted rice and mint leaves, and served with an assortment of veg-ables and glutinous rice.

Mee Kathi หมี่กะทิ—Rice vermicelli served with spicy coconut gravy d garnished with hard-boiled eggs, pea sprouts and yellow bean kes.

Mee Kropp หมี่กรอบ— Crispy fried rice-vermicelli mixed with pork, awns, egg, yellow bean curds, onions and chilies, served with ion grass, pea sprouts and lemon juice.

Mou Daeng หมูแดง— Long strips of pork roasted with sweet spicy uce. Red in color, it is available in most markets.

Mou Kropp (or Mou Yaang) หมูกรอบ (หรือหมูย่าง)— Crispy roast pork.

Mou-phad Phrik-khing หมูผัดพริกขิง— Pork fried with pounded dry awns, dried chilies, garlic, coriander root, lemon grass and galingale root, slightly sweetened.

Mou-phad Priao-wann หมูผัดเปรี้ยวหวาน— Sweet-and-sour fried pork.

Mou Pha-lo หมูพะโล้ — Pork boiled with Chinese black sauce, some spices and aniseed.

Mou-thawd Krathien Phrikthai หมูทอดกระเทียมพริกไทย— Fried pork seasoned with coriander root, garlic, salt and pepper.

Murtaba มะตะบะ— An Indian pancake loaded with ground beef, egg and onions, served with chicken or beef curry.

Narm-phrik Kapi น้ำพริกกะปิ— Fish paste pounded together with chilies, garlic and onions, then mixed with sugar, fish sauce and lime juice.

Narm-phrik Aung น้ำพริกอ่อง— A northern delicacy made with minced pork, chili, tomato and spices. It's eaten with crispy pork rind and fresh vegetables.

Neua-phad Khing เนื้อผัดขิง— Stirred fried beef with fresh shredded ginger.

Neua-phad Phrik เนื้อผัดพริก— Beef fried with fresh hot chilies.

Neua-thawd Phak Salad เนื้อทอดผักสลัด— Beef seasoned with pounded coriander root, salt and pepper, fried and served with lettuce or cucumber.

Phad-phed Pla-douk ผัดเผ็ดปลาดุก— Fish roasted over a fire, filled and deep-fried to crispy pieces. These are stir-fried with fish sauce and sweet curry paste.

Ped-toun Narm-daeng เป็ดตุ๋นน้ำแดง— Steamed duck in brown sauce

Ped-toun Narm-sai เป็ดตุ๋นน้ำใส— Steamed duck soup.

Ped-yaang เป็ดย่าง— Chinese roast duck.

Phak-boung Fai-daeng ผักบุ้งไฟแดง— "Morning glory" vegetable fried with garlic, seasoned with soy sauce or fermented beans.

Phanaeng Neua or Kai พะแนงเนื้อหรือไก่— Beef or chicken curry cor

ining rich coconut cream and finely cut kaffir-lime leaves.

Pla-chian ปลาเจี๋ยน— Sea-bass cooked with strips of fatty pork, soy uce, vinegar and ginger in gravy.

Pla Kaphong Narm-daeng ปลากะพงน้ำแดง— Fried red snapper with quant brown sauce.

Pla Kaphong Priao-waan ปลากะพงเปรี้ยวหวาน— Red snapper fried veet-and-sour.

Pla Pae-Sah ปลาแป๊ะซะ— Steamed fish garnished with spring onns, shredded lean pork, dried black mushrooms, ginger and Chise parsley.

Pla-phad Priao-waan ปลาผัดเปรี้ยวหวาน— Fish fried sweet-and-sour.

Pla or Koung Thawd ปลาหรือกุ้งทอด— Fish or shrimp dipped in batr and fried in deep oil.

Po-piah (Sod) ปอเปี๊ยะ (สด)— Chili and Chinese plum sauce spread paper-thin pastry. Piled on top are turnips, bamboo shoots, pea routs, yellow bean curds, prawns or Chinese sausages.

Po-piah (Thawd) ปอเปี๊ยะ (ทอด)— A crisp, deep-fried roll stuffed ith pork, prawns and pea sprouts, served with a special chili sauce.

Pou cha ปูจ๋า— Deep-fried stuffed crab meat in the shell.

Sala-pao ซาลาเปา— A doughy bun stuffed with barbecued or minced rk.

Satay (Neua, Kai or Mou) สะเต๊ะ (เนื้อ, ไก่ หรือ หมู)— Highly seasoned ef, chicken or pork skewered on sticks, barbecued over a slow arcoal fire, and served with a spicy sauce made of ground peats and chilies.

Si-khrong Mou Phad Si-iew ซี่โครงหมูผัดซีอิ๊ว— Pork spare-ribs fried ith Chinese black bean sauce.

Si-khrong Mou Phad Priao-waan ซี่โครงหมูผัดเปรี้ยวหวาน— Pork spare-bs fried in sweet-and-sour sauce.

Som Tam ส้มตำ— A northeastern relish composed of sliced gree papaya and pounded dried shrimp, flavored with fish sauce, chili and brown sugar.

Thawd-manh Pla ทอดมันปลา— Patties made of fish pounded wi dried chilies, curry and vegetables, then fried and served.

Tom-kha Kai ต้มข่าไก่— Slightly spicy chicken-coconut soup, fl vored with galingale root, lime juice and chilies.

Tom Yamh ต้มยำ— Spicy and sour pungent soup made fro chicken or beef, fish, prawns or smoked dried fish, flavoured wi kaffir-lime leaves, lemon grass, chili paste and lemon.

Yam Pla Krobb ต้มยำปลากรอบ— Smoked dried fish mixed with le tuce, cucumber, fish sauce, lime juice, mint leaves and chilies.

Yam Yai ยำใ-หญ่— A relish consisting of shrimp, lettuce, slice egg, shredded carrot, thin rice noodles, celery, parsley and the th wavy fungus known in Thai as *Hed Hou Nou* or "Cloud Ears".

(f) Complaints and Paying the Bill

Would you ask the proprietor(manager) to come over?	**Phom khaw phob Thao-kae (Phu-chad-karn)?**	ผมขอพบเถ้าแก่ (ผู้จัดการ)?
I am sorry to complain about the service here.	**Phom sia-chai thi tong phoud reuang borikarn.**	ผมเสียใจที่ต้องพูด เรื่องบริการ
I am sorry, I cannot eat that.	**Phom sia-chai phom tharn nanh mai-dai.**	ผมเสียใจ ผมทานนั่นไม่ไ
The meat is tough (overdone).	**Neua niao(souk) kern pai.**	เนื้อเหนียว (สุก) เกินไป
The pork is hard to cut.	**Neua-Mou niao**	เนื้อหมูเหนียว

he fish is not fresh.	**Pla mai sod.**	ปลาไม่สด
he rice is not cooked.	**Khao mai souk.**	ข้าวไม่สุก
he chicken is hard.	**Neua-kai khaeng**	เนื้อไก่แข็ง
his is too sweet (salty).	**Ni waan-maak pai (khem kern pai).**	นี่หวานมากไป (เค็มเกินไป)
his curry is too hot.	**Kaeng phed-maak.**	แกงเผ็ดมาก
his butter is rancid.	**Neui menh-huen laew.**	เนยเหม็นหืนแล้ว
his is not fresh.	**Ni mai sod.**	นี่ไม่สด
his cup of coffee is tasteless.	**Kafae chued mai-mi rot.**	กาแฟจืดไม่มีรส
ay I change this?	**Phom khaw plian dai-mai?**	ผมขอเปลี่ยนได้ไหม?
lease bring me a new one.	**Karuna plian hai phom mai.**	กรุณาเปลี่ยนให้ผมใหม่
his is too cold.	**A-harn chaan ni yenh shued.**	อาหารจานนี้เย็นชืด
/e did not order this.	**Chaan ni raow mai-dai sang.**	จานนี้เราไม่ได้สั่ง
hat's not what I ordered.	**Phom mai-dai sang hai thamh yaang ni.**	ผมไม่ได้สั่งให้ทำอย่างนี้
his is not mine.	**Chaan-ni mai shai khong phom.**	จานนี้ไม่ใช่ของผม
will not pay this charge.	**Ni khid aow kab phom mai-dai.**	นี่คิดเอากับผมไม่ได้
he tablecloth is not clean.	**Pha pou-toh mai sa-ard.**	ผ้าปูโต๊ะไม่สะอาด
he spoons and	**Shonn-somm laang mai**	ช้อมส้อมล้างไม่สะอาด

forks are not clean.	**sa-ard.**	
How much do I have to pay?	**Phom tong chaai thao-rai?**	ผมต้องจ่ายเท่าไร?
Make out one bill for us.	**Karuna tham bill ruam kanh thang-mod.**	กรุณาทำบิลรวมกัน ทั้งหมด
Please make separate bills.	**Karuna tham bill yaek kanh.**	กรุณาทำบิลแยกกัน
What is the total amount?	**Yawd-ruam thang-mod thao-rai?**	ยอดรวมทั้งหมดเท่าไร?
The total is wrong.	**Yawd-ruam phid, khid sia mai.**	ยอดรวมผิด คิดเสียใหม่
The charges are too high.	**Khid phaeng kern pai.**	คิดแพงเกินไป
Is service included?	**Ruam kha borikarn duai rue-plao?**	รวมค่าบริการด้วยหรือเปล่า?
I made a mistake, I beg your pardon.	**Khaw-thoad, phom khao-chai phid.**	ขอโทษ ผมเข้าใจผิด
May I have a receipt, please?	**Khaw bai-rab hai phom dai-mai?**	ขอใบรับให้ผมได้ไหม?
Thank you.	**Khop-khun.**	ขอบคุณ

(g) Market Produce and Glossary of Local Names

The following lists are based on Bangkok markets; they includ all vegetables, fruits, groceries, meats and poultry, fishes, curry-stuff etc. The lists are not exhaustive, but it is hoped that no importar products have been omitted.

'egetables

sh-pumpkin	**Fak khiao**	ฟักเขียว
sparagus	**Naw-mai Farang**	หน่อไม้ฝรั่ง
amboo shoots	**Naw-mai Thai**	หน่อไม้ไทย
asil	**Bai Maenglak, Bai Horapha**	ใบแมงลัก, ใบโหระพา
ay leaves	**Bai krawaan**	ใบกระวาน
eans	**Thua**	ถั่ว
ean sprouts	**Thua-ngawk hua-yai**	ถั่วงอกหัวใหญ่
eets (Beet root)	**Phak-kard daeng**	ผักกาดแดง
ell pepper	**Phrik-yuak**	พริกหยวก
itter melon	**Marah**	มะระ
lack beans	**Thua-damh**	ถั่วดำ
ottle squash	**Narm-tao**	น้ำเต้า
rinjal (green)	**Makheua-khiao**	มะเขือเขียว
rinjal (purple)	**Makheua-muang**	มะเขือม่วง
'abbage	**Kalam-pli**	กะหล่ำปลี
'arrots	**Khaerot**	แครอท
auliflower	**Dawk kalam**	ดอกกะหล่ำ
elery	**Khuen-shai**	คื่นช่าย
hick-pea (Green gram)	**Thua Khiao**	ถั่วเขียว
hilies (green)	**Phrik Shi-fa(khiao)**	พริกชี้ฟ้า (เขียว)
hilies (red)	**Phrik Shi-fa(daeng)**	พริกชี้ฟ้า (แดง)
hinese green mustard	**Phakkard Khiao**	ผักกาดเขียว
hinese white greens (Pak Choy)	**Phakkard Khao**	ผักกาดขาว
hiniese radish	**Shai-thow**	ไชเท้า

Cucumber	**Taeng-kwa**	แตงกวา
Garlic	**Krathiam**	กระเทียม
Gherkin (Pickle)	**Taeng-nou**	แตงหนู
Groundnut	**Thua li-song**	ถั่วลิสง
Kale (Chinese)	**Kha-na**	คะน้า
Kohlrabi	**Kalam-pom**	กะหล่ำปม
Lady's finger	**Krachiap Khao**	กระเจี๊ยบขาว
Leeks	**Tonh Krathiam**	ต้นกระเทียม
Lentils	**Thua Khaek**	ถั่วแขก
Lettuce	**Phak-kard Homm**	ผักกาดหอม
Loofah (angled)	**Buab-liam**	บวบเหลี่ยม
Mint leaves	**Bai Sara-nae**	ใบสะระแหน่
Mushrooms	**Hed-khone**	เห็ดโคน
Okra	**Krachiap Monn**	กระเจี๊ยบมอญ
Onions	**Homm**	หอม
Pandanus leaf	**Bai teui**	ใบเตย
Parsley (Chinese)	**Phak-shi**	ผักชี
Pea sprouts	**Thua-ngork**	ถั่วงอก
Pigeon peas	**Thua-raeh**	ถั่วแระ
Pig weed	**Phak Khome**	ผักโขม
Pumpkin	**Fak-thong**	ฟักทอง
Radish	**Hua-phakkard Daeng**	หัวผักกาดแดง
Rice bean	**Thua-daeng**	ถั่วแดง
Roselle	**Krachiap-daeng**	กระเจี๊ยบแดง
Soybeans	**Thua leuang**	ถั่วเหลือง
Sponge Squash	**Buab homm**	บวบหอม
Squash (gourd)	**Buab**	บวบ
String beans	**Thua fak-yao**	ถั่วฝักยาว
Sugar pea	**Thua Lan-tao**	ถั่วลันเตา

weet basil	**Bai Horapha**	ใบโหระพา
weet corn	**Khao-phode Waan**	ข้าวโพดหวาน
weet potato	**Manh-thed**	มันเทศ
aro	**Pheuak**	เผือก
omato	**Makheua-thed**	มะเขือเทศ
'egetable marrow	**Faeng**	แฟง
Vater convolvulus	**Phak-boung**	ผักบุ้ง
Vatercress	**Phaeng-phuai**	แพงพวย
Vinged bean	**Thua-phou**	ถั่วพู
'am	**Pheuak Hua-lek**	เผือกหัวเล็ก
'am bean	**Manh-kaew**	มันแกว
'ellow bean	**Thua-thawng**	ถั่วทอง

ruits and Nut

ael	**Ma-toum**	มะตูม
anana	**Kluai**	กล้วย
readfruit	**Sa-ke**	สาเก
ullock's heart	**Noi-nong**	น้อยโหน่ง
antaloupe	**Taeng-laai**	แตงลาย
ashew nuts	**Mamuang Himapharn**	มะม่วงหิมพานต์
oconut	**Ma-phrao**	มะพร้าว
ustard apple	**Noi-na**	น้อยหน่า
urian	**Thurian**	ทุเรียน
uava	**Farang**	ฝรั่ง
ambu ayer (Malay)	**Shomphou-khiao**	ชมภู่เขียว
ackfruit	**Khanoun**	ขนุน
affir-lime Bergamot	**Ma-kround**	มะกรูด
angsad	**Langsaad**	ลางสาด
imau manis (Malay)	**Som-Kliang**	ส้มเกลี้ยง

Lime	**Manao**	มะนาว
Litchi or Lychee	**Linchi**	ลิ้นจี่
Longan	**Lam-yai**	ลำไย
Mandarin orange	**Som-chine**	ส้มจีน
Mango	**Ma-muang**	มะม่วง
Mangosteen	**Mang-khoud**	มังคุด
Manila tamarind	**Makharm-thed**	มะขามเทศ
Marian plum	**Ma-praang**	มะปราง
Muskmelon	**Taeng-thai**	แตงไทย
Neck orange	**Som-chouk**	ส้มจุก
Nipa fruit	**Louk-chaak**	ลูกจาก
Papaya	**Mala-kaw**	มะละกอ
Pineapple	**Sapparot**	สับปะรด
Pomegranate	**Thap-thim**	ทับทิม
Pomelo, shaddock	**Som-Oh**	ส้มโอ
Rambai (Malay)	**Ma-fai**	มะไฟ
Rambutan (Malay)	**Ngaw**	เงาะ
Rose-apple	**Shomphou Narm-dorkmai**	ชมพู่น้ำดอกไม้
Santol	**Krathawn**	กระท้อน
Sapodilla	**Lamoud**	ละมุด
Star gooseberry	**Ma-yom**	มะยม
Tamarind	**Ma-kharm**	มะขาม
Tangerine	**Som-khiao-waan**	ส้มเขียวหวาน
Water chestnut	**Krachap**	กระจับ
Wood-apple	**Ma-kwid**	มะขวิด
Watermelon	**Taeng-Mo**	แตงโม

Meats and Poultry

Back fat	**Manh-Khaeng**	มันแข็ง
Beef shin	**Neua Na-khaeng**	เนื้อหน้าแข้ง
Belly	**Phoung**	พุง
Blood	**Leuad**	เลือด
Bone	**Kra-douk**	กระดูก
Breast	**Na-ok**	หน้าอก
Brisket	**Neua Na-ok**	เนื้อหน้าอก
Broiler	**Kai-onn**	ไก่อ่อน
Calves' feet	**Kha Louk-woa**	ขาลูกวัว
Capon	**Kai-tawn**	ไก่ตอน
Chuck	**Neua-lai**	เนื้อไหล่
Cubed stew meat	**Neua tham-satou**	เนื้อทำสตูว์
Dried beef	**Neua Taak-haeng**	เนื้อตากแห้ง
Duck;duckling	**Ped; Louk-ped**	เป็ด, ลูกเป็ด
Fats	**Manh**	มัน
Filet or tenderloin	**Sanh-nai**	สันใน
Flank	**Neua Si-khaang**	เนื้อสีข้าง
Flare fat	**Manh-pleow**	มันเปลว
Fore shank	**Neua Kha-Na**	เนื้อขาหน้า
Giblets	**Khreuang-nai**	เครื่องใน
Goose	**Haan Tua-mia**	ห่านตัวเมีย
Ground beef	**Neua-bod**	เนื้อบด
Head	**Hua**	หัว
Heart	**Hua-chai**	หัวใจ
Hind shank	**Neua-kha Lang**	เนื้อขาหลัง
Intestine	**Sai**	ไส้
Kidney	**Tai**	ไต
Lamb	**Kaeh**	แกะ

Lard	**Manh Samrap-chiao**	มันสำหรับเจียว
Leg	**Kha**	ขา
Liver	**Tab**	ตับ
Loin	**Neua-sanh Nork**	เนื้อสันนอก
Meat	**Neua**	เนื้อ
Meat scraps	**Sed-neua**	เศษเนื้อ
Minced pork	**Mou-bod, Mou-sap**	หมูบด, หมูสับ
Mutton	**Phaeh**	แพะ
Neck	**Khaw**	คอ
Ox-tail	**Haang-woa**	หางวัว
Ox tongue	**Lin-woa**	ลิ้นวัว
Pig's feet	**Kha Mou**	ขาหมู
Plate	**Neua Na-thawng**	เนื้อหน้าท้อง
Pork loin	**Sanh-Mou Tit-kradouk**	สันหมูติดกระดูก
Pork fillet	**Sanh-Nai Mou**	สันในหมู
Pork Sausage	**Sai-krawk Mou**	ไส้กรอกหมู
Pork skin	**Nang Mou**	หนังหมู
Poultry wing	**Peek-Kai**	ปีกไก่
Pullet	**Kai-noum, Kai-sao**	ไก่หนุ่ม, ไก่สาว
Ribs	**Si-khrong**	ซี่โครง
Round	**Sanh-kha**	สันขา
Rump	**Neua-Sa-phoke**	เนื้อสะโพก
Shank	**Neua Na-khaeng**	เนื้อหน้าแข้ง
Shank knuckle	**Neua Kradouk-khaw**	เนื้อกระดูกคอ
Short loin	**Neua-sanh Tit Si-Khrong**	เนื้อสันติดซี่โครง
Shoulder fillet	**Neua-sanh Lai**	เนื้อสันไหล่
Sirloin	**Neua-sanh Ok**	เนื้อสันอก
Spare ribs	**Si-khrong(onn)**	ซี่โครง (อ่อน)
Standing ribs	**Neua Tit Si-khrong**	เนื้อติดซี่โครง

uckling pig	**Louk-Mou Han**	ลูกหมูหัน
uet	**Manh-khaeng**	มันแข็ง
weetbread	**Tab Onn**	ตับอ่อน
ail	**Haang**	หาง
-bone, Porterhouse	**Neua-sanh Tit Kradouk**	เนื้อสันติดกระดูก
ongue	**Lin**	ลิ้น
urkey	**Kai Nguang**	ไก่งวง
'eal	**Neua Louk-woa**	เนื้อลูกวัว

'ish

nabas	**Pla Maw**	ปลาหมอ
arracuda	**Pla Dork-sark**	ปลาดูอกสาก
arracuda(giant)	**Pla Narm Dorkmaai**	ปลาน้ำดอกไม้
ass	**Pla Kaphong**	ปลากะพง
:arp	**Pla Taphian**	ปลาตะเพียน
:atfish(clarias)	**Pla Douk**	ปลาดุก
:atfish(butter)	**Pla Neua Onn**	ปลาเนื้ออ่อน
:atfish(spotted)	**Pla Kod**	ปลากด
:uttlefish	**Pla Muek Yai**	ปลาหมึกใหญ่
:ybium	**Pla In-see**	ปลาอินทรี
:yprinid	**Pla Tadaeng**	ปลาตาแดง
)orab	**Pla Darb-lao**	ปลาดาบลาว
el(swamp)	**Pla Lai**	ปลาไหล
eatherback	**Pla Kraai; Pla Salard**	ปลากราย, ปลาสลาด
lasher (Brown triple-tail)	**Pla Kaphong Damh**	ปลากะพงดำ
latfish (Florender)	**Pla Ta-diao**	ปลาตาเดียว
;ar	**Pla Kathoung Heow**	ปลากะทุงเหว
;oby	**Pla Bou**	ปลาบู่

Gouramy	**Pla Kradi**	ปลากระดี่
Jewfish	**Pla Chuad**	ปลาจวด
Kingfish (black-banded)	**Pla Samli**	ปลาสำลี
Ladyfish (Mugil)	**Pla Krabork**	ปลากระบอก
Mackerel (rake-gilled)	**Pla Lang**	ปลาลัง
Milkfish	**Pla Nuan Chand**	ปลานวลจันทร์
Mullet (white)	**Pla Thu**	ปลาทู
Pangasius	**Pla Sawaai; Pla The-pho**	ปลาสวาย,ปลาเทโพ
Perch (climbing)	**Pla Maw Thai**	ปลาหมอไทย
Perch (giant sea)	**Pla Kaphong Khao**	ปลากะพงขาว
Perch (striped)	**Pla Kaphong Laai**	ปลากะพงลาย
Pilotfish	**Pla Salid**	ปลาสลิด
Pomfret (black)	**Pla Charamed Damh**	ปลาจะระเม็ดดำ
Pomfret (silver)	**Pla Charamed Khao**	ปลาจะระเม็ดขาว
Probarbus	**Pla Yisok**	ปลายี่สก
Queenfish (slender)	**Pla Si-siad**	ปลาสีเสียด
Ray	**Pla Kraben**	ปลากระเบน
Sardine	**Pla Lang-khiao**	ปลาลังเขียว
Saurel, Scad (banded)	**Pla Si-koun**	ปลาสีกุน
Serpenthead Fish	**Pla Shado; Pla shonn**	ปลาชะโด, ปลาช่อน
Shark	**Pla Shalarm**	ปลาฉลาม
Sole (Oriental)	**Pla Lin Ma**	ปลาลิ้นหมา
Snapper (red)	**Pla Kaphong Daeng**	ปลสกะพงแดง
Squid	**Pla Muek lek**	ปลาหมึกเล็ก
Tasselfish	**Pla Kurao**	ปลากุเรา
Tilapia	**Pla Nin**	ปลานิล
Tuna	**Pla Haang Khaeng**	ปลาหางแข็ง
Tunny	**Pla Oh**	ปลาโอ
Wallago	**Pla Khow**	ปลาเค้า

hitefish(milky)	**Pla Bai Khanoun**	ปลาใบขนุน

ollusks and Crustaceans

balone	**Pao Hue**	เป๋าฮื้อ
erithidea obtusa	**Hoi Chubchaeng**	หอยจุ๊บแจง
lams	**Hoi Karp**	หอยกาบ
lams (sea)	**Hoi Talab**	หอยตลับ
ockles (Ark Shell)	**Hoi Khraeng**	หอยแครง
rab	**Pou**	ปู
rab (horse)	**Pou Thale**	ปูทะเล
rab (horseshoe)	**Maengda Thale**	แมงดาทะเล
rab (purse)	**Pou Ma**	ปูม้า
rawfish	**Koung Naang**	กุ้งนาง
onax faba	**Hoi Siab**	หอยเสียบ
obster (sea)	**Koung Shae-buai**	กุ้งแชบ๊วย
elapenaeus monoceros	**Koung Takard**	กุ้งตะกาด
ussel (horse)	**Hoi Kaphong**	หอยกะพง
ussel (sea)	**Hoi Malaeng-phou**	หอยแมลงภู่
yster	**Hoi Naang-rom**	หอยนางรม
rawns (giant blue-legged)	**Koung Karm-kraam; Koung Naang**	กุ้งก้ามกราม, กุ้งนาง
rawns (tiger)	**Koung Laai**	กุ้งลาย
repang	**Pling Thale**	ปลิงทะเล
ivipara doliaris	**Hoi Khom**	หอยขม

urry-stuffs

ardamom	**Krawaan**	กระวาน
hili powder	**Phrik-ponh**	พริกป่น

Cinnamon	**Ob-sheui**	อบเชย
Cloves	**Karn-phlu**	กานพลู
Coconut milk	**Ka-thih**	กะทิ
Coriander seeds	**Maled phak-shi**	เมล็ดผักชี
Cumin seeds	**Maled yi-ra**	เมล็ดยี่หร่า
Curry powder	**Phong kari**	ผงกะหรี่
Galingale	**Kha**	ข่า
Ginger (green; dried)	**Khing (sod;haeng)**	ขิง (สด, แห้ง)
Kaffir lime	**Makroud**	มะกรูด
Kaffir skin	**Phiew makroud**	ผิวมะกรูด
Kaffir leaf	**Bai makroud**	ใบมะกรูด
Lemon Grass	**Takrai**	ตะไคร้
Mace	**Dork-chand thed**	ดอกจันทน์เทศ
Nutmeg	**Louk-chand thed**	ลูกจันทน์เทศ
Pepper	**Phrik-thai**	พริกไทย
Turmeric	**Khamin leuang**	ขมิ้นเหลือง
Zedoary	**Khamin khao**	ขมิ้นขาว

Groceries

Agar	**Vounh**	วุ้น
Baking powder	**Phong fou**	ผงฟู
Bean-curd cheese (white; yellow)	**Tao-hu (khao; leuang)**	เต้าหู้ (ขาว, เหลือง)
Bread	**Khanom-pang**	ขนมปัง
Butter	**Neui**	เนย
Cheese	**Neui-khaeng**	เนยแข็ง
Chili sauce	**Sauce phrik**	ซอสพริก
Chinese mushrooms	**Hed-homm chine**	เห็ดหอมจีน
Chinese vermicelli	**Mi-sua**	หมี่ซั่ว

Coffee (ground)	**Kafae khua laew**	กาแฟคั่วแล้ว
Coffee (instant)	**Kafae phong samret**	กาแฟผงสำเร็จ
Coffee (seeds)	**Kafae med**	กาแฟเม็ด
Cloud ears	**Hed hou-nou**	เห็ดหูหนู
Dried mussels	**Hoi Taak haeng**	หอยตากแห้ง
Dried and salted fish	**Pla haeng**	ปลาแห้ง
Dried small shrimps	**Koung haeng**	กุ้งแห้ง
Egg (salted)	**Khaikhem**	ไข่เค็ม
Fermented cabbage	**Phakkard khem**	ผักกาดเค็ม
Fermented beans	**Tao-chiao**	เต้าเจี้ยว
Fish paste	**Kapi**	กะปิ
Fish sauce	**Narm-pla**	น้ำปลา
Flour	**Paeng**	แป้ง
Flour rice, glutinous	**Paeng khao-chao, khaoniao**	แป้งข้าวเจ้า, ข้าวเหนียว
Flour sago	**Paeng sakhou**	แป้งสาคู
Flour wheat	**Paeng sali**	แป้งสาลี
Flour tapioca	**Paeng manh**	แป้งมัน
Ghee	**Neui khaek**	เนยแขก
Gourmet powder	**Phong shou-rot**	ผงชูรส
Honey	**Narm-phueng**	น้ำผึ้ง
Margarine	**Neui-thiam**	เนยเทียม
Milk	**Nom**	นม
Milk (cow fresh)	**Nom sod**	นมสด
Milk (sweetened condensed)	**Nom khon waan**	นมข้นหวาน
Milk (unsweetened evaporated)	**Nom sod raheui**	นมสดระเหย
Noodles	**Sen-mi**	เส้นหมี่

Noodles (rice)	**Mai-faan**	ไหมฝั่น
Noodles (flat rice)	**Kwaitiao sen-yai**	ก๋วยเตี๋ยวเส้นใหญ่
Noodles (narrow rice)	**Kwaitiao sen-lek**	ก๋วยเตี๋ยวเส้นเล็ก
Noodles (egg)	**Sen bah-mi**	เส้นบะหมี่
Noodles (yellow egg)	**Sen mi-leuang**	เส้นหมี่เหลือง
Oil (vegetable)	**Narm-manh phued**	น้ำมันพืช
Oil (coconut)	**Narm-manh maphrao**	น้ำมันมะพร้าว
Oil (gingelly)	**Narm-manh nga**	น้ำมันงา
Oil (groundnt)	**Narm-manh thua**	น้ำมันถั่ว
Rice	**Khao**	ข้าว
Rice (white)	**Khao-chao**	ข้าวเจ้า
Rice (white glutinous)	**Khao-niao khao**	ข้าวเหนียวขาว
Rice (black glutinous)	**Khao-niao damh**	ข้าวเหนียวดำ
Rice (unpolished)	**Khao sorm-mue**	ข้าวซ้อมมือ
Salt	**Kleua**	เกลือ
Salt (coarse)	**Kluea med**	เกลือเม็ด
Salt (fine)	**Kleua ponh**	เกลือป่น
Salt (rock)	**Kleua Hin, Kleua Sinthaow**	เกลือหิน, เกลือสินเธาว์
Soy sauce (red, black)	**Si-iew (khao; damh)**	ซีอิ๊ว (ขาว, ดำ)
Sugar	**Narm-tarn**	น้ำตาล
Sugar (brown)	**Narm-tarn si ramh**	น้ำตาลสีรำ
Sugar (palm)	**Narm-tarn puek**	น้ำตาลปึก
Sugar (white crystal)	**Narm-tarn saai khao**	น้ำตาลทรายขาว
Sugar (rock)	**Narm-tarn krouad**	น้ำตาลกรวด
Tamarind (dried)	**Makharm-piak**	มะขามเปียก
Tea dust	**Sha-phong**	ชาผง
Tea (instant)	**Sha-samred**	ชาสำเร็จ
Tea (Chinese)	**Sha-chine**	ชาจีน

ea leaf	**Bai-sha**	ใบชา

General Conversation

want to buy some rambutans.	**Shan tongkarn sue ngaw.**	ฉันต้องการซื้อเงาะ
Have you any big and sweet ones?	**Tongkarn louk yai-yai waan-waan?**	ต้องการลูกใหญ่ ๆ หวาน ๆ?
But these are too small.	**Ni lek pai.**	นี่เล็กไป
want bigger rambutans.	**Tongkarn yai kwa ni.**	ต้องการใหญ่กว่านี้
How do you sell them?	**Khaai yang-rai?**	ขายอย่างไร?
want two bunches of fragrant bananas.	**Chan tongkarn kluai-homm sawng hwi.**	ฉันต้องการกล้วยหอมสองหวี
Do you have some ripe ones?	**Tongkarn thi kamlang-kin?**	ต้องการที่กำลังกิน?
These are not ripe.	**Ni yang mai souk.**	นี่ยังไม่สุก
How much for a bunch?	**Hwi-lah thao-rai?**	หวีละเท่าไร?
Do you have some potatoes?	**Mi manh-farang mai?**	มีมันฝรั่งไหม?
Are these oranges sweet or sour?	**Somh lao-ni waan rue priao?**	ส้มเหล่านี้หวานหรือเปรี้ยว?
prefer oranges to bananas.	**Shan shopp somh maak-kwa kluai.**	ฉันชอบส้มมากกว่ากล้วย
Pick bigger ones for me.	**Leuak louk toh-toh hai shan.**	เลือกลูกโต ๆ ให้ฉัน

That is quite all right.	**Louk-nanh shai dai.**	ลูกนั้นใช้ได้
Are these eggs fresh?	**Khai ni sod mai?**	ไข่นี้สดไหม?
I need a dozen eggs.	**Shan tongkarn khai lo nueng.**	ฉันต้องการไข่โหลหนึ่ง
Isn't that too expensive?	**Mai phaeng pai rue?**	ไม่แพงไปหรือ?
Can you make it cheaper?	**Lod hai noi dai mai?**	ลดให้หน่อยได้ไหม?
I believe that's about all.	**Henh chah phaw laew.**	เห็นจะพอแล้ว
How much are they altogether?	**Ruam thang-mod thao-rai?**	รวมทั้งหมดเท่าไร?
Please wrap them up.	**Karuna haw hai-thi.**	กรุณาห่อให้ที
Put them in my basket, please.	**Proad sai long nai ta-kra.**	โปรดใส่ลงในตะกร้า
I am sorry, I do not have small change.	**Chan mai-mi ngoen-pleek.**	ฉันไม่มีเงินปลีก
Please give me small change.	**Khaw ngoen-pleek hai shan.**	ขอเงินปลีกให้ฉัน
Look, you have given me the wrong change.	**Khun thawn-ngoen hai shan mai khrop.**	คุณทอนเงินให้ฉันไม่ครบ

SHOPPING AND BARGAINING

Shopping in Thailand is always an adventure and frequently a delight. This is so not only because of the varied merchandise you may buy as souvenirs of your visit, but also because of the sheer pleasure of making yourself understood. It's important to know, and to be able to explain, exactly what it is that you want - since, obviously, you won't be able to trot downtown a week later to make an exchange. When shopping in Thailand, the rule should be; stick to local goods. Imported articles carry heavy duty and are therefore expensive. As in most other Asian capitals, locally made products are well worth buying and very cheap by comparison with American and European prices.

The following list should be of some help to you in making your wishes known, whether you are on a shopping spree for the family at home or in urgent need of a basic necessity.

(a) General Conversation

I would like to go shopping.	**Phom chah pai ha sue khong.**	ผมจะไปหาซื้อของ

Will you come with me?	**Pai duai-kan mai?**	ไปด้วยกันไหม?
Where's the main shopping area?	**Yarn-karn-kha you thi nai?**	ย่านการค้าอยู่ที่ไหน?
How far is it from here?	**Klai chaak-ni maak mai?**	ไกลจากนี่มากไหม?
How do I get there?	**Pai kanh dai yang-rai?**	ไปกันได้อย่างไร?
At what time do the stores open?	**Doai pok-kati raan-kha perd ki mong?**	โดยปกติ ร้านค้าเปิดกี่โมง?
Where is ....?	**.......you thi nai?**	.......อยู่ที่ไหน?
- the bookstore	**- raan nangsue**	- ร้านหนังสือ
- the drug store	**- raan khaai ya**	- ร้านขายยา
- the grocery store	**- raan khaai-khong shamh**	- ร้านขายของชำ
- the stationery store	**- raan khreuang khian**	- ร้านเครื่องเขียน
- the sundry goods store	**- raan sinkha bettalet**	- ร้านสินค้าเบ็ดเตล็ด
- the laundry	**- raan sak-rid seua-pha**	- ร้านซักรีดเสื้อผ้า
- the department store	**- haang sappha-sinkha**	- ห้างสรรพสินค้า
- the supermarket	**- supermarket**	- ซูเปอร์มาร์เก็ต
- the goldsmith's shop	**- raan thawng rouppaphan**	- ร้านทองรูปพรรณ
- the jeweler's shop	**- raan khreuang phed**	- ร้านเครื่องเพชร
- the record shop	**- raan chamnaai phaen-siang**	- ร้านจำหน่ายแผ่นเสียง
- the food shop	**- raan a-harn**	- ร้านอาหาร

Where can I get ......?	**Phom chah ha dai thi-nai .....?**	ผมจะหา.......ได้ที่ไหน?
Do you sell ....?	**.......mi khaai mai?**	.......มีขายไหม?
- guide book	**- nangsue namh-thiao**	- หนังสือนำเที่ยว
- map of Thailand	**- phaen-thi Prathed Thai**	- แผนที่ประเทศไทย
- world map	**- phaen-thi loke**	- แผนที่โลก
- matches	**- mai khide-fai**	- ไม้ขีดไฟ
- American cigarettes	**- bouri American**	- บุหรี่อเมริกัน
- writing pad	**- kradaad khian chodmaai**	- กระดาษเขียนจดหมาย
- needles and thread	**- khem yeb pha, daai-lord**	- เข็มเย็บผ้า, ด้ายหลอด
- envelopes	**- sawng chod-maai**	- ซองจดหมาย
- medicated soap	**- sabou ya**	- สบู่ยา
Do you have this kind of goods?	**Sinkha baep-diao kab yang ni mi khaai mai?**	สินค้าแบบเดียวกับอย่างนี้ มีขายไหม?
I want something like this.	**Phom tongkarn khlaai kab yang ni.**	ผมต้องการคล้ายกับ อย่างนี้
Can you show me some more?	**Mi hai dou ik mai?**	มีให้ดูอีกไหม?
Could I see that please?	**Khaw phom dou anh nanh dai-mai?**	ขอผมดูอันนั้นได้ไหม?
Have you got it in yellow?	**Si leuang mi mai?**	สีเหลืองมีไหม?
I want some other colour.	**Si uen mi mai**	สีอื่นมีไหม

I prefer a darker (lighter) colour.	**Phom tongkarn si kae kwa (onn kwa).**	ผมต้องการสีแก่กว่า (อ่อนกว่า)
Show me some other qualities.	**Khaw dou shanid uen.**	ขอดูชนิดอื่น
Have you any better quality?	**Di kwa-ni mai mi rue?**	ดีกว่านี้ไม่มีหรือ?
I will take this piece (pair).	**Phom sue shin ni (khou ni).**	ผมซื้อชิ้นนี้ (คู่นี้)
How much is it?	**Thao-rai?**	เท่าไร?
How much is it a meter (a kilo)?	**Met (kilo) lah thao-rai?**	เมตร (กิโล) ละเท่าไร?
How much for a pair?	**Khou-lah thao-rai?**	คู่ละเท่าไร?
How much if I buy three?	**Tha sue thi-diao sarm aow thao-rai?**	ถ้าซื้อทีเดียวสาม เอาเท่าไร?
That's too expensive.	**Phaeng pai.**	แพงไป
I think it's very expensive.	**Phom khid wa khun khaai phaeng.**	ผมคิดว่าคุณขายแพง
Is this a fixed price?	**Rakha ni taw mai-dai rue?**	ราคานี้ต่อไม่ได้หรือ?
Is that the rock-bottom price?	**Nanh penh rakha tam sout laew rue?**	นั่นเป็นราคาต่ำสุด แล้วหรือ?
I cannot buy at that price.	**Phom mai samart sue rakha nanh.**	ผมไม่สามารถซื้อราคานั้น
If you make it cheaper, I'll buy it.	**Phom chah sue tha lod ik dai.**	ผมจะซื้อถ้าลดอีกได้
Tell me your lowest price.	**Khaw rakha khaad-tua tamh soud.**	ขอราคาขาดตัวต่ำสุด

/hat is your last price (not subject to bargaining)?	**Rakha khaad-tua thao-rai?**	ราคาขาดตัวเท่าไร?
/ell, I'll buy it at that price.	**Phom chah sue tarm rakha nanh.**	ผมจะซื้อตามราคานั้น
ow much is it all together?	**Ruam-kanh thang-mod thao-rai?**	รวมกันทั้งหมดเท่าไร?
ave you got a box?	**Khun mi klong sai mai?**	คุณมีกล่องใส่ไหม?
ave you got a bag (for carrying)?	**Khun mi thoung sai mai?**	คุณมีถุงใส่ไหม?
/ill you wrap them up for me?	**Karuna haw hai-phom dai-mai?**	กรุณาห่อให้ผมได้ไหม?
o you accept credit cards?	**Rap credit kard mai?**	รับเครดิตการ์ดไหม?

b) A Shopping List

ntiques	**Watthu boraan**	วัตถุโบราณ
rtificial flowers	**Dorkmai thiam**	ดอกไม้เทียม
ags (ladies)	**Krapaow thue phuying**	กระเป๋าถือผู้หญิง
ags (traveling)	**Krapaow dernthaang**	กระเป๋าเดินทาง
ags (brief)	**Krapaow ekka-sarn**	กระเป๋าเอกสาร
asket (rattan)	**Takra waai**	ตะกร้าหวาย
asket (laundry)	**Takra seua-pha**	ตะกร้าเสื้อผ้า
asket (waste)	**Takra khaya**	ตะกร้าขยะ
athing Suits	**Shoud ab-narm**	ชุดอาบน้ำ
atteries or dry cells	**Tharn fai-shaai**	ถ่านไฟฉาย
ed sheets	**Pha pou-thi-nonn**	ผ้าปูที่นอน
elts	**Khem-khad**	เข็มขัด
icycles	**Rot chak-krayarn**	รถจักรยาน

Blankets	**Phahom-nonn**	ผ้าห่มนอน
Bolster	**Monn-khaang**	หมอนข้าง
Books	**Nangsue**	หนังสือ
Boots	**Rongthao boots**	รองเท้าบู๊ท
Brassieres	**Seua yok-song**	เสื้อยกทรง
Briefs	**Kangkeng nai**	กางเกงใน
Brief case	**Krapaow ekka-sarn**	กระเป๋าเอกสาร
Brooms	**Mai-kwaad**	ไม้กวาด
Buttons	**Kradoum**	กระดุม
Cameras	**Klong thaai-roup**	กล้องถ่ายรูป
Cane furniture	**Khreuang-reuan waai**	เครื่องเรือนหวาย
Carpets	**Phrom**	พรม
Chairs	**Kao-i**	เก้าอี้
Chinaware	**Thuai, shaam, chaan krabeuang**	ถ้วย, ชาม, จานกระเบื้อง
Cigarette lighters	**fai shack**	ไฟแช็ค
Cloths (cleaning)	**Pha samrap shed**	ผ้าสำหรับเช็ด
Cloths (dish)	**Pha shed-shaam**	ผ้าเช็ดชาม
Cloths (scrubbing)	**Pha thou-phuen**	ผ้าถูพื้น
Cloths (table)	**Pha pou-toh**	ผ้าปูโต๊ะ
Cloths (tray)	**Pha rong-thard**	ผ้ารองถาด
Cooking utensils	**Khreuang khrua**	เครื่องครัว
Cosmetics	**Khreuang Sam-arng**	เครื่องสำอาง
Cotton goods	**Pha faai**	ผ้าฝ้าย
Crockery	**Khreuang thuai-shaam**	เครื่องถ้วยชาม
Crystal ware	**Khreuang-kaew chiara-nai**	เครื่องแก้วเจียรนัย
Cushions	**Bawh**	เบาะ
Detergents	**Phong sak-fawk**	ผงซักฟอก

)inner sets	**Shoud a-harn**	ชุดอาหาร
)isinfectants	**Ya kha sheua-roke**	ยาฆ่าเชื้อโรค
)og medicines	**Ya samrab sunak**	ยาสำหรับสุนัข
)resses	**Seua-pha**	เสื้อผ้า
)resses (little girls')	**Seua-pha dek phoo ying**	เสื้อผ้าเด็กผู้หญิง
)resses (petite juniors')	**Seua-pha dek-sao**	เสื้อผ้าเด็กสาว
)resses (women's)	**Seua-pha phoo ying**	เสื้อผ้าผู้หญิง
lectric appliances	**Khreuang-shai fai-fa**	เครื่องใช้ไฟฟ้า
lowers (fresh)	**Dorkmai sod**	ดอกไม้สด
lowers (artificial)	**Dorkmai thiam**	ดอกไม้เทียม
olding beds	**Kao-i phab**	เก้าอี้พับ
urniture (wood)	**Khreuang-reuan maai**	เครื่องเรือนไม้
;as cookers	**Taow gas**	เตาแก๊ส
;as holders	**Thang gas**	ถังแก๊ส
;lasses (household)	**Khreuang kaew**	เครื่องแก้ว
lats	**Muak**	หมวก
leadwear	**Khreuang pradab-phom**	เครื่องประดับผม
lybrid orchids	**Kluai-mai phasom**	กล้วยไม้ผสม
nsecticides	**Ya kha-malaeng**	ยาฆ่าแมลง
ars	**Toum; Hai**	ตุ่ม, ไห
ewelery (imitation)	**Khreuang-phed thiam**	เครื่องเพชรเทียม
(nitted goods	**Sinkha louk-maai thak**	สินค้าลูกไม้ถัก
ace fabrics	**Louk-maai**	ลูกไม้
ighter flints	**Hin lek-fai**	หินเหล็กไฟ
ighter fuel	**Narm-manh fai-shaek**	น้ำมันไฟแช็ค
ocks and keys	**Kounchae**	กุญแจ
Aanicure articles	**Upakorn taeng-leb**	อุปกรณ์แต่งเล็บ
Aats	**Seua; Sard**	เสื่อ, สาด

Mattresses	**Thi-nonn**	ที่นอน
Mirrors	**Krachok**	กระจก
Mosquito nets	**Moung**	มุ้ง
Musical instrument	**Khreuang don-tri**	เครื่องดนตรี
Niello ware	**Khreuang-thom**	เครื่องถม
Phonograph records	**Phaen-siang**	แผ่นเสียง
Perfumes	**Narm-homm; Narm-ob**	น้ำหอม, น้ำอบ
Percolators	**Khreuang tom-kafae**	เครื่องต้มกาแฟ
Picture frames	**Krobb-roup**	กรอบรูป
Plates and dishes	**Chaan, Shaam**	จาน, ชาม
Pots (cooking)	**Maw houng-tom**	หม้อหุงต้ม
Purses (money)	**Krapaow sai ngoen**	กระเป๋าใส่เงิน
Rainwear	**Seua kan-fonh**	เสื้อกันฝน
Radio	**Vithayu**	วิทยุ
Razor blades	**Bai mide-kone**	ใบมีดโกน
Ready-made clothing	**Seua samret-roup**	เสื้อสำเร็จรูป
Refrigerators	**Tou-yenh**	ตู้เย็น
Sandals	**Rong-thao taeh**	รองเท้าแตะ
Scales	**Khreuang-shang**	เครื่องชั่ง
Scissors	**Kan-krai**	กรรไกร
Screen doors	**Bang-ta**	บังตา
Sewing machines	**Chak yeb-pha**	จักรเย็บผ้า
Shavers (electric)	**Khreuang kone-nuad fai-fa**	เครื่องโกนหนวดไฟฟ้า
Shoes	**Rong-thao**	รองเท้า
Shoelaces	**Sheuak phouk rong-thao**	เชือกผูกรองเท้า
Shoe polish	**Ya khad rong-thao**	ยาขัดรองเท้า
Spectacles	**Waenta**	แว่นตา
Sporting goods	**Khreuang ki-la**	เครื่องกีฬา

tationery	**Khreuang khian**	เครื่องเขียน
uits (ready-made)	**Seua-pha samret-roup**	เสื้อผ้าสำเร็จรูป
uitcases	**Krapaow dern-thaang**	กระเป๋าเดินทาง
able (drop-leaf)	**Toh phab-dai**	โต๊ะพับได้
able (ironing)	**Toh reed-pha**	โต๊ะรีดผ้า
able (lamp)	**Takiang tang-toh**	ตะเกียงตั้งโต๊ะ
able (typewriting)	**Toh phim-dide**	โต๊ะพิมพ์ดีด
eacup & saucers	**Thuai-hou chaan-rong**	ถ้วยหูจานรอง
elevision (black & white)	**T.V. (khao-damh)**	ทีวี (ขาวดำ)
elevision (color)	**T. V. Si**	ทีวีสี
hai cotton	**Pha-faai Thai**	ผ้าฝ้ายไทย
hai silk	**Pha-mai Thai**	ผ้าไหมไทย
iffin carrier	**Pin-to**	ปิ่นโต
rays	**Thard**	ถาด
nderwear	**Shoud shan nai**	ชุดชั้นใน
niforms (ready-made)	**Khreuang-baeb tat-samret**	เครื่องแบบตัดสำเร็จ
acuum cleaners	**Khreuang doud-foun**	เครื่องดูดฝุ่น
atches & clocks	**Nalika**	นาฬิกา
igs	**Wig phom**	วิกผม
indow-curtain fabrics	**Pha tham-marn na-taang**	ผ้าทำม่านหน้าต่าง

(c) Buying Gifts and Souvenirs

Thailand is among the best countries in the Orient for souvenir unting. The geographical peculiarities of the country, which cover wide range in topography and climate, are reflected in the great ariety of handicraft products.

The most sought-after handicrafts are the famous Thai wood carving, ornaments, sculptures and prints, bronze and brass artwares costumed dolls, mythological creatures, ceramic vases, celadon tablewares and decorative pieces that reflect the bold and free spirit of the craftsmen who fashioned them. There are many shops specializing in inlaid mother-of-pearl cabinets, antique jade and Chinese porcelain. Antiques from Thailand cost only one-third of the price they command in Europe or America. Outside Bangkok, tourists will find even greater bargains—but of course they will have to look a little harder than in the capital. Chieng Mai, for instance, is famous for its unique fabrics, among them a blend of Thai silk and cotton, lacquerwares, wood-carving, silverware, sun umbrella and cloisonne. Elsewhere, many villages specialize in one particular local craft such as pottery, bronzeware, niello silverware, carvings custom-crafted furniture, or any of a thousand other items designed to catch the fancy of travelers and separate them from their supply of travelers' checks.

Jewelry

Among its many other charms, Bangkok is a city of jewelery shops. Thai jewelry is rapidly becoming one of the main shopping attractions. Gold is exceptionally cheap in Thailand and the standard of workmanship is high.

In buying gems, remember: You get what you pay for. To ensure good value, it pays to spend a little more money in a reliable shop than to buy cheaper merchandise at unknown places. Gems and precious metals sell by weight as well as by workmanship.

Sapphires. Thailand produces several sapphires, of which the best are Phailin of dark-blue in color without a trace of green. They ommand an excellent price in world markets, unlike the common-st variety, the Bang-Ka-Chah. This is normally a very dark blue; if it ontains any green, it will be extremely cheap.

Rubies. Thai rubies are well-known by the name of 'Siamese ubies'. The majority of qualified rubies are found in Chantaburi. rices depend on the brightness and the redness of the stones.

Zircons are semi-precious stones indigenous to Thailand. They nd a ready export market. These are usually cut round. White stones re the most common and are available in a wide range of sizes. lue stones are rare and consequently command a higher price.

want a small present for my daughter.	**Phom tongkarn khong-khwan samrap louk-sao.**	ผมต้องการของขวัญ สำหรับลูกสาว
Vhat would you suggest?	**Chah hai phom sue arai di?**	จะให้ผมซื้ออะไรดี?
Vill you show me some rings, please?	**Khaw shom waen.**	ขอชมแหวน?
hat's not what I want.	**Yang nanh phom mai tongkarn.**	อย่างนั้นผมไม่ต้องการ
am most interested in a	**Phom sonh-chai ....**	ผมสนใจ.......
- solitaire	**- waen-phed med diao**	- แหวนเพชรเม็ดเดี่ยว
- ring with center stone	**- waen lom phed**	- แหวนล้อมเพชร
- birthstone ring	**- waen wan-kerd**	- แหวนวันเกิด
- two-piece set	**- waen-song-wong khou**	- แหวนสองวงคู่

- cultured pearl ring	**- waen khai-mouk**	- แหวนไข่มุก
Here's a very fine one. I'll try it on.	**Wong ni suai di. Khaw long suam.**	วงนี้สวยดี ขอลองสวม
I think it is slightly big for my finger.	**Yai pai noi (or luam pai noi).**	ใหญ่ไปหน่อย (หรือ หลวมไปหน่อย)
I think it is the right size.	**Phom khid wa kha-nard phaw-di.**	ผมคิดว่าขนาดพอดี
I suppose the price is as nice as the ring.	**Rakha khong chah phaw-di meuan waen.**	ราคาคงจะพอดีเหมือน แหวน
Can't you make it a bit smaller for me?	**Tham wong hai lek long ik dai mai?**	ทำวงให้เล็กลงอีกได้ไหม?
Can you get my initials engraved on it?	**Salak shue hai dai mai?**	สลักชื่อให้ได้ไหม?
My initials are S.K.	**Shue khong phom S.K.**	ชื่อของผม เอส.เค
Do you have a really nice ring with......	**Khun mi waen pradab duai......**	คุณมีแหวนประดับด้วย ......
- alexandrite sapphire	**- phloi sarm si**	- พลอยสามสี
- amethyst	**- phloi si muang**	- พลอยสีม่วง
- aquamarine	**- phloi si fa nam thale**	- พลอยสีฟ้าน้ำทะเล
- diamond	**- phed thae**	- เพชรแท้
- emerald	**- maw-rakot**	- มรกต
- jade	**- yok**	- หยก
- onyx	**- hinh yok (or mora)**	- หินหยก (หรือโมรา)
- rubies	**- thab-thim**	- ทับทิม

- star ruby	**- thab-thim saraek**	- ทับทิมสาแหรก
- sapphires	**- nil si khraam**	- นิลสีคราม
- topaz	**- phloi si leuang**	- พลอยสีเหลือง
- turquoise	**- phloi khiao**	- พลอยเขียว
- white spinel	**- phloi khao**	- พลอยขาว
- zircon	**- phe-thaai**	- เพทาย
- yellow zircon	**- ko-men si leuang**	- โกเมนสีเหลือง
Do you have a ring with a (n) ......?	**Khun mi .... mai?**	คุณมี......ไหม?
- oval-shaped stone	**- waen-phed roup khai**	- แหวนเพชรรูปไข่
- round stone	**- waen-phed med klom**	- แหวนเพชรเม็ดกลม
- rectangular-shaped stone	**- waen-phed med si-liam phuen pha**	- แหวนเพขรเม็ดสี่เหลี่ยมผืนผ้า
- a good zircon	**- waen phe-thaai narm di**	- แหวนเพทายน้ำดี
Do you have a ....?	**Khun mi .... mai?**	คุณมี...........ไหม?
- Nine-stone ring	**- waen nopha kao**	- แหวนนพเก้า
- ring with a ruby set between two diamonds	**- waen fang thab-thim rawaang phed song med**	- แหวนฝังทับทิมระหว่าง - เพชรสองเม็ด
What is the cost of this diamond ring?	**Waen-phed wong ni rakha thao-rai?**	แหวนเพชรวงนี้ราคาเท่าไร?
These diamonds are beautifully cut.	**Phed chia-ra-nai dai suai di.**	เพชรเจียรนัยได้สวยดี
What is that stone?	**Nanh hinh arai?**	นั่นหินอะไร?
What carat?	**Ki karat?**	กี่กะรัต?

I believe these stones are genuine?	**Khong chah penh khong thae?**	คงจะเป็นของแท้?
Are these stones guaranteed against chipping or scratching?	**Khun rap-rawng dai mai wa mai mi tam-ni?**	คุณรับรองได้ไหม ว่าไม่มีตำหนิ?
I want to buy	**Phon tongkarn sue........**	ผมต้องการซื้อ........
- earrings	**- toum-hou**	- ตุ้มหู
- a gold necklace	**- soi-khaw thong-kham**	- สร้อยคอทองคำ
- a diamond pendant	**- chi phed**	- จี้เพชร
- a chain bracelet	**- kamlai onn**	- กำไลอ่อน
- an Indian-style bracelet	**- kamlai khaeng**	- กำไลแข็ง
- a heart-picture locket	**- locket roup hua-chai**	- ล็อกเก็ตรูปหัวใจ
Please show me something in 18-carat gold of exquisite workmanship.	**Khaw-dou thong-roupa-phan sib-paed karat.**	ขอดูทองรูปพรรณ - สิบแปดกะรัต
I suppose you'll guarantee the gold.	**Khun rab-rong khunna-phab thong mai.**	คุณรับรองคุณภาพทองไหม
My ring is growing old-fashioned.	**Khong phom la-samai laew.**	ของผมล้าสมัยแล้ว
Can I get a trade-in for a higher priced diamond ring?	**Phom chah laek aow waen-phed, rakha phaeng-kwa, dai mai?**	ผมจะแลกเอาแหวนเพชร ราคาแพงกว่าได้ไหม?

Vhat would you allow me for it, in exchange for.... ?	**Khun ti rakha thao-rai, tha plian penh ....?**	คุณตีราคาเท่าไร ถ้าเปลี่ยนเป็น.......?
Vill you let me weigh it?	**Phom khaw shang dou dai mai?**	ผมขอชั่งดูได้ไหม?
)o you accept returns?	**Khun rab sue khuen mai?**	คุณรับซื้อคืนไหม?
)o you make all these things yourself?	**Khong thang-mod tham thi-ni rue?**	ของทั้งหมดทำที่นี่หรือ?
'ou might pack these all neatly for me.	**Proad haw hai di-di.**	โปรดห่อให้ดี ๆ
ɪere is a check for the amount of your bill.	**Ni penh cheque tarm rakha thi khun tongkarn.**	นี่เป็นเช็คตามราคาที่คุณต้องการ
am staying at the Dusit Thani.	**Phom phak thi rongraem Dusit Thani.**	ผมพักที่โรงแรมดุสิตธานี

'hai Silk

Pershaps the best known of all the good "buys" is the exotic ıand-woven Pha-Mai Thai or Thai silk. No woman can resist this ɪeautiful material. Apart from the dresses and suits, the heavier-veight Thai silks are used a great deal by interior decorators through ɪut the world. Thai silk is a practical fabric, being very durable, olor-fast and non-shrinking. Usually it is dry-cleaned but it can ɪlso be washed.

There are different qualities of Thai silk, i.e. lightweight (LW), nedium weight(MW), heavy weight(HW) and extra heavy weight

(EW) one-ply, two-ply, four-ply and six-ply respectively. Thai silk sold by the yard and by the meter. From 2.5 to 3 yards are usual required for a dress. There are solid colors, plaids, stripes, check brocaded and prints. Prices vary with the different qualities.

I would like to buy ...	**Phom tongkarn seu .....**	ผมต้องการซื้อ**.......**
- lightweight, plain-color Thai silk	**- pha-mai Thai shanid baang, si riap-riap**	- ผ้าไหมไทยชนิดบาง สีเรียบ ๆ
- heavyweight silk printed with a floral design	**- pha-mai Thai shanid na, laai dork-mai**	- ผ้าไหมไทยชนิดหนา ลายดอกไม้
- extra heavy weight silk for upholstery	**- pha-mai Thai shanid na phised, samrab tham bawh.**	- ผ้าไหมไทยชนิดหนา - พิเศษ สำหรับทำเบาะ
What is the price ....?	**Khid rakha yang-rai ....?**	คิดราคาอย่างไร**.......**?
- per meter	**- taw medh**	- ต่อเมตร
- per yard	**- taw la**	- ต่อหลา
What colors do you have?	**Khun mi si arai?**	คุณมีสีอะไร?
I'd like to have it in....	**Phom yaak dai .....**	ผมอยากได้**.......**
- green	**- si-khiao bai maai**	- สีเขียวใบไม้
- jade green	**- si khiao yok**	- สีเขียวหยก
- indigo	**- si khraam**	- สีคราม
- grey	**- si thaow**	- สีเทา
- dark grey	**- si thaow kae**	- สีเทาแก่
- blue	**- si narm ngoen**	- สีน้ำเงิน
- sky blue	**- si khiao fa**	- สีเขียวฟ้า

- dark blue	**- si nam ngoen khem**	- สีน้ำเงินเข้ม
- light purple	**- si muang onn**	- สีม่วงอ่อน
- dark purple	**- si muang kae**	- สีม่วงแก่
- yellow	**- si leuang**	- สีเหลือง
- black	**- si dam**	- สีดำ
- red	**- si daeng**	- สีแดง
- scarlet	**- si leuad-mou**	- สีเลือดหมู
- white	**- si khao**	- สีขาว
- ivory	**- si nga-shaang**	- สีงาช้าง
- pink	**- si shom-phu**	- สีชมพู
)o you have it in striped?	**Khun mi shanid laai mai?**	คุณมีชนิดลายไหม?
:an you match this color?	**Si Khao kap si-ni mi mai?**	สีเข้ากับสีนี้มีไหม?
'his color is too loud.	**Si ni shoud-shard kern pai.**	สีนี้ฉูดฉาดเกินไป
how me something quieter.	**Khaw dou si riap kwa-ni ....**	ขอดูสีเรียบกว่านี้
don't care for that color.	**Si nanh phom mai shopp.**	สีนั้นผมไม่ชอบ
'hey are	**Manh ....**	มัน.......
- out of date	**- mod sa-mai laew**	- หมดสมัยแล้ว
- too common	**- thama-da kern pai**	- ธรรมดาเกินไป
- discolored	**- tok (or si-tok)**	- ตก (หรือ สีตก)
- an old design	**- laai kaow borarn**	- ลายเก่าโบราณ
- stained	**- mi roi peuan**	- มีรอยเปื้อน
)o you have an orange-colored one?	**Phom yaak dai si som?**	ผมอยากได้สีส้ม?

Is it colorfast?	**Si tok mai ?**	สีตกไหม?
Do you have it in red?	**Si daeng mi mai?**	สีแดงมีไหม?
Have you more of this color?	**Si yang ni mi ik mai?**	สีอย่างนี้มีอีกไหม?
I don't like this one.	**Phom mai shopp si ni.**	ผมไม่ชอบสีนี้
May I see something better?	**Phom khaw dou thi di-kwa ni?**	ผมขอดูที่ดีกว่านี้?
I like this one.	**Phom shopp laai ni.**	ผมชอบลายนี้
Do you deliver the goods?	**Khun song khawng thueng baan mai?**	คุณส่งของถึงบ้านไหม?
Please have it double-wrapped in plastic and in brown paper	**Proad haw sawng-shan, duai plastic na-na lae kradard na ik shan nueng.**	โปรดห่อสองชั้นด้วย พลาสติกหนา ๆ และกระดาษหนาอีกชั้ หนึ่ง
Please pack it in a carton	**Laew ban-chu klong kradaad**	แล้วบรรจุกล่องกระดาษ

Skin and Leather Products

Bangkok is world famous as a center for the manufacture of fas ionable accessories out of reptile skins. Shoes, briefcases, handbag belts, purses, wallets, watchbands, and even ties are made here fro python, crocodile, water monitor, iguana, brown lizard, and oth beautiful skin. Some of these are dyed to produce a wide range fashionable colors. Others, usually more expensive, are left to di play their natural markings in the most effective way. These high prized fashion luxuries are probably cheaper in Bangkok than an where else in the world.

ould you show me ....?	**Khaw phom shom ....?**	ขอผมชม**.......**?
- handbags made from crocodile skin	**- krapaow-nang chora-khe**	- กระเป๋าหนังจระเข้
- handbags made from python skin	**- krapaow-nang ngou-leuam**	- กระเป๋าหนังงูเหลือม
- from brown lizard	**- nang takuad**	- หนังตะกวด
would like to see ...	**Phom khaw shom ......**	ผมขอชม**.......**
- shoes	**- rawng-thao**	- รองเท้า
- slippers	**- rawng-thao taeh**	- รองเท้าแตะ
...made from animal and reptile skins.	**.....tham duai nang-sat lae nang ngou.**	**.......**ทำด้วยหนังสัตว์ และหนังงู
it hand-made?	**Tham duai mue shai-mai?**	ทำด้วยมือใช่ไหม?

old and Silver

nklets	**Kamlai thao**	กำไลเท้า
sh tray	**Thi khia buri**	ที่เขี่ยบุหรี่
angles	**Kamlai kho mue**	กำไลข้อมือ
eer tankard	**Kaew beer**	แก้วเบียร์
elt	**Khem-khad**	เข็มขัด
owl	**Shaam khome**	ชามโคม
racelet	**Kamlai khaeng**	กำไลแข็ง
rooch	**Khem-klad**	เข็มกลัด
uckle	**Hua khemkhad**	หัวเข็มขัด
igar box	**Klong cigar**	กล่องซิการ์
igarette case	**Sawng buri**	ซองบุหรี่

Coffee,tea set	**Shoud Kafae, sha**	ชุดกาแฟ, ชา
Cold water jug	**Yeuak-narm**	เหยือกน้ำ
Cross Crucifix	**Kang-khen**	กางเขน
Cuff links	**Doum shirt**	ดุมเชิ้ต
Earrings	**Toum-hou**	ตุ้มหู
Flower vase	**Chae-kanh**	แจกัน
Fork, spoon	**Somm, shonn**	ส้อม, ช้อน
Fruit stand	**Phaan pholamai**	พานผลไม้
Gold necklace	**Soi thongkham**	สร้อยทองคำ
Hair pins	**Pin pak-phom**	ปิ่นปักผม
Ice bucket	**Thang narm-khaeng**	ถังน้ำแข็ง
Incense burner	**Thi pak thoup**	ที่ปักธูป
Key chain	**Phuang kounchae**	พวงกุญแจ
Locket	**Locket**	ล็อกเก็ต
Match case	**Klong mai-khid**	กล่องไม้ขีด
Napkin ring	**Huang pha-ched-paaak**	ห่วงผ้าเช็ดปาก
Pen knife	**Mede perd sawng chodmaai**	มีดเปิดซองจดหมาย
Pendant	**Chi**	จี้
Photo frame	**Kropp roup**	กรอบรูป
Powder compact	**Talab paeng**	ตลับแป้ง
Ring(engagement)	**Waen manh**	แหวนหมั้น
Ring(wedding)	**Waen salak-shue**	แหวนสลักชื่อ
Rosary	**Louk prakham**	ลูกประคำ
Silver bowl	**Khan ngoen**	ขันเงิน
Silver casket	**Pha-ob ngoen**	ผะอบเงิน
Silver tray	**Thard ngoen**	ถาดเงิน
Snuff bottle	**Khuad ya-nat**	ขวดยานัตถุ์
Tie pin	**Khem-klad thye**	เข็มกลัดไท
Tie clip	**Khem-neep thye**	เข็มหนีบไท

ronze and Brass

ronze statuettes	**Roup salak**	รูปสลัก
rass or bronze table lamps	**Takiang tang-toh**	ตะเกียงตั้งโต๊ะ
andle holders	**Sherng thian**	เชิงเทียน
arved brass table lamps	**Khome-fai salak**	โคมไฟสลัก
ss-stick holders	**Thi pak-thoup**	ที่ปักธูป
alt and pepper set	**Khreuang-shoud kleua phrikthai**	เครื่องชุดเกลือพริกไทย
poons, forks and knives with carved handles	**Somm,shonn, mide mi daam salak**	ส้อม ช้อน มีดมีด้ามสลัก
emple bells	**Rakhang thongleuang**	ระฆังทองเหลือง

eramics and Stone wares

asserole dishes	**Shaam-khome**	ชามโคม
owls and dishes (Bencharong)	**Thuai, shaam Bencharong**	ถ้วย, ชามเบญจรงค์
rchids and flower pots	**Krathaang kluai-mai**	กระถางกล้วยไม้
oup pots	**Maw-kaeng**	หม้อแกง
eapots	**Ka-narm**	กาน้ำ
ases; jars	**Chae-kanh; hai**	แจกัน, ไห

Voodcraft

ltar tables	**Toh bousha, toh-phra**	โต๊ะบูชา, โต๊ะพระ
etel tray sets	**Shoud maak-phlu**	ชุดหมากพลู

Carved chess pieces	**Tua maak-rouk**	ตัวหมากรุก
Elephant chairs	**Koup**	กูบ
Rocking chairs	**Kao-i yoke**	เก้าอี้โยก
Linen chest	**Tou seua-pha**	ตู้เสื้อผ้า
Wood screens	**Bang-ta**	บังตา
Traditional Thai dining room sets	**Toh a-harn baeb Thai-thai**	โต๊ะอาหารแบบไทย
Carved statuettes	**Roup-salak maai**	รูปสลักไม้
Carved elephants, buffaloes	**Shaang-maai, khwaai-maai**	ช้างไม้, ควายไม้
Food canisters	**Klong a-harn maai**	กล่องอาหารไม้
Fruit-and-salad bowls	**Shaam pholamai; Shaam salad**	ชามผลไม้, ชามสลัด
Lazy Susan (revolving tray)	**Thard moun**	ถาดหมุน
Snack tray	**Thard a-harn waang**	ถาดอาหารว่าง

Hill-tribe Handicrafts

Hill-tribe dolls	**Touk-kata shao-khao**	ตุ๊กตาชาวเขา
Embroidered jackets	**Seua jacket laai pak**	เสื้อแจ๊กเก็ตลายปัก
Shoulder bags	**Yarm saphaai shao-khao**	ย่ามสะพายชาวเขา
Reed mouth organ	**Khaen**	แคน
Reed flute	**Khlui**	ขลุ่ย
Drums	**Klong**	กลอง

Miscellaneous

Ayuthaya feather fans	**Phad khon-nok Ayuthaya**	พัดขนนกอยุธยา
Ban Chiang artifacts	**Watthu borarn Baan Chiang**	วัตถุโบราณบ้านเชียง

Chanthaburi gems	**Phloi Chanthaburi**	พลอยจันทบุรี
Chiang Mai cotton fabrics	**Pha-faai Chiang Mai**	ผ้าฝ้ายเชียงใหม่
Insect whisks	**Sae pad malaeng**	แส้ปัดแมลง
Dolls in Thai costumes	**Touk-kata shoud Thai**	ตุ๊กตาชุดไทย
Dramatic masks	**Hua-khone**	หัวโขน
Fish mobiles	**Pla taphian bai-laan**	ปลาตะเพียนใบลาน
Gilt-bordered mirrors	**Krachok krob-thawng**	กระจกกรอบทอง
Hammocks	**Ple-yuan**	เปลญวน
Paintings of Thai scenes	**Pharb-khian view Thai**	ภาพเขียนวิวไทย
Models of Thai houses, boats and furniture	**Reuan lae khreuang-reuan chamlong baeb Thai.**	เรือนและเครื่องเรือน จำลองแบบไทย
Ceramic wares of Samut Sakhon	**Thuai-shaam krabeuang Samut Sakhon**	ถ้วย-ชามกระเบื้อง สมุทรสาคร
Stuff animals and birds	**Sat staff lae nok**	สัตว์สตั๊ฟและนก
Tiger's head	**Hua seua**	หัวเสือ
Thai umbrellas	**Rom Thai**	ร่มไทย
Thai silk shirts	**Shirt Mai Thai**	เชิ้ตไหมไทย
Ladies' scarves	**Pha khloum-phom**	ผ้าคลุมผมลายไทย
Transparencies for shadow play	**Nang Talung**	หนังตะลุง
Sangkhalok wares	**Thuai shaam Sangkhalok**	ถ้วยชามสังคโลก

Crafts Conversation

Do you have a genuine piece of carving?	**Khun mi sinkha mai-salak fi-mue yiam khaai mai?**	คุณมีสินค้าไม้สลักฝีมือเยี่ยมขายไหม?
Is it all hard wood?	**Pen mai neua-khaeng thangmod rue?**	เป็นไม้เนื้อแข็งทั้งหมดหรือ
I am looking for a bronze incense burner.	**Khun mi thi pak-thoup thong-samrit khaai mai?**	คุณมีที่ปักธูปทองสำริดขายไหม?
Do you have a very rare land-scape drawing by a famous artist?	**Khun mi pharb-view waad doai chittrakorn mi shue khaai mai?**	คุณมีภาพวิววาดโดยจิตรกรมีชื่อขายไหม?
I don't care for any of these.	**Laow-ni phom mai sonh chai.**	เหล่านี้ผมไม่สนใจ
What do these creatures represent?	**Ni pen tua a-rai?**	นี่เป็นตัวอะไร?
These are called Kinnari, half human, half bird.	**Ni riak Kinnari, khrueng khon, khrueng nok.**	นี่เรียกกินรี ครึ่งคน ครึ่ง นก
Have you nice lacquered cabinet?	**Khun mi tou long-rak pid-thong khaai mai?**	คุณมีตู้ลงรักปิดทองขายไหม?
It shoud be gold lacquer work inlaid with ivory and mother-of pearl.	**Phom tongkarn thi pradab duai nga-shaang lae hoi-mouk.**	ผมต้องการที่ประดับด้วยงาช้างและหอยมุก

Will you guarantee that the lacquer won't peel off?	**Khun rab-rong dai mai wa si-rak chah mai lawk?**	คุณรับรองได้ไหมว่าสีรักจะไม่ลอก?
What is that vase?	**Nanh chae-kanh a-rai?**	นั่นแจกันอะไร?
How old is it?	**Ayu narn sak thao-rai?**	อายุนานสักเท่าไร?
Can you take them down from the shelf?	**Aow long ma chaak tou hai dou dai mai?**	เอาลงมาจากตู้ให้ดูได้ไหม?
They look quite new.	**Dou pen khong mai.**	ดูเป็นของใหม่
They look to me simply made to sell to foreigners.	**Dou khlaai kab-wa phlit khuen pheua khaai shao tang-prathed.**	ดูคล้ายกับว่าผลิตขึ้นเพื่อขายชาวต่างประเทศ
They look like regular modern imitation rubbish.	**Phom wa pen khong-thiam.**	ผมว่าเป็นของเทียม
What are these bowls and dishes?	**Thuai shaam laow-ni pen khong kao rue?**	ถ้วยชามเหล่านี้เป็นของเก่าหรือ?
This is a set of Sangkhalok wares introduced by potters in the court of Kublai Khan.	**Ni pen shoud Sangkhalok nai samnak Kublai Khan.**	นี่เป็นชุดสังคโลกในสำนักกุบไลข่าน
It is so rare that I really don't like to part with it.	**Ni pen shoud thi ha yaak phom thaeb mai yaak khaai.**	นี่เป็นชุดที่หายากผมแทบไม่อยากขาย
These are reproductions of the famous Ban Chiang artifacts.	**Laow-ni pen khong chamlong khong boraan Baan Chiang.**	เหล่านี้เป็นของจำลองของโบราณบ้านเชียง

I'll buy some of them, but you must pack them very carefully.	**Phom chah sue tae khun tong haw duai khwaam ramat-rawang.**	ผมจะซื้อ แต่คุณต้องห่อด้วยความระมัดระ
How would you like this screen?	**Khun shob bang-ta ni mai?**	คุณชอบบังตานี่ไหม?
I will buy this screen, if you will sell it for 2,000 baht.	**Phom chah sue bang-ta ni tha khun khaai song-phan Baht.**	ผมจะซื้อบังตานี้ถ้าคุณขายสองพันบาท
I think that is enough today.	**Phom khid-wa wanni phaw laew.**	ผมคิดว่าวันนี้พอแล้ว
Please have all things packed very carefully.	**Proad haw khong thang-mod hai di.**	โปรดห่อของทั้งหมดให้ดี
Put this mark on the box (boxes).	**Tham khreuang-maai ni thouk heep-haw.**	ทำเครื่องหมายนี้ทุกหีบห่อ
Send the things to my hotel.	**Proad song khong thang-mod pai thi rongraem.**	โปรดส่งของทั้งหมดไปที่โรงแรม
I am going away on the ...... so you must get the things packed by that time.	**Phom chah pai wan-thi .... shanan tong banchu khong song thanh konn vela.**	ผมจะไปวันที่.....ฉะนั้นต้องบรรจุของส่งทันก่อนเวลา
They are going a long way to the United States.	**Khong tong pai klai thueng Saharat America.**	ของต้องไปไกลถึงสหรัฐอเมริกา

they are not very carefully packed they will smash enroute.	**Tha mai-haw hai di khong chah taek rawaang thaang.**	ถ้าไม่ห่อให้ดี ของจะแตก ระหว่างทาง
ıe box must be ironbound.	**Tong shai lek-sen khaad heep-haw hai naen-na.**	ต้องใช้เหล็กเส้นคาดหีบ ห่อให้แน่นหนา

d) Books and Stationery

In Thailand, bookshops and stationers are usually separate shops, ›ough the latter will often sell paperbacks or ballpoint pens. News- apers and magazines are sold at news stands and kiosks.

ookshop	**Raan nangsue**	ร้านหนังสือ
:ationer's store	**Raan khreuang khian**	ร้านเครื่องเขียน
lews stand	**Raan khaai nangsue phim**	ร้านขายหนังสือพิมพ์
ibrary	**Hong samud**	ห้องสมุด
want to buy	**Phom tongkarn sue ......**	ผมต้องการซื้อ.......
- a copy of The Nation	**- nangsue phim The Nation nueng shabab**	- หนังสือพิมพ์เดอะเนชั่น หนึ่งฉบับ
- a map of Thailand	**- phaen-thi prathed Thai nueng phaen**	- แผนที่ประเทศไทย หนึ่งแผ่น
- an English-Thai dictionary	**- phochana-nukrom angkrit-Thai nueng lem**	- พจนานุกรมอังกฤษ-ไทย หนึ่งเล่ม
allpoint pens	**Pakka louk-luen**	ปากกาลูกลื่น
allpoint refills	**Sai-nai pakka louk-luen**	ไส้ในปากกาลูกลื่น

Bookends	**Thi khan nangsue**	ที่คั่นหนังสือ
Colored pencils	**Dinsaw-si**	ดินสอสี
Crayons (coluored)	**Si thran**	เครยอง (สี), สีเทียน
Diary	**Diary**	ไดอารี่
Drawing set	**Upakorn waad khian**	อุปกรณ์วาดเขียน
Envelopes	**Sawng**	ซอง
Envelopes (large)	**Sawng(yai)**	ซอง (ใหญ่)
Envelopes (small)	**Sawng(lek)**	ซอง (เล็ก)
Eraser (ink)	**Yaang lob(muek)**	ยางลบ (หมึก)
Eraser (pencil)	**Yaang lob(dinsaw)**	ยางลบ (ดินสอ)
Fountain pen	**Parkka muek-suem**	ปากกาหมึกซึม
Glue (liquid)	**Kaow(narm)**	กาว (น้ำ)
Ink (endorsing)	**Muek(tra-yaang)**	หมึก (ตรายาง)
Ink (stencils)	**Muek(add samnaow)**	หมึก (อัดสำเนา)
Ink (fountain pen)	**Muek(parkka muek suem)**	หมึก (ปากกาหมึกซึม)
Ink (black)	**Muek(damh)**	หมึก (ดำ)
Ink (red)	**Muek(daeng)**	หมึก (แดง)
Letter file (hard)	**Faem(shanid khaeng)**	แฟ้ม (ชนิดแข็ง)
Letter file (soft)	**Faem(shanid onn)**	แฟ้ม (ชนิดอ่อน)
Map	**Phaen-thi**	แผนที่
Metal paper punch	**Khreuang choh kradard**	เครื่องเจาะกระดาษ
Mucilage	**Kaow leow**	กาวเหลว
Newspaper	**Nangsue phim**	หนังสือพิมพ์
Nibs	**Tua parkka**	ตัวปากกา
Notebook	**Samud banthuek**	สมุดบันทึก
Paper	**Kradard**	กระดาษ
- Blotting paper	**- Kradard sab**	- กระดาษซับ
- Carbon paper	**- " carbon**	- กระดาษคาร์บอน

- Copying paper	- " **copy**	- กระดาษกอปปี้
- Drawing paper	- " **waad khian**	- กระดาษวาดเขียน
- Duplicating paper	- " **add sam-naow**	- กระดาษอัดสำเนา
- Imitation art paper	- " **art thiam**	- กระดาษอาร์ตเทียม
- Coloured paper	- " **si**	- กระดาษสี
- Photocopy paper	- " **phim khiao**	- กระดาษพิมพ์เขียว
- Newsprint paper	- " **nangsue phim**	- กระดาษหนังสือพิมพ์
- Toilet paper	- " **shamrah**	- กระดาษชำระ
- Tracing paper	- " **lawk-baeb**	- กระดาษลอกแบบ
- Typewriting paper	- " **phim**	- กระดาษพิมพ์
- Wrapping paper	- " **haw-khawng**	- กระดาษห่อของ
Paper clips	**Clip tid kradard**	คลิปติดกระดาษ
Paper napkin	**Kradard shed paak**	กระดาษเช็ดปาก
Paperweight	**Thi-thap kradard**	ที่ทับกระดาษ
Pen and pencil	**Parkka lae dinsaw**	ปากกาและดินสอ
Pen holder	**Daam parkka**	ด้ามปากกา
Pencils	**Dinsaw**	ดินสอ
Pencil sharpener	**Khreuang lao dinsaw**	เครื่องเหลาดินสอ
Postcards	**Praisani-batt**	ไปรษณียบัตร
Postal scale	**Khreuang-shang praisani-phand**	เครื่องชั่งไปรษณียภัณฑ์
Rubber	**Yarng-lob**	ยางลบ
Ruler (foot)	**Mai banthat**	ไม้บรรทัด
Scissors	**Kan-krai**	กรรไกร
Sealing wax	**Khrang**	ครั่ง
Stapler	**Khreuang yeb kradard**	เครื่องเย็บกระดาษ
Staples	**Luad yeb kradard**	ลวดเย็บกระดาษ
String	**Sheuak**	เชือก

(e) Cosmetics and Personal Accessories

Acne cream	**Cream raksa siew**	ครีมรักษาสิว
After-shave lotion	**Narm-homm lang kone-nuad**	น้ำหอมหลังโกนหนวด
Anti-bacterial soap	**Sabu kha sheua**	สบู่ฆ่าเชื้อ
Astringent cream	**Cream samarn phiew**	ครีมสมานผิว
Baby powder	**Paeng dek**	แป้งเด็ก
Barber shears	**Kankrai tat phom**	กรรไกรตัดผม
Bath essence	**Narm-homm phasom narm arb**	น้ำหอมผสมน้ำอาบ
Bath oil	**Narm-manh shalome tua**	น้ำมันชะโลมตัว
Bleaching cream	**Cream lawk na**	ครีมลอกหน้า
Brilliantine	**Narm-manh sai phom**	น้ำมันใส่ผม
Calamine	**Ya raksa phiew**	ยารักษาผิว
Cleansing cream	**Cream laang na**	ครีมล้างหน้า
Comb	**Wi**	หวี
Complexion milk	**Narm-manh khad phiew**	น้ำมันขัดผิว
Cuticle remover	**Ya laang khob leb**	ยาล้างขอบเล็บ
Deodorant	**Ya khamchad klin-tua**	ยากำจัดกลิ่นตัว
Dry shampoo	**Shampoo sah phom**	แชมพูสระผม
Eyeliner pencil	**Dinsaw khian khiew**	ดินสอเขียนคิ้ว
Eye-darkener	**Si tha khon-ta/khiew**	สีทาขนตา, คิ้ว
Eye-shadow	**Si tha pleuak-ta**	สีทาเปลือกตา
Face powder	**Paeng phad na**	แป้งผัดหน้า
Foundation cream	**Cream rawng-phuen**	ครีมรองพื้น
Hair bleach preparation	**Ya kat si phom**	ยากัดสีผม
Hair brush	**Praeng praeng-phom**	แปรงแปรงผม

air conditioner	**Cream nuad phom**	ครีมนวดผม
air cream	**Cream sai phom**	ครีมใส่ผม
and cream	**Cream tha mue**	ครีมทามือ
air dye	**Ya yomm phom**	ยาย้อมผม
air dryer	**Khreuang pow phom**	เครื่องเป่าผม
air and scalp condition	**Cream bamrung phom**	ครีมบำรุงผม
air pommade	**Cream taeng phom**	ครีมแต่งผม
air remover	**Ya kamchad khon**	ยากำจัดขน
air spray	**Spray shide phom**	สเปรย์ฉีดผม
air tint	**Si taem phom**	สีแต้มผม
ormone cream	**Cream phasom hormone**	ครีมผสมฮอร์โมน
p pencil	**Dinsaw waad khop paak**	ดินสอวาดขอบปาก
ipstick	**Lipstick**	ลิปสติค
lanicure set	**Shoud tham leb**	ชุดทำเล็บ
lascara	**Si tha khon ta(Mascara)**	สีทาขนตา (มัสคาร่า)
ledicated soap	**Sabu ya**	สบู่ยา
lilk lotion	**Cream narm nom**	ครีมน้ำนม
lail brush	**Praeng khad leb**	แปรงขัดเล็บ
lail color	**Si tha leb**	สีทาเล็บ
lail enamel	**Ya tha leb**	ยาทาเล็บ
lail enamel remover	**Ya laang leb**	ยาล้างเล็บ
lail file	**Tabai leb**	ตะไบเล็บ
lail polish	**Ya khad leb**	ยาขัดเล็บ
lail scissor	**Kankrai tat leb**	กรรไกรตัดเล็บ
lail varnish	**Narm-manh khleuap leb**	น้ำมันเคลือบเล็บ
erfume; lotion	**Narm-ob;Narm-homm**	น้ำอบ, น้ำหอม

Permanent wave curler	**Lawd muan phom**	หลอดม้วนผม
Powder compact	**Paeng talab**	แป้งตลับ
Razor	**Mide kone**	มีดโกน
Razor blades	**Bai mide kone**	ใบมีดโกน
Shampoo cream	**Shampoo cream**	แชมพูครีม
Shampoo oil	**Shampoo narm-manh**	แชมพูน้ำมัน
Skin cream	**Cream laang phiew**	ครีมล้างผิว
Shaving brush	**Praeng tha nuad**	แปรงทาหนวด
Shaving soap	**Sabu kone nuad**	สบู่โกนหนวด
Soap	**Sabu**	สบู่
Sponge	**Fawng-narm**	ฟองน้ำ
Setting lotion	**Narm-homm set phom**	น้ำหอมเซ็ทผม
Straight razor	**Mide-kone mi darm**	มีดโกนมีด้าม
Talcum powder	**Paeng roai-tua**	แป้งโรยตัว
Toothbrush	**Praeng si-fanh**	แปรงสีฟัน
Toothpaste	**Ya si-fanh**	ยาสีฟัน
Vitamin cream	**Cream vitamin**	ครีมวิตามิน

(f) At the Seamstress

I have been recommended to you by a friend who tells me that you are an excellent dress-maker and your charges are most reasonable.	**Pheuan nae-namh shan wa khun penh shang-seua fi-mue di rakha mai phaeng.**	เพื่อนแนะนำฉันว่าคุณเป็นช่างเสื้อฝีมือดีราคาไม่แพง

My name is Mrs. Jones.	**Shan shue Mrs. Jones.**	ฉันชื่อมิสซิสโจนส์
Thank you, won't you come in, please?	**Khob-khun! Shern khaang nai.**	ขอบคุณ เชิญข้างใน
I'll sit down here if you don't mind.	**Tha mai-rangkiat, shan khaw nang thi-ni.**	ถ้าไม่รังเกียจ ฉันขอนั่งที่นี่
I had to walk some distance to find your place.	**Ha raan khun shan tong dern klai.**	หาร้านคุณ ฉันต้องเดินไกล
Foolishly, I had jotted down your address incorrectly.	**Sapphrao maak, Shan chod thi-you khun phid.**	สะเพร่ามาก ฉันจดที่อยู่คุณผิด
I have brought material for two dresses which I want you to make for me.	**Shan sue pha ma hai khun tat seua song tua.**	ฉันซื้อผ้ามาให้คุณตัดเสื้อสองตัว
I'm afraid that I am too busy to make any dresses for you.	**Khanah-ni shan mi ngarn maak tham a-rai mai dai.**	ขณะนี้ฉันมีงานมากทำอะไรไม่ได้
It's close to the Christmas and New Year holidays.	**Christmas lae Pi-mai kamlang klai khow ma.**	คริสต์มาสและปีใหม่กำลังใกล้เข้ามา
I'll be glad to do any minor alterations for you.	**Ngarn kae lek-lek noi-noi phaw tham hai dai.**	งานแก้เล็ก ๆ น้อย ๆ พอทำให้ได้

Perhaps you can buy something ready-made and leave the dresses go until after the holidays.	**Baangthi khun sue seua tat-samret roup pai konn. Pi-mai phaan pai chueng tat mai.**	บางทีคุณซื้อเสื้อตัดสำเร็จรูป ไปก่อน ปีใหม่ผ่าน ไปจึงตัดใหม่
They have some very pretty dresses in the stores now.	**Seua-pha suai-suai mi-maak nai raan.**	เสื้อผ้าสวย ๆ มีมากในร้าน
I suppose it really is difficult for a stout person.	**Khon ouan ha seua-pha sai lam-baak.**	คนอ้วนหาเสื้อผ้าใส่ลำบาก
What was the dress you wanted me to fix for you?	**Khun chah hai tham a-rai kap seua khong khun?**	คุณจะให้ทำอะไรกับเสื้อ ของคุณ?
Would you care to slip it on?	**Khun lawng sai hai dou thi rue?**	คุณลองใส่ให้ดูทีรึ?
This is a dress that's gotten too tight for me.	**Seua tua-ni khap maak samrap shan.**	เสื้อตัวนี้คับมากสำหรับฉัน
Do you think you can let it out a little? Can you open the seams?	**Tham hai luam noi dai mai? Lawh ta-kheb awk**	ทำให้หลวมหน่อยได้ไหม? เลาะตะเข็บออก
It's also a little tight through the back and shoulders.	**Thi lang lae lai kaw khap duai.**	ที่หลังและไหล่ก็คับด้วย
I think you should change the neckline.	**Shan khid wa plian khor seua chah di-kwa.**	ฉันคิดว่าเปลี่ยนคอเสื้อ จะดีกว่า

Instead of buttons down the front, you would have a V neckline.	**Thaen tit kradoum daan-na, tham khaw baeb tua V sia.**	แทนติดกระดุมด้านหน้า ทำคอแบบตัววีเสีย
Would you prefer a round neckline?	**Rue khun shob baeb khaw klom?**	หรือคุณชอบแบบคอกลม?
Either one will be all right.	**Yaang-dai yaang-nueng kaw dai.**	อย่างใดอย่างหนึ่งก็ได้
Don't you want the long back zipper closing?	**Khun mai tong-karn zip daan lang rue?**	คุณไม่ต้องการซิบด้านหลังหรือ?
Before you take the dress off, let me mark the hemline.	**Konn thawd seua awk, khaw tham khreuang-maai thi takheb.**	ก่อนถอดเสื้อออก ขอทำเครื่องหมายที่ตะเข็บ
It hangs a little low in the back.	**Daan lang yawn nid-noi.**	ด้านหลังหย่อนนิดหน่อย
How long do you generally wear your skirts?	**Doai pok-katih kraprong khun yao thao-rai?**	โดยปกติกระโปรงคุณยาวเท่าไร?
I like them about 12 or 13 inches from the floor.	**Shan shob pramarn sib-song rue sib-sarm niew chaak phuen.**	ฉันชอบประมาณสิบสองหรือสิบสามนิ้วจากพื้น
Do you want to have a pleat or pleatless?	**Khun tong-karn mi cheep mai ?**	คุณต้องการมีจีบไหม?
By the way, I am looking for a short-sleeved dress.	**Shan kamlang mawng ha seua khaen sanh you.**	ฉันกำลังมองหาเสื้อแขนสั้นอยู่

I will show you some. What do you think of this one?	**Shan chah hai shom song-sarm tua. Baeb ni di mai?**	ฉันจะให้ชุมสองสามตัว แบบนี้ดีไหม?
The style is all right, but the size, I am afraid,is a little bit too small.	**Baeb di, tae khanard dou lek pai.**	แบบดี แต่ขนา ดดูเล็กไป
I want to try on the two frocks I ordered.	**Shan tong-karn lawng seua-kraprong thi dai sang tat wai.**	ฉันต้องการลองเสื้อ กระโปรงที่ได้สั่งตัดไว้
Not too bad.	**Mai leow.**	ไม่เลว
A little too tight over the hips.	**Khap pai noi thi sa-phoke.**	คับไปหน่อยที่สะโพก
I will let that out a bit. And how is it for length?	**Shan chah kae hai luam. Suan yao di rue yang?**	ฉันจะแก้ให้หลวม ส่วนยาวดีหรือยัง?
Just the slightest bit too long, don't you think?	**Dou yao pai noi, khun henh duai mai?**	ดูยาวไปหน่อย คุณเห็นด้วยไหม?
Perhaps it is. I'll shorten it by one centimeter.	**Kaw penh dai. Shan chah tham hai sanh long ik nueng cent.**	ก็เป็นได้ ฉันจะทำให้ สั้นลงอีกหนึ่งเซ็นต์
As to the rest, it needs no alteration.	**Thi uen, mai tong kae.**	ที่อื่นไม่ต้องแก้
Please come in on Friday afternoon for a second fitting.	**Proad ma Wan Souk ton baai, pheua lawng ik khrang.**	โปรดมาศุกร์ตอนบ่าย เพื่อลองอีกครั้ง

Vide-leg trousers	**Karng-keng kha baan.**	กางเกงขาบาน
hirt dresses	**Seua khaw-shirt**	เสื้อคอเชิ้ต
ong dresses	**Kraprong yao**	กระโปรงยาว
asual dresses	**Seua sai-lenh**	เสื้อใส่เล่น
uit dresses	**Seua shoud**	เสื้อชุด
-neck	**Khaw tua V**	คอตัววี
quare neckline	**Khaw si-liam**	คอสี่เหลี่ยม
oat-shaped neckline	**Khaw paad**	คอปาด
eter Pan collar	**Pok khaw bua**	ปกคอบัว
rew neck	**Khaw kalasi**	คอกลาสี
leeveless dress	**Seua mai-mi khaen**	เสื้อไม่มีแขน
tretch panty	**Karngkeng rat-sa-phoke**	กางเกงรัดสะโพก

g) At the Tailor

want to have a new suit made.	**Phom tong-karn tat seua-karngkeng nueng shoud.**	ผมต้องการตัดเสื้อกางเกงหนึ่งชุด
how me the style book, please.	**Phom khaw dou baeb-seua.**	ผมขอดูแบบเสื้อ
how me some samples of cloth.	**Khaw dou tua-yaang pha.**	ขอดูตัวอย่างผ้า
ould you show me...	**Khaw dou ...**	ขอดู...
- some of the serges	**- pha serd**	- ผ้าเสิร์จ
- some of the twills	**- pha laai sawng**	- ผ้าลายสอง
- some of your tweeds	**- sakka-lard na**	- สักหลาดหนา

- flannels	**- sakka-lard baang**	- สักหลาดบาง
- gabardines	**- garbadines**	- การ์บาดีน (หรือ ก๋ามะดิน)
- corduroy	**- pha riew**	- ผ้าริ้ว
- orlon	**- orlon**	- ออร์ล่อน
This is artificial serge.	**Ni pen pha serge thiam.**	นี่เป็นผ้าเสิร์จเทียม
These cloths are too thick.	**Pha ni na maak.**	ผ้านี้หนามาก
I want something thinner.	**Phom tong-karn baang kwa ni.**	ผมต้องการบางกว่านี้
I want something for evening wear.	**Phom tong-karn suam vela yenh.**	ผมต้องการสวมเวลาเย็น
I like this pattern.	**Phom shobb pha baeb ni.**	ผมชอบผ้าแบบนี้
I don't like this pattern.	**Phom mai shobb baeb ni.**	ผมไม่ชอบแบบนี้
I like this dark grey with stripes.	**Phom shobb si thow-kae, mi laai.**	ผมชอบสีเทาแก่ มีลาย
Take my measurements.	**Wat tua phom sih.**	วัดตัวผมซิ
Where's the fitting room?	**Hong lawng you nai?**	ห้องวัดตัวอยู่ไห?
Do you want it double or single-breasted?	**Tong-karn kradoum song-thaew rue thaew-diao?**	ต้องการกระดุมสองแถว หรือแถวเดียว?
Single, with only two buttons.	**Thaew-diao, kradoum song med.**	แถวเดียว กระดุมสองเม็ด
I like the coat a little loose.	**seua luam nid-noi kaw di.**	เสื้อหลวมนิดหน่อยก็ดี

o not make the coat too tight.	**Seua ya hai khap maak.**	เสื้ออย่าให้คับมาก
ıe sleeves can be a little bit long.	**Khaen yao noi.**	แขนยาวหน่อย
ɔout a half-inch longer will be enough.	**Yao ik pramarn khrueng-niew kaw-phaw.**	ยาวอีกประมาณครึ่งนิ้วก็พอ
want the suit lined with good lining.	**Sab-nai tong shai pha di.**	ซับในต้องใช้ผ้าดี
ow about your trousers?	**Laew kang-keng laow?**	แล้วกางเกงเล่า?
don't want them too long nor too big.	**Phom mai tong-karn yao rue yai maak.**	ผมไม่ต้องการยาวหรือใหญ่มาก
ıake deep inside pockets.	**Tham krapow-nai hai luek.**	ทำกระเป๋าในให้ลึก
vo flap pockets.	**Krapow mi fa song krapow.**	กระเป๋ามีฝาสองกระเป๋า
ıree set-in pockets.	**Krapow mai-mi fa sarm krapow.**	กระเป๋าไม่มีฝาสามกระเป๋า
think it is a little tight in the waist.	**Phom wa aew khap pai nid-noi.**	ผมว่าเอวคับไปนิดหน่อย
ow long do you take to finish it?	**Meua-rai chah set?**	เมื่อไรจะเสร็จ?
/hen shall I come for a fitting?	**Chah hai phom ma lawng meua-rai?**	จะให้ผมมาลองเมื่อไร?
want to buy a ready-made suit.	**Phom tong-karn sue seua samret roup.**	ผมต้องการซื้อเสื้อสำเร็จรูป

Can you show me the one in the window?	**Khaw dou tua thi you nai tou-show?**	ขอดูตัวที่อยู่ในตู้โชว์?
I like this coat. May I try this on?	**Phom shobb tua ni. Khaw lawng dai mai?**	ผมชอบตัวนี้ ขอลองได้ไหม?
It fits very well.	**Sai dai phaw di.**	ใส่ได้พอดี
What's the price of this?	**Rakha thao-rai?**	ราคาเท่าไร?
This suit doesn't look very good on me.	**Shoud-ni mai mawh samrap phom.**	ชุดนี้ไม่เหมาะสำหรับผม
This coat is a little	**Seua ni ....**	เสื้อนี้....
- tight at the waist	**- khap thi aew**	- คับที่เอว
- tight under the arms	**- khap thi taai khaen**	- คับที่ใต้แขน
- tight at the shoulders	**- khap thi lai**	- คับที่ไหล่
The arm-holes appear rather tight.	**Khaen dou tueng kern pai.**	แขนดูตึงเกินไป
Will you enlarge the arm-holes a little?	**Chah khayaai khaen hai kwaang ik dai mai?**	จะขยายแขนให้กว้างอีกได้ไหม?
It wrinkles between the shoulders.	**Rawaang lai sawng-khaang, pha manh yonh.**	ระหว่างไหล่สองข้าง ผ้ามันย่น
The sleeves are	**Khaen .....**	แขน.....
- too long	**- yao kern pai**	- ยาวเกินไป
- too wide	**- kwaang pai**	- กว้างไป
- too narrow	**- khaep pai**	- แคบไป

on't you think the sleeves are rather short?	**Khaen mai sanh pai rue?**	แขนไม่สั้นไปหรือ?
I like to have them about half-inch shorter.	**Phom yaak hai sanh ik pramarn khrueng niew.**	ผมอยากให้สั้นอีกประมาณ ครึ่งนิ้ว
ie trousers are	**Kang-keng ......**	กางเกง....
- long	**- yao**	- ยาว
- short	**- sanh**	- สั้น
- loose	**- luam**	- หลวม
- tight	**- khap**	- คับ
ease let them out a bit.	**Tham hai luam ik-noi.**	ทำให้หลวมอีกหน่อย
ie waist is too full (wide).	**Aew luam maak.**	เอวหลวมมาก
ike the trousers high in the waist.	**Phom shobb kang-keng aew soung.**	ผมชอบกางเกงเอวสูง
ease make all these alterations.	**Proad kae tarm ni.**	โปรดแก้ตามนี้

) At the Shoemaker

want to buy a pair of shoes.	**Phom tongkarn sue rong-thao.**	ผมต้องการซื้อรองเท้า
hat kind of shoes do you prefer?	**Khun tongkarn rong-thao shanid nai?**	คุณต้องการรองเท้า ชนิดไหน?
I like to have a pair of	**Phom tongkarn rong-thao ....**	ผมต้องการรองเท้า.......
- brown leather shoes	**- nang si narm-tarn**	- หนังสีน้ำตาล

- black leather shoes	**- nang si dam**	- หนังสีดำ
- tan leather shoes	**- nang fawk, si narm-tarn**	- หนังฟอก สีน้ำตาล
- box calf balmorals	**- nang louk wua**	- หนังลูกวัว
- squared toe	**- hua liam**	- หัวเหลี่ยม
- rounded toe	**- hua klom**	- หัวกลม
- flat squared toe	**- hua baen-liam**	- หัวแบนเหลี่ยม
- tapered toe	**- hua laem**	- หัวแหลม
These shoes are too small for me.	**Rong-thao lao-ni lek pai.**	รองเท้าเหล่านี้เล็กไป
They are a little tight.	**Khap nid-noi.**	คับนิดหน่อย
They are too narrow (large; broad).	**Khaep(yai; kwaang) pai.**	แคบ (ใหญ่, กว้าง) ไป
I cannot get my foot in.	**Phom sai mai dai.**	ผมใส่ไม่ได้
They hurt my feet.	**Sai laew cheb thao.**	ใส่แล้วเจ็บเท้า
Show me another pair, please.	**Khaw phom dou ik khou nueng.**	ขอผมดูอีกคู่หนึ่ง
This pair fits me well.	**Khou ni suam phaw-di.**	คู่นี้สวมพอดี
I like this style.	**Phom shob baep ni.**	ผมชอบแบบนี้
How much a pair?	**Khou-lah thao rai?**	คู่ละเท่าไร?
I would rather advise you to let us make a pair for you.	**Phom wah khun tad mai di kwa.**	ผมว่าคุณตัดใหม่ดีกว่า
Have you any special wishes as to how the shoes are to be made?	**Chah hai phom tham style arai?**	จะให้ผมทำสไตล์อะไร?

want rubber heels put on the shoes.	**Phom tongkarn sonh yaang.**	ผมต้องการส้นยาง
.ll right, please make a new pair of shoes for me.	**Tok-long, tad rong-thao mai hai nueng khou.**	ตกลง รองเท้าใหม่ให้หนึ่งคู่
Vhen will they be ready?	**Meuarai chah set?**	เมื่อไรจะเสร็จ?
will be good if you could finish them next week.	**Chah di maak tha khun tham hai set a thit na.**	จะดีมาก ถ้าคุณทำให้เสร็จอาทิตย์หน้า

i) At the barber

lease give me a haircut.	**Phom tongkarn tat phom.**	ผมต้องการตัดผม
lease cut it short (very short).	**Tat hai sanh (sanh maak-maak).**	ตัดให้สั้น (สั้นมาก ๆ)
eave it (fairly) long.	**Ploi hai yao (phaw som-khuan).**	ปล่อยให้ยาว (พอสมควร)
)on't cut it too short..	**Ya tat hai sanh maak ..**	อย่าตัดให้สั้นมาก.........
- at the back	**- thi daan lang**	- ที่ด้านหลัง
- on top	**- khang-bonh**	- ข้างบน
- in front	**- khang na**	- ข้างหน้า
- at the sides	**- khang-khaang (or daan khaang)**	- ข้าง ๆ (หรือ ด้านข้าง)
:ut a little more	**Tat awk ik nid ....**	ตัดออกอีกนิด.........
- of the top	**- bonh si-sah**	- บนศีรษะ
- of the sides	**- daan khaang**	- ด้านข้าง
'lease don't take too much	**Ya tat awk hai maak .....**	อย่าตัดออกให้มาก.........

- of the top	**- bonh si-sah**	- บนศรีษะ
- of the sides	**- daan khaang**	- ด้านข้าง
You already cut too much of the back.	**Khun tat khang-lang sanh maak pai.**	คุณตัดข้างหลังสั้นมากไป
Please give me a mirror.	**Khaw dou krachok.**	ขอดูกระจก
I don't want any oil.	**Ya sai narm manh**	อย่าใส่น้ำมัน
Please give me a shave.	**Phom tongkarn kone-nuad.**	ผมต้องการโกนหนวด
Please shave my neck.	**Karuna kone tonh-khaw.**	กรุณาโกนต้นคอ
Would you trim ......?	**Lem(or kanh)...hai duai?**	เล็ม (หรือกัน...ให้ด้วย)?
- the beard	**- khrao**	- เครา
- the moustache	**- nuad**	- หนวด
I'd like to have a	**Phom tongkarn.......**	ผมต้องการ......
- face massage	**- nuad na**	- นวดหน้า
- shampoo	**- sah phom duai shampoo**	- สระผมด้วยแชมพู
- scalp massage	**- nuad nang si-sah**	- นวดหนังศรีษะ
- manicure	**- tham leb**	- ทำเล็บ

(j) At the Beautician

I'd like to have my hair done.	**Shan tongkarn tham phom.**	ฉันต้องการทำผม
I want to have a permanent wave.	**Shan tong-karn dad-phom hai you dai naan-naan.**	ฉันต้องการดัดผม ให้อยู่ได้นาน ๆ

Vhich hair style do you prefer?	**Khun shobb song-phom baeb nai?**	คุณชอบทรงผมแบบไหน?
don't know which style suits me.	**Shan mai-saab baeb nai chah di.**	ฉันไม่ทราบแบบไหนจะดี
lease select a style to suit my face.	**Karuna leuak baeb thi moh kap na khong-shan.**	กรุณาเลือกแบบที่เหมาะ กับหน้าของฉัน
our hair is very long. You must have your hair cut first.	**Phom khun yao maak.Tong tat-awk sia konn.**	ผมคุณยาวมาก ต้องตัดออกเสียก่อน
fter that a wet shampoo.	**Laew sah duai shampoo.**	แล้วสระด้วยแชมพู
I have time you can give me a wave.	**Tha mi vela phaw, kaw dad dai leui.**	ถ้ามีเวลาพอก็ ดัดได้เลย
want	**Shan tongkarn ....**	ฉันต้องการ.........
- a shampoo and set	**- sah lae set-phom**	- สระและเซ็ทผม
- a bleach	**- kad si phom**	- กัดสีผม
- a colour rinse	**- khleuap si phom, kroke-phom**	- เคลือบสีผม, โกรกผม
- a dye	**- yomm phom**	- ย้อมผม
- a perm	**- dad phom**	- ดัดผม
- a tint	**- taem si-phom**	- แต้มสีผม
- a touch up	**- yomm khone-phom**	- ย้อมโคนผม
want	**Shan tongkarn ....**	ฉันต้องการ.........
- the same color	**- si-meuan derm**	- สีเหมือนเดิม
- a darker color	**- si khem kwa derm**	- สีเข้มกว่าเดิม

- lighter color	**- si on kwa derm**	- สีอ่อนกว่าเดิม
- auburn	**- si namtarn daeng**	- สีน้ำตาลแดง
- blond	**- si thong**	- สีทอง
- brunette	**- si narm-tarn khem**	- สีน้ำตาลเข้ม
I want it	**Shan tongkarn ....**	ฉันต้องการ.........
- with bangs	**- phom ma**	- ผมม้า
- in a bun	**- phom muai**	- ผมมวย
- in curls	**- dad pen lon**	- ดัดเป็นลอน
- frizz style	**- dad hai yik**	- ดัดให้หยิก
- a razor cut and shaping	**- soi phom**	- ซอยผม
- a scissor cut	**- tat duai kan-krai.**	- ตัดด้วยกรรไกร
- a(complete) re-style	**- plian song phom mai**	- เปลี่ยนทรงผมใหม่
- with ringlets	**- tham phom penh lord**	- ทำผมเป็นหลอด
- with waves	**- phom set lawn**	- ผมเซ็ทลอน
Would you put a ....on for me?	**Sai .... hai dai mai?**	ใส่.........ให้ได้ไหม?
- hair piece	**- hair piece**	- แฮร์พีซ
- wig	**- wig**	- วิก
- half wig	**- half wig**	- ฮาล์ฟวิก
Could I have ....?	**Shan khaw hai khun ....?**	ฉันขอให้คุณ.........?
- a semi-wave	**- dad phom yaang onn**	- ดัดผมอย่างอ่อน
- a manicure	**- taeng leb mue**	- แต่งเล็บมือ
- a pedicure	**- taeng leb thao**	- แต่งเล็บเท้า
- a facial and skin pack	**- nuad lae phawk na**	- นวดและพอกหน้า

- a face massage	- **nuad na**	- นวดหน้า
- bridal makeup	- **taeng baeb chao-sao**	- แต่งแบบเจ้าสาว
- hair-removal wax	- **wax khon**	- แว็กซ์ขน
- eyebrow shaping	- **kan khiew**	- กันคิ้ว
- special steaming for dry hair	- **ob phom duai aye-narm**	- อบผมด้วยไอน้ำ
- curly-hair straightening	- **yend phom**	- ยืดผม
- Form cutting	- **Tat hai penh song**	- ตัดให้เป็นทรง
- Hot-oil perm	- **Ob narm-manh**	- อบน้ำมัน

k) Photography

There are no restrictions on photography in Thailand, except in 'eas controlled by the Armed Services (and thus out of bounds to e public).

t a Camera Shop

y camera doesn't work.	**Klong khawng-phom sia**	กล้องของผมเสีย
he shutter won't close.	**Shutter mai pid.**	ชัตเตอร์ไม่ปิด
can't rewind the film.	**Film muan klab mai dai.**	ฟิล์มม้วนกลับไม่ได้
an you fix it?	**Khun kae dai mai?**	คุณแก้ได้ไหม?
need .... rolls of color film.	**Phom tongkarn film-si.........muan.**	ผมต้องการฟิล์มสี.....ม้วน

Do you have movie film?	**Mi film thaai pharb-phayon mai?**	มีฟิล์มถ่ายภาพยนตร์ไหม
Do you have any flashbulbs?	**Mi lawd flash light mai?**	มีหลอดแฟลชไลท์ไหม?
I'd like(five) rolls of film.	**Phom tongkarn film (ha) muan.**	ผมต้องการฟิล์ม (ห้า) ม้ว
Will you develop (and print) this roll?	**Karuna laang film(lae add-pharb)hai dai-mai?**	กรุณาล้างฟิล์ม (และอัดภาพ) ให้ได้ไหม?
Will you put in the film?	**Karuna sai film hai duai?**	กรุณาใส่ฟิล์มให้ด้วย?
Would you please take the film out of the camera for me?	**Karuna thawd film hai duai?**	กรุณาถอดฟิล์มให้ด้วย?
Can you have this film developed?	**Laang film hai phom?**	ล้างฟิล์มให้ผม?
I want three prints of each negative.	**Phom tongkarn ard pharb yaang-lah sarm pharb.**	ผมต้องการอัดภาพอย่างละสามภาพ
Can I have these negatives enlarged?	**Khayaai pharb hai dai mai?**	ขยายภาพ ให้ได้ไหม?
Can you make a black-and-white(color) enlargement?	**Proad khayaai pharb khao-dam(pharb si) hai phom?**	โปรดขยายภาพขาวดำ (ภาพสี) ให้ผม?
How much will it cost for an 8 X 10 enlargement?	**Khayaai pharb paed khoun sib khid thao rai?**	ขยายภาพแปดคูณสิบคิดเท่าไร?

Film and Accessories

A black-and-white film	**Film khao-dam**	ฟิล์มขาวดำ
A color film	**Film si**	ฟิล์มสี
A fast(fine) grain film	**Film shanid wai saeng**	ฟิล์มสีชนิดไวแสง
Please let me have	**Phom tongkarn ....**	ผมต้องการ....
- some flash bulbs	**- lawd-fai flash**	- หลอดไฟแฟลช
- an exposure meter	**- khreuang wat saeng**	- เครื่องวัดแสง
- a tripod	**- sarm-kha**	- สามขา

Taking Pictures

Excuse me, may I take a picture of you?	**Khaw anuyart phom thaai-pharb khun dai-mai?**	ขออนุญาตผมถ่ายภาพคุณได้ไหม?
Please stay there for a moment.	**Karuna yuen ning-ning.**	กรุณายืนนิ่ง ๆ
Please look this way, but directly into the camera.	**Han-na thang ni, ta mawng klong.**	หันหน้าทางนี้ ตามองกล้อง
Now, a big smile.	**Yim maak-maak.**	ยิ้มมาก ๆ
Smile, please	**Yim noi.**	ยิมหน่อย
Now, come closer.	**Khow ma klai ik noi.**	เข้ามาใกล้อีกหน่อย
Look this way, please	**Karuna mawng thang-ni.**	กรุณามองทางนี้
Please go a few steps farther.	**Thoi lang pai ik sawng-sarm kao.**	ถอยหลังไปอีกสองสามก้าว
Not so close to one another.	**Ya yuen hai chid kanh.**	อย่ายืนให้ชิดกัน

Walk towards me, please.	**Dern ma thang phom.**	เดินมาทางผม
Thank you, I'll send you a copy of this picture.	**Khob khun.Phom chah song pharb ma hai.**	ขอบคุณ ผมจะ ส่งภาพมาให้
What is your address?	**Khaw shue lae thi-you Khong khun dai mai?**	ขอชื่อและที่อยู่ของคุณ ได้ไหม?

MAKING FRIENDS

(a)Meeting People

Do you know that lady?	**Khun rouchak supharb-satri khon-nanh mai?**	คุณรู้จักสุภาพสตรีคนนั้นไหม?
Yes. I know her. She is Wanthani Chulaphand.	**Rouchak, theu shue Wanthani Chulaphand**	รู้จัก เธอชื่อวันทนีย์ จุลพันธุ์
Introduce me to her, please.	**Karuna nae-namh phom hai rouchak theu noi.**	กรุณาแนะนำผมให้รู้จัก เธอหน่อย
Wanthani, allow me to introduce my friend, Charles Smith.	**Wanthani, khaw nae-namh hai rouchak pheuan phom Charles Smith.**	วันทนีย์ ขอแนะนำให้รู้จัก เพื่อนผม ชาร์ลส์ สมิธ
Charlie, this is Khun Wanthani.	**Charlie, ni Khun Wanthani**	ชาลี นี่คุณวันทนีย์
Sawadi, Khun Wanthani. How do you do?	**Sawadi, Khun Wanthani, khun sabaai di rue?**	สวัสดี คุณวันทนีย์ คุณสบายดีหรือ?

I am pleased to know (to meet) you.	**Phom yin-di thi rouchak (phob) khun.**	ผมยินดีที่รู้จัก (พบ) คุณ
I've heard John speak about you often.	**John kheui-phoud thueng khun sameu.**	จอห์นเคยพูดถึงคุณเสมอ
I am afraid my Thai pronunciation is very poor.	**Phom phoud Thai mai keng.**	ผมพูดไทยไม่เก่ง
I love your Thai language, but most people speak so fast. I don' t understand it completely.	**Phom shob phasa-Thai thae wâ khon suan-maak phoud réow phom fang. keuap mai thanh.**	ผมชอบภาษาไทย แต่ว่าคนส่วนมาก พูดเร็ว ผมฟังเกือบไม่ทัน
Where did you learn to speak Thai?	**Khun rian-phoud Thai dai yaang-rai?**	คุณเรียนพูดไทยได้อย่างไร?
I picked it up from my Thai friends in Australia.	**Phom rian chak pheuan Thai nai Australia.**	ผมเรียนจากเพื่อนไทย ในออสเตรเลีย
You can' t learn Thai well unless you try to speak it.	**Khun chah phoud Thai mai-dai di tha mai phaya-yaam hadd phoud.**	คุณจะพูดไทยไม่ได้ดี ถ้า ไม่พยายามหัดพูด
Perhaps you're right.	**Art-thouk khong khun.**	อาจถูกของคุณ
Where are you staying now?	**Diao-ni khun phak you thi nai?**	เดี๋ยวนี้คุณพักอยู่ที่ไหน?
I am staying at the Dusit Thani hotel.	**Phom phak you thi rongraem Dusit Thani.**	ผมพักอยู่ที่โรงแรมดุสิตธานี
How long will you be there?	**Khun chah you thi-ni naan thao-rai?**	คุณจะอยู่ที่นี่นานเท่าไร?

Another week or so.	**Ik nueng a-thit rue rao-rao nanh.**	อีกหนึ่งอาทิตย์หรือราว ๆ นั้น
Is this your first visit to Thailand?	**Ni pen khrang-raek shai-mai thi khun ma meuang Thai?**	นี่เป็นครั้งแรกใช่ไหมที่คุณ มาเมืองไทย?
This is the third time I've been to Bangkok.	**Phom ma Krungthep sarm khrang laew.**	ผมมากรุงเทพฯ สามครั้งแล้ว
You're on holiday, Aren' t you?	**Khrao-ni khun ma pheua phak-phonn shai-mai?**	คราวนี้คุณมาเพื่อพัก ผ่อนใช่ไหม?
I'm here on a business trip.	**Phom ma tham thurah.**	ผมมาทำธุระ
What kind of business are you in?	**Khun tham kit thurah arai?**	คุณทำกิจธุระอะไร?
I trade in ready-made garments and some Thai-made products.	**Phom sue-khaai seua-pha samret-roupe lae sinkha Thai baang shanid.**	ผมซื้อขายเสื้อผ้าสำเร็จรูป และสินค้าไทยบางชนิด
I'm a journalist. I'm here on assignment to my magazine.	**Phom pen nak-khian reuang. Phom ma pheua tham-reuang hai maek-ka-sin phom.**	ผมเป็นนักเขียนเรื่อง ผมมาเพื่อ ทำเรื่องให้แมกกาซีนผม
Are you enjoying your stay?	**Khun rou-suek sanuk mai rawaang you thi ni?**	คุณรู้สึกสนุกไหม ระหว่างอยู่ที่นี่?

Yes, I like Thai food and Thai friendliness.	**Khrab, Phom shob a-harn Thai lae mitr-maitri khon Thai.**	ครับ, ผมชอบอาหารไทยและมิตรไมตรีคนไทย
Have you seen Thai boxing?	**Khun kheui dou Muai Thai mai?**	คุณเคยดูมวยไทยไหม?
No. Is it different from Western boxing?	**Yang. Manh taek-taang kab Muai Farang yang rai?**	ยัง มันแตกต่างกับมวยฝรั่งอย่างไร?
Thai boxers use their elbows, knees, feet to inflit punishment.	**Nak-muai Thai shai sawk, khaow, thao kab khou taw-sou.**	นักมวยไทยใช้ศอกเข่าเท้ากับคู่ต่อสู้
When are you planning to leave?	**Khun khid chah klab meua-rai?**	คุณคิดจะกลับเมื่อไร?
I plan to leave Bangkok the day after tomorrow.	**Phom khid chah awk chaak Krungthep wan maruen ni.**	ผมคิดจะออกจากกรุงเทพฯ วันมะรืนนี้
I'm glad to have made your acquaintance. Your English is very good.	**Phom di-chai thi mi o'kaad rou-chak khun. Phasa angkrit khun yiam maak.**	ผมดีใจที่มีโอกาสรู้จักคุณ ภาษาอังกฤษคุณเยี่ยมมาก
I hope I shall have the pleasure of meeting you again.	**Phom wang wa khong chah mi o'kaad dai phob khun ik.**	ผมหวังว่าคงจะมีโอกาสได้พบคุณอีก

ʼlay I have your name and address in English?	**Karuna khaw shue lae thi-you khun hai phom pen phasa angkrit?**	กรุณาขอชื่อและที่อยู่คุณให้ผมเป็นภาษาอังกฤษ?
you cannot write in English, please write it in Thai.	**Tha khun khian angkrit mai-dai, proad khian pen phasa Thai.**	ถ้าคุณเขียนอังกฤษไม่ได้ โปรดเขียนเป็นภาษาไทย
ll write to you first.	**Phom chah khian thueng khun konn.**	ผมจะเขียนถึงคุณก่อน
's getting late now. I think I 'd better leave. Good night.	**Diao-ni duek laew. Phom khid wa phom khuan klab dai laew. Sawadi Khrab.**	เดี๋ยวนี้ดึกแล้ว ผมคิดว่าผมควรกลับได้แล้ว สวัสดีครับ

b)With a Girlfriend

ʼho is there?	**Nanh khrai?**	นั่นใคร?
ʼh. very good. I told the boy to call you here.	**Aw, di-maak, phom bawk boy pai shern khun ma.**	อ้อ ดีมาก ผมบอกบ๋อยไปเชิญคุณมา
ome in please.	**Shern khaang-nai.**	เชิญข้างใน
can' t remember you very well.	**Khaw-thoad, khwaam-cham phom mai di.**	ขอโทษ ความจำผมไม่ดี
ʼhat is your name please?	**Khun shue arai?**	คุณชื่ออะไร?
ʼly name is John Snookums.	**Phom shue John Snookums.**	ผมชื่อจอห์น สนุคัมส์

This is Mr. Jack Lambkin, a good friend of mine.	**Khon-ni shue Jack Lambkin, pheuan phom.**	คนนี้ชื่อแจ๊ค แลมบ์กิน เพื่อนผม
I want to learn Thai.	**Phom yaak-rian phasa Thai.**	ผมอยากเรียนภาษาไทย
For a long time I have wanted a Thai teacher.	**Naan-laew phom ha-khrou sawn mai-dai.**	นานแล้ว ผมหาครูสอน ไม่ได้
Is the Thai language difficult to learn?	**Phasa Thai khong rian yaak?**	ภาษาไทยคงเรียนยาก?
Can I learn Thai from you?	**Phom yaak rian Thai kap khun dai mai?**	ผมอยากเรียนไทยกับคุณ ได้ไหม?
I think you could be my teacher.	**Phom khid-wa khun chah sawn phom dai.**	ผมคิดว่าคุณจะสอนผมไ
I think I can learn Thai better with you than anyone else.	**Phom rian Thai kap khun di-kwar ian kap khon-uen.**	ผมเรียนไทยกับคุณ ดีกว่าเรียนกับคนอื่น
You are such a pretty girl and your name is beautiful too.	**Khun suai lae shue phraw.**	คุณสวยและชื่อเพราะ
How much would you ask for teaching me Thai?	**Khun chah khid kha-sonn yaang rai?**	คุณจะคิดค่าสอนอย่างไร
- by the hour	**- pen shua-mong**	- เป็นชั่วโมง
- by the day.	**- pen wan**	- เป็นวัน
What would you like to have?	**Khun tongkarn duem arai?**	คุณต้องการดื่มอะไร?

- a glass of beer	- **beer nueng kaew**	- เบียร์หนึ่งแก้ว
- a bottle of orangenade	- **narm-som**	- น้ำส้ม
- a glass of black iced coffee	- **owe-liang**	- โอเลี้ยง
- whisky and soda	- **whisky lae soda**	- วิสกี้และโซดา
Do you smoke?	**Khun soub buri mai?**	คุณสูบบุหรี่ไหม?
Would you like to listen to music?	**Khun yaak fang phleng mai?**	คุณอยากฟังเพลงไหม?
Do you like to dance?	**Khun shob ten-ramh mai?**	คุณชอบเต้นรำไหม?
Can you dance?	**Khun ten-ramh pen mai?**	คุณเต้นรำเป็นไหม?
I can teach you how to dance.	**Phom yin-di sawn hai khun ten-ramh.**	ผมยินดีสอนให้คุณเต้นรำ
What is your hobby?	**Vela-waang khun tham arai?**	เวลาว่างคุณทำอะไร?
By the way, where are you living?	**Aw, baan khun you thi-nai?**	อ้อ, บ้านคุณอยู่ที่ไหน?
How do I get there?	**Chah pai baan khun dai yaang rai?**	จะไปบ้านคุณได้อย่างไร?
- by minibus	- **Rot tuk-tuk**	- รถตุ๊ก ตุ๊ก
- by bus	- **Rot pracham-thaang**	- รถประจำทาง
Is there a bus stop near your house?	**Klai-klai baan mi paai rot pracham-thaang mai?**	ใกล้ ๆ บ้าน มีป้ายรถประจำทางไหม?
Do you have a telephone at home?	**Thi baan mi thorasab mai?**	ที่บ้านมีโทรศัพท์ไหม?

What's your telephone number?	**Beur arai?**	เบอร์อะไร?
Do you live with your family ?	**Khun khong-chah you kap khrob-khrua?**	คุณคงจะอยู่กับครอบครัว
Or do you live alone?	**Rue you khon-diao?**	หรืออยู่คนเดียว?
Please come and sit here.	**Ma nang-thi-ni di kwa.**	มานั่งที่นี่ดีกว่า
What are you planning to do on Sunday?	**Wan Athit khun tham arai?**	วันอาทิตย์คุณทำอะไร?
Will you be home on Sunday afternoon?	**Wan Athit tawn-baai you baan mai?**	วันอาทิตย์ตอนบ่ายอยู่บ้านไหม
Do you have an engagement for next Saturday?	**Sao na khun waang mai?**	เสาร์หน้าคุณว่างไหม?
I am still a bachelor.	**Phom yang penh sode.**	ผมยังเป็นโสด
How about going to see the cinema with me this evening?	**Yen-ni pai dou nang kan mai?**	เย็นนี้ไปดูหนังกันไหม?
Or do you prefer to go shopping?	**Rue khun yaak pai sue khong?**	หรือคุณอยากไปซื้อของ?
Do you want to come along?	**Khun chah pai duai-kanh mai?**	คุณจะไปด้วยกันไหม?
Take me with you.	**Shan pai duai khon.**	ฉันไปด้วยคน
How about having dinner with me tonight?	**Khuen ni tharn-aharn kan mai?**	คืนนี้ทานอาหารกันไหม?

Vould you like to go for a drive?	**Khun yaak nang rot thiao duai-kan mai?**	คุณอยากนั่งรถเที่ยวด้วยกันไหม?
)id you have a good dinner?	**Aharn a-roi mai?**	อาหารอร่อยไหม?
'hank you for the treat.	**Khop khun samrab a-harn mue ni.**	ขอบคุณสำหรับอาหารมื้อนี้
Vhere are you going?	**Khun chah pai nai?**	คุณจะไปไหน?
'ou don't have to leave now, do you?	**khun yang mai klap mi-shai rue?**	คุณยังไม่กลับมิใช่หรือ?
.et's go home.	**Klab baan kanh therd.**	กลับบ้านกันเถิด
'hall we go?	**Raow pai kanh rue yang?**	เราไปกันหรือยัง?
am tired.	**Phom phlia. Phom neuai.**	ผมเพลีย. ผมเหนื่อย
am very sleepy.	**Phom nguang-nonn.**	ผมง่วงนอน

LIVING IN THAILAND

(a) Renting a House

Is this house to be let?	**Baan ni hai show rue?**	บ้านนี้ให้เช่าหรือ?
Do you know of any other houses to be let?	**Khun saab mai thi-nai mi baan-hai-shao?**	คุณทราบไหม ที่ไหนมีบ้า ให้เช่า?
Who is the landlord, please?	**Khrai penh chao-khong?**	ใครเป็นเจ้าของ?
May I see it?	**Phom khaw dou baan?**	ผมขอดูบ้าน?
How many rooms are there?	**Thang-mod mi ki hong?**	ทั้งหมดมีกี่ห้อง?
I would like to see the rooms.	**Phom yaak shom thouk hong.**	ผมอยากชมทุกห้อง
Does the house have a garage?	**Mi rong rot mai?**	มีโรงรถไหม?
How much is the rent?	**Khid kha-shao yaang-rai?**	คิดค่าเช่าอย่างไร?
Ten thousand baht a month.	**Deuan-lah muen Baht.**	เดือนละหมื่นบาท

How many months rent do you want me to pay in advance?	**Tong chaai luang-nâ ki deuan?**	ต้องจ่ายล่วงหน้ากี่เดือน?
prefer to pay by the month.	**Phom phaw-chai hai kha-shao penh rai-deaun.**	ผมพอใจให้ค่าเช่าเป็นรายเดือน
cannot decide now.	**Phom yang tat-sin chai arai mai-dai.**	ผมยังตัดสินใจอะไรไม่ได้
Let me think it over.	**Phom khaw khid dou konn.**	ผมขอคิดดูก่อน
When do you want me to move in?	**Meua-rai phom cha yaai khow ma dai?**	เมื่อไรผมจะย้ายเข้ามาได้?
will take it from the first of next month.	**Phom chah shao tang-tae, wan-thi-nueng deuan na.**	ผมจะเช่าตั้งแต่, วันที่หนึ่งเดือนหน้า
Will you put in electric light and water for me?	**Khun proad taw fai lae narm khow baan?**	คุณโปรดต่อไฟและน้ำเข้าบ้าน?
The roof ought to be repaired.	**Lang-kha khuan somm hai duai.**	หลังคาควรซ่อมให้ด้วย
Please let me have a full set keys.	**Khaw kounchae hai phom khrob shoud.**	ขอกุญแจให้ผมครบชุด
I'll sign the formal contract tomorrow.	**Phom chah senh sanya wan phroung-ni.**	ผมจะเซ็นสัญญาวันพรุ่งนี้

(b) Employing a Servant

Who are you and what do you want?	**Theu pen khrai, tongkarn arai?**	เธอเป็นใคร ต้องการอะไร?

Oh, you are hunting for a job?	**Oh, ma ha ngârn tham rue?**	อ้อ, มาหางานทำหรือ?
What kind of job can you do?	**Tham arai dai baang?**	ทำอะไรได้บ้าง?
What's your name, please?	**Theu sheu arai?**	เธอชื่ออะไร?
Do you know.......?	**Theu.......?**	เธอ.......?
- how to cook Thai food	**- tham a-harn Thai dai mai**	- ทำอาหารไทยได้ไหม
- how to look after babies	**- liang dek dai mai**	- เลี้ยงเด็กได้ไหม
- how to look after the flower garden	**- tham suan dai mai**	- ทำสวนได้ไหม
- how to wash and iron clothes	**- sak-reed pen mai**	- ซักรีดเป็นไหม
Are you from upcountry?	**Ma chaak tâng-changwad rue?**	มาจากต่างจังหวัดหรือ?
Where do you live now?	**Kha-nah ni phak you thi-nai?**	ขณะนี้พักอยู่ที่ไหน?
Where have you worked before and for how long?	**Kheui tham-ngârn thi-nai ma konn, lae tham narn thao-rai?**	เคยทำงานที่ไหนมาก่อน และทำนานเท่าไร?
I shall employ you and your salary will be 1300 Baht a month.	**Shan charng theu lae hai kha charng deuan lah phan sarm-roi Baht.**	ฉันจ้างเธอ และให้ค่าจ้างเดือนละพันสามร้อยบาท

Vill you be kind enough to give me 1500 Baht?	**Karuna hai phom phan ha-roi mai dai rue?**	กรุณาให้ผมพันห้าร้อยไม่ได้หรือ?
ll right, but you must work well.	**Kaw daai, tae tong khayanh tham-ngarn.**	ก็ได้ แต่ต้องขยันทำงาน
:an you start work here tomorrow?	**Rerm tham-ngarn tae phroung-ni dai mai?**	เริ่มทำงานแต่พรุ่งนี้ได้ไหม?
'lease clean all the rooms upstairs and downstairs.	**Shuai pad-kwaad hong khang-bonh lae khang-laang.**	ช่วยปัดกวาดห้องข้างบน และข้างล่าง
:hange the table cloth and flowers.	**Plian phâ-pou-toh lae dork-mai.**	เปลี่ยนผ้าปูโต๊ะและดอกไม้
idy the kitchen.	**Pad, kwaad, thou khrua hai sa-ard.**	ปัด กวาด ถูครัวให้สะอาด
'ut the rubbish in the garbage can.	**Thing kha-yah long nai thang kha-yah**	ทิ้งขยะลงในถังขยะ
ll dirty clothes must be washed.	**Phâsok-kaprok tong keb sak mod.**	ผ้าสกปรกต้องเก็บซักหมด
)o not forget to put a little starch on the dresses.	**Ya-luem sheed spray nid-noi nai seua-phâ lao-ni.**	อย่าลืมฉีดสเปรย์นิดหน่อย ในเสื้อผ้าเหล่านี้
'ants are to be neatly pressed.	**Kang-kéng tong reed hai riap.**	กางเกงต้องรีดให้เรียบ
ilk dresses should be sent to a dry cleaner.	**Seua-phâ phrae khuan song pai raan sak haeng.**	เสื้อผ้าแพรควรส่งไปร้าน สักแห้ง
'here is a stain on my shirt and it won' t come out.	**Shirt mi roi-peuân sak mai awk.**	เชิ้ตมีรอยเปื้อนซักไม่ออก

Try to take it out.	**Phaya-yarm sak hai awk.**	พยายามซักให้ออก
Please iron this shirt for me.	**Reed shirt tua-ni hai noi.**	รีดเชิ้ตตัวนี้ให้หน่อย
We always eat lunch at noon.	**Tawn thiang raow mak tharn a-harn klaang-wan.**	ตอนเที่ยง เรามักทานอาหารกลางวัน
Is the water hot enough to make tea?	**Narm ronn phaw shong shâ dai-mai?**	น้ำร้อนพอชงชาได้ไหม?
If you are making tea, I like a strong brew.	**Thâ shah tham narm-shâ khaw hai shong kae-kae.**	ถ้าจะทำน้ำชา ขอให้ชงแก่ ๆ
Have you bathe the child?	**Theu ab-narm dek laew rue yang?**	เธออาบน้ำเด็กแล้วหรือยัง?
Why don' t you tie on his bib when he eats?	**Tham-mai mai phouk-iam meua dek kamlang kin nom?**	ทำไมไม่ผูกเอี๊ยมเมื่อเด็กกำลังกินนม?
On your visit to town, please stop at the bakery to buy some bread.	**Véla pai khaang-nawk sue khanom-pang ma duai.**	เวลาไปข้างนอก ซื้อขนมปังมาด้วย
This evening I shall not dine at home. I have been invited out.	**Yen-ni shan mai tharn a-harn thi baan. Mi khon shern kin liang.**	เย็นนี้ฉันไม่ทานอาหารที่บ้าน มีคนเชิญกินเลี้ยง
Lock up the house and put out all the lamps but one.	**Sai klonn-pratou hai mid-shit lae pid fai mod. Leua wai duang diao.**	ใส่กลอนประตูให้มิดชิด และปิดไฟหมดเหลือไว้ดวงเดีย

.nd don't leave the house.	**Laew ya awk-pai nok baan.**	แล้วอย่าออกไปนอกบ้าน
Vatch the house.	**Tong you dou-lae baan hai di.**	ต้องอยู่ดูแลบ้านให้ดี
heard the doorbell rings.	**Khrai kod kring thi pratou.**	ใครกดกริ่งที่ประตู
omeone is knocking at the door.	**Mi khon khaw pratou.**	มีคนเคาะประตู
;o and see who comes and ask for his name.	**Pai dou-si khrai ma laew tharm shue duai.**	ไปดูซิใครมา แล้วถามชื่อด้วย
e sure to bolt the door.	**Ya luem pid sai klonn sia-duai.**	อย่าลืมปิดใส่กลอนเสียด้วย
)o you want some thing?	**Theu tong-karn a-rai rue?**	เธอต้องการอะไรหรือ?
would like a little loan.	**Phom khaw berk luang-nâ.**	ผมขอเบิกล่วงหน้า
Vhat do you want a loan for?	**Aow luang-nâ pai tham a-rai ?**	เอาล่วงหน้าไปทำอะไร?
'ou have just received your wages.	**Theu phueng rap ngoen-deuan pai yok-yok**	เธอเพิ่งรับเงินเดือนไปหยก ๆ
low much do you want to borrow?	**Tong-karn berk sak thao-rai?**	ต้องการเบิกสักเท่าไร?
'ou can have 400 baht.	**Aow pai si-roi Baht dai.**	เอาไปสี่ร้อยบาทได้
wish to ask for a day's leave.	**Phom khaw yout ngârn nueng wanh.**	ผมขอหยุดงานหนึ่งวัน

Why do you want leave?	**Yout pai tham a-rai?**	หยุดไปทำอะไร?
My mother is ill.	**Khun-mae phom mai sabaai.**	คุณแม่ผมไม่สบาย
You are slack at your work.	**Theu tham-ngarn mai di. Tong tang chai maak kwa ni.**	เธอทำงานไม่ดี, ต้องตั้งใ มากกว่านี้
You'd better take care.	**Chong rawang ya kiat khraan.**	จงระวังอย่างเกียจคร้าน
Here, take your wages and leave my service.	**Aow kha-chaang khong theu pai lae mai tong ma ik.**	เอาค่าจ้างของเธอไป และไม่ ต้องมาอีก

AT A DOCTOR'S OFFICE

(a) Parts of the Body

Ankle	**Khaw-thao**	ข้อเท้า
Appendix	**Sai-ting**	ไส้ติ่ง
Arm	**Khaen**	แขน
Armpit	**Rak-rae**	รักแร้
Arteries	**Sen leuad; Sen lo-hit daeng**	เส้นเลือด, เส้นโลหิตแดง
Back	**Lang**	หลัง
Belly	**Phoung**	พุง
Blood	**Leuad**	เลือด
Bones	**Kradouk**	กระดูก
Bowels	**Thawng**	ท้อง
Brain	**Samong**	สมอง
Breast	**Na-ok; Taow-nom**	หน้าอก, เต้านม
Calf	**Nong**	น่อง
Cheek	**Kaem**	แก้ม
Chest	**Na-ok**	หน้าอก

Chin	**Khaang**	คาง
Collarbone	**Kradouk hai-plarâ**	กระดูกไหปลาร้า
Cornea	**Kaew-tâ, Krachok-tâ**	แก้วตา, กระจกตา
Ear	**Hou**	หู
Elbow	**Khaw-sawk**	ข้อศอก
Epidermis	**Nang kam-phrâ**	หนังกำพร้า
Esophagus	**Lawd a-harn**	หลอดอาหาร
Eyes	**Tâ**	ตา
Eyeball	**Louk-tâ**	ลูกตา
Eyelashes	**Khon-tâ**	ขนตา
Eyebrow	**Khon-khiew**	ขนคิ้ว
Face	**Nâ**	หน้า
Finger	**Niew**	นิ้ว
Forehead	**Nâ-phaak**	หน้าผาก
Foot,feet	**Thao**	เท้า
Gall bladder	**Thoung narm-di**	ถุงน้ำดี
Glands	**Tawm**	ต่อม
Gullet	**Khaw-hoi; Lawd a-harn**	คอหอย, หลอดอาหาร
Gum	**Ngeuak**	เหงือก
Hands	**Mue**	มือ
Head	**Si-sah or Hua**	ศีรษะ หรือหัว
Heart	**Hua-chai**	หัวใจ
Heel	**Sonh-thao**	ส้นเท้า
Hip	**Sa-phoke**	สะโพก
Intestines	**Lam-sai**	ลำไส้
Jaw	**Khâ kan-krai**	ขากรรไกร
Joints	**Khaw-taw**	ข้อต่อ
Kidneys	**Tai**	ไต

;nee; Kneecap	**Khow; Sabah hua-khow**	เข่า, สะบ้าหัวเข่า
egs	**Khâ**	ขา
ips	**Rim fi-paak**	ริมฝีปาก
iver	**Tab**	ตับ
ung	**Pord**	ปอด
Aoustache	**Nuad**	หนวด
Aouth	**Paak**	ปาก
Auscles	**Klaam-neua**	กล้ามเนื้อ
Neck	**Khaw**	คอ
Nerves	**Prasaad**	ประสาท
Nose	**Cha-mouk**	จมูก
'ancreas	**Tab-onn**	ตับอ่อน
'upil	**Louk-tâ damh**	ลูกตาดำ
;ectum	**Thawaan nak**	ทวารหนัก
;etina	**Yeua louk-tâ**	เยื่อลูกตา
;ibs	**Si-khrong**	ซี่โครง
;oots of hair	**Raak-phom**	รากผม
crotum	**Thoung an-thah**	ถุงอัณฑะ
houlder	**Lai**	ไหล่
kin	**Phiew-nang; Nang**	ผิวหนัง, หนัง
kull	**Kraloke si-sah**	กระโหลกศีรษะ
pine	**Sanh-lang**	สันหลัง
pleen	**Maam**	ม้าม
tomach	**Thawng or Thong**	ท้อง
weat glands	**Tawm-ngeua**	ต่อมเหงื่อ
ole of the foot	**Fâ-thao**	ฝ่าเท้า
'emples	**Kha-mab**	ขมับ
'endon	**Enh**	เอ็น

Testicles	**An-thah**	อัณฑะ
Thumb	**Niew hua-mae-mue**	นิ้วหัวแม่มือ
Thigh	**Khâ-onn**	ขาอ่อน
Throat	**Lam-khaw**	ลำคอ
Toe	**Niew-thao**	นิ้วเท้า
Tongue	**Linh**	ลิ้น
Tooth, teeth	**Fanh**	ฟัน
Torso	**Lam-tua**	ลำตัว
Veins	**Sen lo-hit damh**	เส้นโลหิตดำ
Waist	**Banh-éow**	บั้นเอว
Womb	**Mod-louk**	มดลูก
Wrist	**Khaw-mue**	ข้อมือ

(b) Common Diseases

Abscesses	**Fi hua-yai**	ฝีหัวใหญ่
Acne	**Siew**	สิว
Angina Pectoris	**Rôke hua-chai**	โรคหัวใจ
Apoplexy(Stroke)	**Tok-leuad nai samong**	ตกเลือดในสมอง
Appendicitis	**Rôke sai-ting ak-seb**	โรคไส้ติ่งอักเสบ
Arthritis	**Khaw akseb**	ข้ออักเสบ
Asphyxia	**Haai-chai mai saduak**	หายใจไม่สะดวก
Asthma	**Hued**	หืด
Beriberi	**Neb-shâ**	เหน็บชา
Boils	**Fi hua-lek**	ฝีหัวเล็ก
Bronchitis	**Lawd-lom akseb**	หลอดลมอักเสบ
Cancer	**Mareng**	มะเร็ง
Chickenpox	**I-souk I-sai**	อีสุกอีใส

Cholera	**A-hiwâ**	อหิวาต์
Convulsions	**Lom-shak**	ลมชัก
Cramps	**Takhriew**	ตะคริว
Diabetis	**Bao-waan**	เบาหวาน
Diarrhea	**Thong-ruang**	ท้องร่วง
Diphtheria	**Khaw-teep**	คอตีบ
Dysentery	**Bid mi-tua**	บิดมีตัว
Eczema	**Khi-klaak lek**	ขี้กลากเล็ก
Encephalitis	**Samong akseb**	สมองอักเสบ
Food poisoning	**A-harn pen-phit**	อหารเป็นพิษ
Gallstones (Bladder stones)	**Niew nai thoung narm-di**	นิ่วในถุงน้ำดี
Gastritis	**Kraphaw a-harn akseb**	กระเพาะอาหารอักเสบ
Goiter	**Rôke khaw-phawk**	โรคคอพอก
Gonorrhea	**Gonorrhea**	โกโนเรีย
Heart failure	**Hua-chai waai**	หัวใจวาย
Hemorrhoids (Stroke)	**Rit si-duang**	ริดสีดวง
Hemorrhage	**Tok-leuad**	ตกเลือด
Hepatitis	**Tab-khaeng**	ตับแข็ง
Hernia (Rupture)	**Sai-leuan**	ไส้เลื่อน
Hives(Nettle rash)	**Lom-phit**	ลมพิษ
Hypertension	**Khwaam-danh lohit soung**	ความดันโลหิตสูง
nfluenza	**Khai Wad-yai**	ไข้หวัดใหญ่
ch	**Rôke khanh**	โรคคัน
idney stones	**Niew nai-tai**	นิ่วในไต
umbago	**Puad lang**	ปวดหลัง
Malaria	**Khai chab-sanh**	ไข้จับสั่น

Measles	**Had**	หัด
Mumps	**Khaang thoum**	คางทูม
Neuralagia	**Puad prasard**	ปวดประสาท
Nosebleed(Epistaxis)	**Leuad kamdao awk**	เลือดกำเดาออก
Pharyngitis (sore throat)	**Khaw akseb**	คออักเสบ
Pleurisy	**Yeua houm-pord akseb**	เยื่อหุ้มปอดอักเสบ
Pneumonia	**Pord akseb (Pneumonia)**	ปอดอักเสบ (นิวมอเนีย)
Poliomyelitis	**Khai san-lang akseb**	ไขสันหลังอักเสบ
Rash	**Phod-phuen**	ผดผื่น
Rabies(Hydrophobia)	**Rôke klua-narm**	โรคกลัวน้ำ
Ringworm	**Khi-klaak**	ขี้กลาก
Scabies	**Shanna-tu**	ชันนะตุ
Scarvy	**Rôke lak-pid lak-perd**	โรคลักปิดลักเปิด
Smallpox	**Khai thoraphit**	ไข้ทรพิษ
Sprue (Tropical Diarrhea)	**Thong-sia, a-harn mai yoi**	ท้องเสีย, อาหารไม่ย่อย
Stroke	**Rôke lom patchu-ban**	โรคลมปัจจุบัน
Sunstroke	**Pen-lom phae-daed**	เป็นลมแพ้แดด
Syphilis	**Syphilis**	ซิฟิลิส
Tetanus	**Bart-thayak**	บาดทะยัก
Tonsilitis	**Tom tonsil akseb**	ต่อมทอนซิลอักเสบ
Tuberculosis	**Wanna-rôke**	วัณโรค
Typhoid	**Khai thai-foi**	ไข้ไทฟอยด์
Typhus	**Khai raak-sard noi**	ไข้รากสาดน้อย
Ulcers	**Phlae lek**	แผลเล็ก
Varicose veins	**Sen leuad khord**	เส้นเลือดขอด

nereal Disease	**Kama rôke**	กามโรค
hooping cough	**Rôke aye-kron**	โรคไอกรน
ws	**Khud tharaad**	คุดทะราด

) First-aid Kit and Home Medicine Chest

ti bacterial soaps	**Sabou khâ cheua**	สบู่ฆ่าเชื้อ
hesive tape	**Plaster**	พลาสเตอร์
erile gauze	**Phâ-goss**	ผ้าก๊อส
sorted sterile compresses	**Phâ phan-phlae**	ผ้าพันแผล
bber bag for hot water	**Krapow narm-ronn**	กระเป๋าน้ำร้อน
rn ointment	**Khi-phueng raksa phlae fai-luak**	ขี้ผึ้งรักษาแผลไฟลวก
lastic tourniquet	**Saai-rat harm leuad**	สายรัดห้ามเลือด
inter forceps	**Paak-khipe**	ปากคีบ
ller bandages	**Muan phâ phan-phlae**	ม้วนผ้าพันแผล
dpan	**Maw samrap thaai**	หม้อสำหรับถ่าย
sorbent cotton	**Sam-li**	สำลี
omatic spirits of ammonia	**Ammonia klanh**	แอมโมเนียกลั่น
lamine lotion	**Narm Calamine**	น้ำคาลาไมน์
mphorated oil	**Narm-manh karaboun**	น้ำมันการบูร
d liver oil	**Narm-manh tab plâ**	น้ำมันตับปลา
stor oil	**Narm-manh la-houng**	น้ำมันละหุ่ง
nical thermometer, mouth style	**Prodd wadd-khai**	ปรอทวัดไข้

Compound tincture of benzion	**Tincture benzoin**	ทิงเจอร์เบนโซอิน
Earache drops	**Ya yawd hou**	ยาหยอดหู
Epsom salts	**Di-kleau**	ดีเกลือ
Eucalyptus oil	**Narm-manh eucalyp**	น้ำมันยูคาลิป
Eye-washing glass	**Kaew laang-tâ**	แก้วล้างตา
Measuring glass	**Kaew tuang ya**	แก้วตวงยา
Medicine droppers	**Thi yord-tâ**	ที่หยอดตา
Medicine glass	**Kaew yâ**	แก้วยา
Oil of cloves	**Narm-manh karn-phlu**	น้ำมันกานพลู
Potassium permanganate	**Daang thab-thim**	ด่างทับทิม
Rubbing alcohol	**Alcohol laang phlae**	อัลกอฮอล์ล้างแผล
Safety pins	**Khem-sonn-plaai**	เข็มซ่อนปลาย
Scissors	**Kan-krai**	กรรไกร

(d) General Conversation

What is the matter with you?	**Khun penh arai?**	คุณเป็นอะไร?
I don' t feel well. I need a doctor.	**Phom mai sabaai. Phom tong phob maw.**	ผมไม่สบาย ผมต้องพบหม
Is there a drugstore near here?	**Thaew-ni mi raan khaai-yâ mai?**	แถวนี้มีร้านขายยาไหม?
Where is the hospital ?	**Rong phaya-barn you thi-nai?**	โรงพยาบาลอยู่ที่ไหน?
Please send me to a hospital.	**Karuna song phom pai rong phaya-barn.**	กรุณาส่งผมไปโรงพยาบ

ıll the ambulance, please.	**Proad riak rot-phaya-barn mâ.**	โปรดเรียกรถพยาบาลมา
ıave a headache and pains in all my bones and joints.	**Phom puad si-sah, puad kradouk lae khaw-taw.**	ผมปวดศีรษะ ปวดกระดูก และข้อต่อ
ıave diahrrea and gripping pain in the abdomen.	**Thong ruang, lae puad-thong maak.**	ท้องร่วง และปวดท้อง มาก
'ho is the best doctor in this place?	**Khun rou-chak maw di-di mai?**	คุณรู้จักหมอดี ๆ ไหม?
ıon' t feel very well, doctor.	**Maw, phom mai sabaai maak.**	หมอ ผมไม่สบายมาก
ıffer from sleeplessness.	**Phom nonn mai-lab.**	ผมนอนไม่หลับ
ɛel a little tired.	**Phom rou-suek neuai lae phlia.**	ผมรู้สึกเหนื่อยและเพลีย
lso have some pain occasionally.	**Baang-thi mi a-karn puad.**	บางทีมีอาการปวด
night be.......	**Ach-penh duai.....**	อาจเป็นด้วย.....
- rheumatism	- **roke puad khaw puad klaam-neua**	- โรคปวดข้อปวดกล้ามเนื้อ
- neurits	- **rôke prasaad ak-seb**	- โรคประสาทอักเสบ
- kidney trouble	- **roke tai**	- โรคไต
- heart trouble	- **roke hua-chai**	- โรคหัวใจ
ɔw is your appetite?	**Tharn a-harn dai mai?**	ทานอาหารได้ไหม?
ave hardly eaten anything these two days.	**Phom mai yaak tharn a-rai song-wan laew.**	ผมไม่อยากทานอะไร สองวันแล้ว

I am suffering from constipation.	**Thong phouk.**	ท้องผูก
I have rheumatic pains in my joints.	**Puad tarm khaw-kradouk.**	ปวดตามข้อกระดูก
Where do you feel pain now?	**Puad thi trong nai?**	ปวดที่ตรงไหน?
I have a pain here.	**Phom puad thi-ni.**	ผมปวดที่นี่
Have you a pain in your chest?	**Puad nâ-ok mai?**	ปวดหน้าอกไหม?
I have a pain in my back.	**Phom puad lang.**	ผมปวดหลัง
I have pains in my stomach.	**Phom puad-thong.**	ผมปวดท้อง
Let me examine your chest.	Khaw **turad na-ok.**	ขอตรวจหน้าอก
Lie down, please.	**Proad nonn-long.**	โปรดนอนลง
I want to check your blood pressure.	**Phom chah truad Khwaam-dan lo-hit.**	ผมจะตรวจความดันโล
Your bloood-pressure is slightly above normal. Nothing to worry about.	**Khwaam-dan soung lek-noi. Mai-mi a-rai na wi-tok.**	ความดันสูงเล็กน้อย ไม่มีอะไรน่าวิตก
I feel pains in my side, and I breath with difficulty.	**Phom rousuek cheb-siad thi daan khaang, haai-chai mai saduak.**	ผมรู้สึกเจ็บเสียดที่ด้าน หายใจไม่สะดวก
Let me feel your pulse.	**Khaw truad shipachonn.**	ขอตรวจชีพจร
Your pulse is a little fast.	**Shipachonn ten raeng lek-noi.**	ชีพจรเต้นแรงเล็กน

ave you any fever?	**Mi khai mai?**	มีไข้ไหม?
o, I have no fever.	**Mai-mi khai.**	ไม่มีไข้
o you cough at all?	**Aye baang mai?**	ไอบ้างไหม?
how me your tongue.	**Khaw dou linh.**	ขอดูลิ้น
must take your temperature.	**Tong truad unha-phoum. Tong wat khai.**	ต้องตรวจอุณหภูมิ, ต้องวัดไข้
have a sore throat.	**Phom cheb khaw.**	ผมเจ็บคอ
o you feel nausea?	**Rou suek khluen-sai mai?**	รู้สึกคลื่นไส้ไหม?
feel a slight nausea.	**Mi baang.**	มีบ้าง
suffer from indigestion.	**A-harn tharn laew mai yoi.**	อาหารทานแล้วไม่ย่อย
nything wrong with the urine?	**Passa-wah penh yaang-rai?**	ปัสสาวะเป็นอย่างไร?
es,it is red and developes a deposit.	**Passa-wah daeng, mi ta-kon.**	ปัสสาวะแดง, มีตะกอน
am suffering from constipation.	**Mi a-karn thong phouk.**	มีอาการท้องผูก
have been shivering all night long.	**Nao san talawd khuen.**	หนาวสั่นตลอดคืน
ow long have you felt ill?	**Mai sa-baai nann laew rue?**	ไม่สบายนานแล้วหรือ?
began the day before yesterday by a shivering fit.	**Rerm meua waan-suen ni, doai mi a-karn nao satharn.**	เริ่มเมื่อวานซืนนี้ ด้วยมีอาการหนาวสะท้าน

Then I perspired profusely and have been ill ever since.	**Taw ma mi ngeuâ awk maak, laew phom mai sabai tae wanh-nan.**	ต่อมามีเหงื่อออกมาก แล้วผ ไม่สบายแต่วันนั้น
You must take a little medicine.	**Khun tong tharn yâ nid-noi.**	คุณต้องทานยานิดหน่อย
Do you think my illness is dangerous?	**A-karn puai khong-phom raai-raeng mai?**	อาการป่วยของผมร้ายแรงไหม
If you take care of yourself, you'll be feeling better soon.	**Thâ khun raksa tua di, mai-shâ khun chah pen pokati.**	ถ้าคุณรักษาตัวดี ไม่ช้าคุณจะ เป็นปกติ
Here are some pills.	**Aow yâ lao-ni pai tharn.**	เอายาเหล่านี้ไปทาน
How often must I take these pills?	**Rap-pratharn yaang-rai khrap?**	รับประทานอย่างไรครับ?
Three times a day. Take one each after meals.	**Wan-lah sarm véla. Yang-lah nueng med lang a-harn.**	วันละสามเวลา อย่างละหนึ่ง เม็ดหลังอาหาร
In two or three days. you will be quite well.	**Nai sawng rue sarm wan khun kaw chah haai.**	ในสองหรือสามวัน คุณก็จะ หาย

OST, TELEGRAPH ND TELEPHONE

a) Postal Terms

ir letter	**Chodmai akaad**	จดหมายอากาศ
ir mail	**Praisani akaad**	ไปรษณีย์อากาศ
ir mail rates	**Attra praisani thaang akaad**	อัตราไปรษณีย์ทางอากาศ
.O.D. parcel	**Phasadu keb-ngoen plaai thâng**	พัสดุเก็บเงินปลายทาง
ountry of destination	**Meuang plaai thaang**	เมืองปลายทาง
omestic mail	**Mail nai prathed**	เมล์ในประเทศ
press	**Duan**	ด่วน
press charge	**Khâ tham-niam song-douan**	ค่าธรรมเนียมส่งด่วน
eneral Post Office (G.P.O.)	**Praisani klaang**	ไปรษณีย์กลาง
etters	**Chodmaai**	จดหมาย
ocked bags	**Thoung Praisani**	ถุงไปรษณีย์
oney Order	**Thana-Nat**	ธนาณัติ

Parcel post	**Phasadu praisani**	พัสดุไปรษณีย์
Postal clerk/official	**Phanak-ngârn praisani**	พนักงานไปรษณีย์
Post and Telegraph Office	**Thi thamkarn Praisani Thoralek**	ที่ทำการไปรษณีย์โทรเล
Post Card	**Praisani Bat**	ไปรษณีย์บัตร
Postman	**Bourut praisani**	บุรุษไปรษณีย์
Postage stamps	**Duang trâ praisaniya-korn**	ดวงตราไปรษณียากร
Postal Services	**Karn praisani**	การไปรษณีย์
Printed Matter	**Sing Phim**	สิ่งพิมพ์
Private Letters Boxes	**Tou-shaow praisani**	ตู้เช่าไปรษณีย์
Registered	**Long-thabian**	ลงทะเบียน
Registered letters	**Chodmaai long-thabian**	จดหมายลงทะเบียน
Registered parcels	**Phasadu long-thabian**	พัสดุลงทะเบียน
Registered charge	**Khâ long-thabian**	ค่าลงทะเบียน
To weigh	**Shang narm-nak**	ชั่งน้ำหนัก
Weight	**Narm-nak**	น้ำหนัก

(b) At the Post Office

In Thailand, a Post Office is indicated by an emblem. All ma boxes are painted red. Opening hours: 8:30 a.m. to 4:30 p.m. wee days, and 9 to 11 a.m. on Saturdays, Sundays and all government ho days.

I want to go to the Post Office.	**Phom tongkarn pai thi tham-karn Praisani.**	ผมต้องการไปที่ทำการไปรษณีย์
Can you tell me how to get to the Post Office?	**Thi tham-karn Praisani you nai? Phom chah pai dai yaang rai?**	ที่ทำการไปรษณีย์อยู่ไหน ผมจะไปได้อย่างไร?

d like to send this letter to the United States of America.	**Phom tongkarn song chodmaai ni pai America.**	ผมต้องการส่งจดหมายนี้ ไปอเมริกา
is is to go by air mail.	**Song thang a-kaad.**	ส่งทางอากาศ
ow much postage do I need?	**Tong pid stamp thao-rai?**	ต้องปิดแสตมป์เท่าไร?
et me have 10 two-baht stamps.	**Phom khaw stamp duang la sawng-baht sib duang.**	ผมขอแสตมป์ดวงละสอง บาทสิบดวง
ease let me have all different stamps.	**Karuna khaw stamp thi mai samh kan.**	กรุณาขอแสตมป์ที่ไม่ ซ้ำกัน
hat's the postage for an air mail to Australia?	**Chodmaai song thang-akaad pai Australia pid stamps thao-rai?**	จดหมายส่งทางอากาศไป ออสเตรเลียปิดแสตมป์ เท่าไร?
hen will this letter get there?	**Meuarai chod-maai ni chah thueng?**	เมื่อไรจดหมายนี้จะถึง?
want to send this parcel packet.	**Phom tongkarn song phasadu ni (haw ni).**	ผมต้องการส่งพัสดุนี้ (ห่อนี้)
hat does it contain?	**Khaang-nai mi arai?**	ข้างในมีอะไร?
ooks only.	**Nangsue thao-nanh.**	หนังสือเท่านั้น
an this be registered?	**Long thabian dai-mai?**	ลงทะเบียนได้ไหม?
ease send it as a registered parcel.	**Proad song pen phasadu long-thabian.**	โปรดส่งเป็นพัสดุ ลงทะเบียน
here do I cash money orders?	**Rap-ngoen thananat thi nai?**	รับเงินธนาณัติที่ไหน?

(c) At the Telegraph Office

At the Post Office you will find seperate counters for sending tel- grams. In Bangkok, overseas telegraph and telephone services are avai able round-the-clock in the General Post office.

I'd like to send a telegram to New York.	**Phom tongkarn song thoralek pai New York.**	ผมต้องการส่งโทรเลขไปนิวยอร์ค
May I have a form, please?	**Khaw form-thoralek nueng bai?**	ขอฟอร์มโทรเลขหนึ่งใบ?
How much is it per word?	**Kham-lah thao-rai?**	คำละเท่าไร?
How long will a telegram to New York take?	**Thoralek song pai New York meuarai chah thueng?**	โทรเลขส่งไปนิวยอร์คเมื่อไรจะถึง?
Inland telegram	**Thoralek nai prathed**	โทรเลขในประเทศ
Minimum charge	**Attra yaang-tam**	อัตราอย่างต่ำ
First 10 words	**Sib-kham raek**	สิบคำแรก
Additional word	**Kham taw pai**	คำต่อไป
Number of words	**Chamnuan kham**	จำนวนคำ
Per word	**Kham-lah**	คำละ

(d) Telephone Conversation

Only in Bangkok will you find public telephone booth scatt around. The streets phones are known in Thai as Thorasab Satharana

Where may I telephone?	**Phoud thora-sab dai thi-nai?**	พูดโทรศัพท์ได้ที่ไหน?

ay I use your telephone, please?	**Karuna khaw phom thora-sab dai mai?**	กรุณาขอผมโทรศัพท์ได้ไหม?
ave you got a telephone directory?	**Mi samud thora-sab mai?**	มีสมุดโทรศัพท์ไหม?
ease help me get this name.	**Karuna ha shue ni hai phom.**	กรุณาหาชื่อนี้ให้ผม
am sorry, I cannot speak Thai.	**Sia chai, phom phoud Thai mai-dai.**	เสียใจ, ผมพูดไทยไม่ได้
an you answer the phone for me?	**Shuai phoud thaen phom noi?**	ช่วยพูดแทนผมหน่อย?
can't hear you, please speak louder.	**Phom mai-dai yin, proad phoud dang-dang.**	ผมไม่ได้ยิน โปรดพูดดัง ๆ
/e have a very bad connection.	**Mi siang rob-kuan maak.**	มีเสียงรบกวนมาก
don' t understand.	**Phom fang mai rou-reuang.**	ผมฟังไม่รู้เรื่อง
ll try to connect you again.	**Laew phom chah thoh ma-mai.**	แล้วผมจะโทรมาใหม่
lease call someone who can speak English.	**Karuna riak khon phoud angkrit dai ma phoud kap phom.**	กรุณาเรียกคนพูดอังกฤษได้มาพูดกับผม
1ay I speak to Mr. Anderson?	**Phom khaw phoud kab khun Anderson?**	ผมขอพูดกับคุณแอนเดอร์สัน?
lo, he's gone for the day.	**Khow mai you thang wanh.**	เขาไม่อยู่ทั้งวัน
)o you want to leave a message?	**Khun tongkarn sang arai mai?**	คุณต้องการสั่งอะไรไหม?

No. thanks, I'll call on him later.	**Mai, laew chah thoh ma ik.**	ไม่, แล้วจะโทรมาอีก
What is the telephone number there?	**Thorasab khun beur arai?**	โทรศัพท์คุณเบอร์อะไร?
I am speaking from a public telephone booth.	**Phom phoud chaak thorasab Sathara-nah.**	ผมพูดจากโทรศัพท์สาธารณะ
Will you write the number down?	**Khun chod beur thorasab wai dai mai?**	คุณจดเบอร์โทรศัพท์ไว้ได้ไหม?
At what time would you suggest that I call him again?	**Sak-ki mong khun khid wa phom khuan thoh ma-mai?**	สักกี่โมง คุณคิดว่าผมควรโทรมาใหม่?
Wait a moment, I think Mr. Anderson is coming now.	**Khoi pra-diao, phom khid wa khun Anderson klap ma laew.**	คอยประเดี๋ยว ผมคิดว่าคุณแอนเดอร์สันกลั มาแล้ว
Please do not hang up.	**Ya waang hou.**	อย่าวางหู
Will it take very long?	**Narn maak mai?**	นานมากไหม?
Who's speaking please?	**Khrai phoud?**	ใครพูด?
This is Joe Smith speaking.	**Ni Joe Smith phoud.**	นี่ โจสมิธ พูด
Well, just tell him that I called, please.	**Di-laew, proad bawk wa phom thorasab ma.**	ดีแล้ว โปรดบอกว่าผมโทรศัพท์มา
Telephone	**Thorasab**	โทรศัพท์
Telephone book	**Samud Thorasab**	สมุดโทรศัพท์
To dial	**Moun**	หมุน
Call charges	**Kha phoud thorasab**	ค่าพูดโทรศัพท์

verseas Telephone Service	**Thorasab thâng-klai tarng prathed**	โทรศัพท์ทางไกล ต่างประเทศ
ong Distance Calls	**Thorasab thâng klai nai prathed**	โทรศัพท์ทางไกล ในประเทศ
xchange Office	**Shoum-saai thorasab**	ชุมสายโทรศัพท์
ervice hours	**Véla borikarn**	เวลาบริการ
rong numbers	**Taw-phid beur**	ต่อผิดเบอร์
ait a moment	**Khoi sak khrou**	คอยสักครู่

MINISTRIES AND GOVERNMENT DEPARTMENTS

Office of the Prime Minister
Samnak Nayok Ratha-Montri

Executive office of the Prime Minister	**Samnak Thamniap Nayok Ratha-Montri**	สำนักทำเนียบนายกรัฐมนตรี
The Secretariat of the Cabinet	**Samnak-ngarn Lekhathikarn Khana Ratha-Montri**	สำนักงานเลขาธิการคณะรัฐมนตรี
Budget Office	**Samnak Ngob Pramarn**	สำนักงบประมาณ
Office of the National Economic and Social Development Board	**Samnak-ngarn Khana Kammakarn Phathanakarn Sehthakit lae Sangkhom**	สำนักงานคณะกรรมการพัฒนาการเศรษฐกิจแล สังคม
Office of the Civil Service Commision	**Samnak-ngarn Khana Kammakarn Kha-rajakarn Pholareuan**	สำนักงานคณะกรรมการข้าราชการพลเรือน

ffice of National Research Council of Thailand Committee	**Samnak-ngarn Khana Kammakarn Vichai**	สำนักงานคณะกรรมการวิจัย
ffice of the Board of Investment	**Samnak-ngarn Songserm Karn Long-thoun**	สำนักงานส่งเสริมการลงทุน
ational Energy Authority	**Samnak-ngarn Phlang-ngarn**	สำนักงานพลังงาน
ffice of National Statistics	**Samnak-ngarn Sathi-ti**	สำนักงานสถิติ
ublic Relations Department	**Krom Prasha Samphan**	กรมประชาสัมพันธ์
entral Intelligence Department	**Krom Pramuan Khao Klaang**	กรมประมวลข่าวกลาง
echnical Economic Cooperative (TEC) Department	**Krom Withed Saha-karn**	กรมวิเทศสหการ

inistry of Defence
rasuang Kalâ-Home

upreme Command Headquarters	**Kawng Banshâ-karn Tha-harn Soung-sout**	กองบัญชาการทหารสูงสุด
ilitary Research and Development Center	**Soun Vichai lae Phathana-karn Tha-harn**	ศูนย์วิจัยและพัฒนาการทหาร
rmy Signal Department	**Krom Karn Sue-sarn Tha-harn**	กรมการสื่อสารทหาร

Operations Directorate Department	**Krom Yuthakarn Tha-harn**	กรมยุทธการทหาร
Military Intelligence Department	**Krom Khao Tha-harn**	กรมข่าวทหาร
Communist Suppression Center	**Kawng Amnuai-karn Pong-kanh lae Praab-praam Communist**	กองอำนวยการป้องกันและปราบปรามคอมมูนิสต์
Central Security Division	**Kawng Amnuai-karn Raksâ Khwaam Plawd-phai**	กองอำนวยการรักษาควา ปลอดภัย
Armed Forces Industrial Department	**Krom Karn Utsaha-kam Tha-harn**	กรมการอุตสาหกรรมทหาร

Ministry of Interior
Krasuang Mahaad Thai

Administration Department	**Krom Karn Pok-Khrong**	กรมการปกครอง
Community Development Department	**Krom Karn Phathana Shoum-shon**	กรมการพัฒนาชุมชน
Office of Accelerated Rural Development	**Samnak-ngarn Reng-rat Phathana Shonna-bot**	สำนักงานเร่งรัดพัฒนาชนบท
Land Department	**Krom Thi-din**	กรมที่ดิน
Public Welfare Department	**Krom Prasha Songkhraw**	กรมประชาสงเคราะห์

ublic Municipal Works Department	**Krom Yotha-thikarn**	กรมโยธาธิการ
orrecttions Department	**Krom Raja-thanh**	กรมราชทัณฑ์
abor Department	**Krom Raeng-ngarn**	กรมแรงงาน
ublic Prosecution Department	**Krom Aye-karn**	กรมอัยการ
olice Department	**Krom Tamruat.**	กรมตำรวจ
oreign Affairs Division	**Kawng Karn Tang-Prathed**	กองการต่างประเทศ
ommunication Division	**Kawng Karn Sue-sarn**	กองการสื่อสาร
egal Affairs Division	**Kawng Khadi**	กองคดี
nmigration Division	**Kawng Truad Khon Khow-meuang**	กองตรวจคนเข้าเมือง
ire Brigade Headquarters	**Kawng Tamruat Dab-phloeng**	กองตำรวจดับเพลิง
lighway Patrol Division	**Kawng Tamruat Thaang-luang**	กองตำรวจทางหลวง
1arine Police	**Kawng Tamruat Narm**	กองตำรวจน้ำ
orestry Police Division	**Kawng Tamruat Pâ Mai**	กองตำรวจป่าไม้
ailway Police Division	**Kawng Tamruat Rot-Fai**	กองตำรวจรถไฟ
pecial Branch Police Division	**Kawng Tamruat Santi-barn**	กองตำรวจสันติบาล
egistration Division	**Kawng Thabian**	กองทะเบียน
lien Registration and Tax Division	**Kawng Thabian Tang-Dao lae Phasi Akorn**	กองทะบียนต่างด้าวและภาษีอากร

Criminal Record Office	**Kawng Thabian lae Pravat Ashaya-korn**	กองทะเบียนและประวัติอาชญากร
Traffic Police Division	**Kawng Tamruat Chara-chorn**	กองตำรวจจราจร
Metropolitan Police Commisioner Division	**Kawng Bansha-karn Tamruat Nakhorn-Barn**	กองบัญชาการตำรวจนครบาล
Provisional Police Division	**Kawng Tamruat Phu-thorn**	กองตำรวจภูธร
Border Police Division	**Kawng Tamruat Phu-thorn Shaai-daen**	กองตำรวจภูธรชายแดน
Central Investigation Bureau	**Kawng Tamruat Sobb-suan Klaang**	กองตำรวจสอบสวนกลาง
Police Education Division	**Kawng Tamruat Suek-sâ**	กองตำรวจศึกษา
Crime Suppression Division	**Kawng Praab-praam**	กองปราบปราม
Logistics Division	**Kawng Phala-thikarn**	กองพลาธิการ
Identification Division	**Kawng Phisout Lak-tharn**	กองพิสูจน์หลักฐาน
Medical Division	**Kawng Phaed**	กองแพทย์
Research and Planning Division	**Kawng Vichai lae Waang-phaen**	กองวิจัยและวางแผน
Technical Division	**Kawng Visha-karn**	กองวิชาการ

Ministry of Foreign Affairs
Krasuang Karn Taang Prathed

Treaty Department	**Krom Sonthi Sanyâ**	กรมสนธิสัญญา
Political Department	**Krom Pithi Karn Thout**	กรมพิธีการทูต
Economic Department	**Krom Sehthakit**	กรมเศรษฐกิจ
Protocol Department	**Krom Karn Meuang**	กรมการเมือง
Information Department	**Krom Sara-Nithed**	กรมสารนิเทศ
International Organization	**Krom Ong-karn Taang Prathed.**	กรมองค์การต่างประเทศ

Ministry of Education
Krasuang Suek-sa Thi-karn

Education Technical Department	**Krom Vishâ-karn**	กรมวิชาการ
Education Training Technical Department	**Krom Karn Fuek-hat Khru**	กรมการฝึกหัดครู
Elementary and Adult Education Department	**Krom Visamanh Suek-sa**	กรมวิสามัญศึกษา
Fine Arts Department	**Krom Silapa-korn**	กรมศิลปากร
Physical Education Department	**Krom Phala-Sueksa**	กรมพลศึกษา
Religious Affairs Department	**Krom Karn Sasana**	กรมการศาสนา

Secondary Education Department	**Krom Samanh Sueksa**	กรมสามัญศึกษา
Vocational Education Department	**Krom A-shiva Sueksa**	กรมอาชีวศึกษา

Ministry of Finance
Krasuang Karn Khlang

Comptroller General Department	**Krom Banshi Klaang**	กรมบัญชีกลาง
Crown Property Department	**Samnak-ngarn Sab-sin Suan Phra Maha Kasat**	สำนักงานทรัพย์สินส่วนพระมหากษัตริย์
Customs Department	**Krom Sulka-korn**	กรมศุลกากร
Excise Duties Department	**Krom Sanpha Samit**	กรมสรรพสามิต
Revenue Department	**Krom Sanpha Korn**	กรมสรรพากร
Treasury Department	**Krom Thana-rak**	กรมธนารักษ์

Ministry of Industry
Krasuang Utsaha Kam

Industrial Promotion Department	**Krom Songserm Utsaha Kam**	กรมส่งเสริมอุตสาหกรรม
Industrial Works Department	**Krom Rong-ngarn Utsaha-kam**	กรมโรงงานอุตสาหกรรม
Mineral Resources Department	**Krom Sab-phayakorn Thorani**	กรมทรัพยากรธรณี
Science Department	**Krom Withayasart**	กรมวิทยาศาสตร์

Ministry of Commerce
Krasuang Phanit

Commercial Relations Department	**Krom Phanid Samphan**	กรมพาณิชย์สัมพันธ์
Commercial Registration Department	**Krom Thabian Karn Khâ**	กรมทะเบียนการค้า
Domestic Trade Department	**Krom Karn Khâ Phaai-nai**	กรมการค้าภายใน
Foreign Trade Department	**Krom Karn Khâ Taang Prathed**	กรมการค้าต่างประเทศ
Economic Commercial Department	**Krom Seththakit Karn Phanid**	กรมเศรษฐกิจการพาณิชย์

Ministry of Agriculture
Krasuang Kaset lae Saha-korn

Agriculture Technical Department	**Krom Visha Karn Kaset**	กรมวิชาการเกษตร
Agriculture Extension Department	**Krom Songserm Karn Kaset**	กรมส่งเสริมการเกษตร
Cooperative Promotion Department	**Krom Songserm Sahakorn**	กรมส่งเสริมสหกรณ์
Fisheries Department	**Krom Pramong**	กรมประมง
Irrigation Department	**Krom Shola-pratharn**	กรมชลประทาน
Land Development Department	**Krom PhathanaThi-din**	กรมพัฒนาที่ดิน

Livestock Department	**Krom Pa-su-sat**	กรมปศุสัตว์
Royal Forest Department	**Krom Pâ Mai**	กรมป่าไม้

Ministry of Communication
Krasuang Khommana-khom

Commercial Aviation Department	**Krom Karn Bin Phanid**	กรมการบินพาณิชย์
Harbor Department	**Krom Chao Thâ**	กรมเจ้าท่า
Highway Department	**Krom Thaang Luang**	กรมทางหลวง
Land Transport Department	**Krom Karn Khon-song Thaang Bok**	กรมการขนส่งทางบก
Meteorology Department	**Krom Ou-tu Niyom Vithaya**	กรมอุตุนิยมวิทยา
Post and Telegraph Department	**Krom Praisani Thoralek**	กรมไปรษณีย์โทรเลข

Ministry of Public Health
Krasuang Satharana-suk

Health Promotion Department	**Krom Songserm Satharana suk**	กรมส่งเสริมสาธารณสุข
Medical Science Department	**Krom Vithayasart Karn-Phaed**	กรมวิทยาศาสตร์การแพทย์
Medical and Health Department	**Krom Karn-Phaed lae A-namai**	กรมการแพทย์และอนามัย

Bangkok Metropolis
Krungthep Maha Nakhorn

Governor	**Phu-Wa-rasha-karn**	ผู้ว่าราชการ
Central Division	**Kawng Klaang**	กองกลาง
Education Division	**Kawng Karn Sueksa**	กองการศึกษา
Finance Division	**Kawng Karn Ngoen**	กองการเงิน
Public Works Division	**Kawng Karn Yotha**	กองการโยธา
Public Health Division	**Kawng Satharana-suk**	กองสาธารณสุข
Refuse and Nightsoil Disposal Office	**Samnak-ngarn Kamchad Moun-foi lae Sing-patikul**	สำนักงานกำจัดมูลฝอย และสิ่งปฏิกูล

Other Government Organizations

Electricity Generating Authority	**Karn Fai-fa Fai Phlit**	การไฟฟ้าฝ่ายผลิต
Express Transportation Organization	**Ong-karn Rab-Song Sinkha lae Phasadu-phan**	องค์การรับ-ส่งสินค้า และพัสดุภัณฑ์
Fish Marketing Organization	**Ong-karn Saphan Plâ**	องค์การสะพานปลา
Forest Industry Organization	**Ong-karn Utsaha-kam Pâ Mai**	องค์การอุตสาหกรรมป่าไม้
Petroleum Authority of Thailand	**Karn Pitroliam haeng Prathed Thai**	การปิโตรเลี่ยมแห่ง ประเทศไทย
Pharmaceutical Organization	**OnOg-karn Phesat**	องค์การเภสัช

Guru Sabha Trade Organization	**Ong-karn Khâ Guru Sabha**	องค์การค้าคุรุสภา
Metropolitan Electricity Authority	**Karn Fai-fa Nakhorn Luang**	การไฟฟ้านครหลวง
Metropolitan Waterworks	**Karn Pra-pâ Nakhorn Luang**	การประปานครหลวง
Port Authority of Thailand	**Karn Tha-reua**	การท่าเรือ
Provincial Electricity Authority	**Karn Fai-fa Suan Phumi-phaak**	การไฟ้ฟ้าส่วนภูมิภาค
Sports Promotion Organization of Thailand	**Ong-karn Songserm Kilâ**	องค์การส่งเสริมกีฬา
State Lottery	**Samnak-ngarn Salaak Kin Baeng Rathabarn**	สำนักงานสลากกินแบ่งรัฐบาล
State Railway of Thailand	**Karn Rot-fai haeng Prathed Thai**	การรถไฟแห่งประเทศไทย
Telephone Organization of Thailand	**Ong-karn Thorasab**	องค์การโทรศัพท์
Tourism Authority of Thailand	**Ong-karn Songserm Karn Thongthiao**	องค์การส่งเสริมการท่องเที่ยว
Thailand Tobacco Monopoly	**Rong-ngarn Yâ Soub**	โรงงานยาสูบ
War Veterans Organization	**Ong-karn Song-khraw Thaharn Phaan Suek**	องค์การสงเคราะห์ทหารผ่านศึก
Warehouse Organization	**Ong-karn Khlang Sinkhâ**	องค์การคลังสินค้า

Some Official Titles

The Prime Minister	**Nayok Ratha-Montri**	นายกรัฐมนตรี
Deputy Prime Minister	**Rawng Nayok Ratha-Montri**	รองนายกรัฐมนตรี
Provincial Governor	**Phu-wâ Rajakarn-Changwad**	ผู้ว่าราชการจังหวัด
Deputy Governor	**Rawng Phu-wâ Rajakarn-Changwad**	รองผู้ว่าราชการจังหวัด
Governor's Private Secretary	**Aksorn-lek**	อักษรเลข
Provincial Clerk	**Châ-Changwad**	จ่าจังหวัด
Personnel and Procurement Officer	**Samian-tra Changwad**	เสมียนตราจังหวัด
Commune Headman	**Kamnan**	กำนัน
Village Headman	**Phuyai-Baan**	ผู้ใหญ่บ้าน
District Officer	**Nai Amphur**	นายอำเภอ
Deputy District Officer	**Palad Amphur**	ปลัดอำเภอ
Minister	**Ratha-montri**	รัฐมนตรี
Secretary to Minister	**Lekhanukarn Ratha-Montri**	เลขานุการรัฐมนตรี
Under Secretary of State	**Palad Krasuang**	ปลัดกระทรวง
Deputy Under Secretary of State	**Rawng Palad Krasuang**	รองปลัดกระทรวง
Director General	**Athi-bodi**	อธิบดี
Deputy Director	**Rawng Athi-bodi**	รองอธิบดี
Chief of Division	**Hua-Na Kawng**	หัวหน้ากอง
Chief of Section	**Hua-na Phanaek**	หัวหน้าแผนก

ENGLISH-THAI VOCABULARY

able (to be able)	sa-mart	สามารถ
about	pramarn; keuab	ประมาณ
above	neua; bonh; kern-kwâ	เหนือ, บน, เกินกว่า
abroad	nawk prathed	นอกประเทศ
abcess	fi	ฝี
absent	mai-mâ; mai you	ไม่มา, ไม่อยู่
absent-minded	chai-loi	ใจลอย
absurd	mai-nâ-cheua	ไม่น่าเชื่อ
abuse	dâ	ด่า
accent	samniang	สำเนียง
accept	rab; yomm-rab	รับ, ยอมรับ
accompany	pai pen-pheuan	ไปเป็นเพื่อน
accessories	u-pakorn	อุปกรณ์
according	tarm-tae	ตามแต่
accident	u-batti-het	อุบัติเหตุ

account (narrative)	reuang-rao;	เรื่องราว
(on his account)	nai banshi khong khow	ในบัญชีของเขา
accuse	klao hâ	กล่าวหา
accused	cham-leui	จำเลย
accuser	chôde	โจทก์
ache	puad	ปวด
acid	krod	กรด
across	kharm; you trong-kharm	ข้าม, อยู่ตรงข้าม
act (do)	tham	ทำ
(on stage)	sadaeng	แสดง
add (increase)	buak, pherm	บวก, เพิ่ม
active	wong-wai	ว่องไว
actor	nak sadaeng	นักแสดง
address	thi-you	ที่อยู่
admire	shuen-shom; leuam-sai	ชื่นชม, เลื่อมใส
administration	karn-pok-khrong	การปกครอง
admit (let in)	yomm hai khow	ยอมให้เข้า
(acknowledge)	yomm rab	ยอมรับ
advance (0f money)	luang-nâ	ล่วงหน้า
To pay in advance:	chaai luang-nâ	จ่ายล่วงหน้า
adventure	phachon-phai	ผจญภัย
advertise	khosana	โฆษณา
advise	nae-namh	แนะนำ
advice	kham nae-nam	คำแนะนำ
affair	kit-thurah	กิจธุระ
affect	krathop-kratheuan	กระทบ กระเทือน
affectionate	pen-thi rak	เป็นที่รัก
afford	phaw-hai dai	พอให้ได้

afraid	kluâ	กลัว
after	phai-lang, thi-lang	ภายหลัง, ทีหลัง
afternoon	véla baai	เวลาบ่าย
afterwards	phaai-lang	ภายหลัง
again	ik; ik-thi	อีก, อีกที
age (length of life)	a-yuh	อายุ
(a very long time)	kao-kae	เก่าแก่
old age:	ayuh-maak	อายุมาก
aged	kae	แก่
agent	tua-thaen	ตัวแทน
secret agent:	sai-labb	สายลับ
agreement	khaw tok-long	ข้อตกลง
aggression	karn rouk-rarn	การรุกราน
aggressor	phou rouk-rarn	ผู้รุกราน
ago	luang-laew; thi phaan ma laew	ล่วงแล้ว, ที่ผ่านมาแล้ว
agree (to contract)	tok-long	ตกลง
(to consent)	yin-yomm	ยินยอม
agreeable	khow-kann dai	เข้ากันได้
agreement (contract)	san-yâ; khaw tok-long	สัญญา, ข้อตกลง
agriculture	karn ka-set	การเกษตร
agriculturist	kasikorn	กสิกร
ahead	khang-nâ	ข้างหน้า
aid	karn shuai-leua	การช่วยเหลือ
aim	khwam moung maai	ความมุ่งหมาย
air (atmosphere)	a-kas	อากาศ
(tune)	tham-nawng	ทำนอง
(to air clothes)	phueng-lom	ผึ่งลม
(in the open air)	klaang-chaeng	กลางแจ้ง

rcraft	khreuang-binh	เครื่องบิน
ike	khlaai-kanh	คล้ายกัน
ive	yang-you	ยังอยู่
l	thang-mod	ทั้งหมด
all right:	di- laew	ดีแล้ว
all over:	sin-soud kanh-thi	สิ้นสุดกันที
most	keuab-chah	เกือบจะ
low	yomm-hai; a-nuyart	ยอมให้, อนุญาต
one (of a man)	khon-diao	คนเดียว
ong	tarm	ตาม
oud	dang-dang	ดัง ๆ
phabet	tua-aksorn	ตัวอักษร
ready	laew; riab-roi	แล้ว, เรียบร้อย
so	duai	ด้วย
ter	plian-plaeng	เปลี่ยนแปลง
though	mae-wâ	แม้ว่า
together	phrom-kanh thangmod	พร้อมกัน
mbulance	rot phayabarn	รถพยาบาล
ways	sameu	เสมอ
mbassador	ék-akkha-rajathout	เอกอัครราชทูต
mong	nai rawaang	ในระหว่าง
mount	cham-nuan	จำนวน
musing	khob-khanh	ขบขัน
ncestor	banpha-bourut	บรรพบุรุษ
ncient	kao-kae; boraan	เก่าแก่, โบราณ
nd	lae; kab	และ, กับ
ngel	théva-thout	เทวทูต
ngry	krôde	โกรธ
nimal	satt	สัตว์

announce	prakaad	ประกาศ
annoy	kuan-chai	กวนใจ
annual	pracham-pi	ประจำปี
another (one more)	ik-anh nueng	อีกอันหนึ่ง
answer	tobb	ตอบ
anxious	pen-huang; penkang-vonh	เป็นห่วง, เป็นกังวล
any	khrai-khrai; dai-dai	ใคร ๆ, ใด ๆ
anyone will do:	anh-nai kaw dai	อันไหนก็ได้
anybody:	khrai kaw dai	ใครก็ได้
anything:	sing-dai sing nueng	สิ่งใดสิ่งหนึ่ง
anything else:	a-rai ik	อะไรอีก
anywhere:	thi-nai kaw dai	ที่ไหนก็ได้
apologize	khaw thode	ขอโทษ
appeal	ou-thawn; rong-rian	อุทธรณ์, ร้องเรียน
appear	prakod tua	ปรากฏตัว
apply	samak	สมัคร
appoint	taeng-tang	แต่งตั้ง
appreciate	rou khun khâ	รู้คุณค่า
approach	prachid tua	ประชิดตัว
approve	a-nuyart; henh-duai	อนุญาติ, เห็นด้วย
approximately	pramaan	ประมาณ
area	khet	เขต
aren' t = are not	mai penh	ไม่เป็น
argue	tô-thiang	โต้เถียง
art	silpa	ศิลปะ
artificial	thiam; mai-thae	เทียม, ไม่แท้
as	thow-kab; dang-thi	เท่ากับ, ดังที่
as from:	nab-tae	นับแต่
as usual:	shén-kheui	เช่นเคย

shamed	abb-aye; kradaakchai	อับอาย, กระดากใจ
sk	tharm	ถาม
sleep	nonn-lab	นอนหลับ
ssault	tham-rai raang-kaai	ทำร้ายร่างกาย
ssemble (meet together)	mâ ruam kanh	มารวมกัน
sset	sin-sab	สินทรัพย์
ssign	mob-maai nâ-thi	มอบหมายหน้าที่
ssignment	tamnaeng nâ-thi	ตำแหน่งหน้าที่
ssist	shuai-leua	ช่วยเหลือ
ssistance	karn shuai-leua	การช่วยเหลือ
ssistant	phu-shuai	ผู้ช่วย
ttempt	khwaam phaya-yarm	ความพยายาม
ttend (to look after)	rab-shai	รับใช้
ttendant	khon rab-shai	คนรับใช้
ttention	khwaam aow chai-sai	ความเอาใจใส่
ttire	taeng-tua; seua-phâ	แต่งตัว,เสื้อผ้า
ttitute	thasanah-khatih	ทัศนคติ
ttractive	shuan-hai-mawng	ชวนให้มอง
uction	leh-lang	เลหลัง
uthority	am-nart na-thi	อำนาจหน้าที่
udience	khon-fang; khon-dou	คนฟัง, คนดู
uditorium	haw prashoum	หอประชุม
uthor	phu-praphand reuang	ผู้ประพันธ์เรื่อง
uthority(power)	am-nart	อำนาจ
(government)	chao na-thi	เจ้าหน้าที่
utomatic	attano-matt	อัตโนมัติ
utomobile	rot-yonh	รถยนต์
vailable	phaw-ha ma-dai	พอหามาได้

average	suan cha-lia	ส่วนเฉลี่ย
aviator	nak-binh	นักบิน
avoid	leek-liang	หลีกเลี่ยง
awake	tuen; mai-lab	ตื่น, ไม่หลับ
award	raang-wanh	รางวัล
away	pai; chaak-pai	ไป, จากไป

B

Bachelor	shaai-sôde	ชายโสด
back	lang; khaang-lang; klab	หลัง, ข้างหลัง, กลับ
to be back:	klab-ma	กลับมา
go back:	klab-pai	กลับไป
send back	song klab pai	ส่งกลับไป
bad(wicked)	léow; shua; mai-di	เลว, ชั่ว, ไม่ดี
bag	thoung	ถุง
paper bag	thoung kradaad	ถุงกระดาษ
baggage	krapow dern-thaang	กระเป๋าเดินทาง
bail	prakanh-tua	ประกันตัว
bait	yeuâ	เหยื่อ
bake	ping	ปิ้ง
balance	suan thi leua	ส่วนที่เหลือ
(scales)	ta-shang	ตาชั่ง
bald	hua-laan	หัวล้าน
ball	louk ball	ลูกบอล
ballroom	hong-ten-ramh	ห้องเต้นรำ
bamboo	maiphai	ไม้ไผ่
banana	kluai	กล้วย

and (company of people)	mou; phuak	หมู่, พวก
(musicalmen)	wong-dontri	วงดนตรี
andit	chône phu-raai	โจรผู้ร้าย
ank (of river)	fang-maenam	ฝั่งแม่น้ำ
(for money)	thana-kharn	ธนาคาร
ank-note	thanabat	ธนบัตร
ankrupt	lomh la-laai	ล้มละลาย
arbarian	a-naraya-shon	อนารยชน
arber	shaang tat-phom	ช่างตัดผม
argain	taw rakha	ต่อราคา
ark(of a dog)	haow	เห่า
ase	tharn-thab; Thaan	ฐานทัพ, ฐาน
asin	âng	อ่าง
ath(bath room)	hong narm	ห้องน้ำ
(to have a bath)	ab-narm	อาบน้ำ
attle	karn-rob	การรบ
attle field	sanarm-rob	สนามรบ
ay	âow	อ่าว
e(existence)	penh; you	เป็น, อยู่
each	shaai-haad	ชายหาด
ean	thuâ	ถั่ว
ear (animal) (to carry)	mi; thue	หมี, ถือ
eard	nuad; khrao	หนวด, เครา
east	sat dérat-shaan	สัตว์เดรัจฉาน
eat	ti; khian; tob; shana	ตี, เฆี่ยน, ตบ, ชนะ
eautiful (of women)	suai, ngârm	สวยงาม
eauty salon	hong serm-suai	ห้องเสริมสวย

because	phraw-wa	เพราะว่า
	penh phraw	เป็นเพราะ
become	klaai-penh	กลายเป็น
bed	thi-nonn	ที่นอน
bedroom:	hong nonn	ห้องนอน
to go to bed:	pai-nonn	ไปนอน
bedstead	tiang-nonn	เตียงนอน
beef	neua-woa	เนื้อวัว
before	konn; konn-ni;	ก่อน, ก่อนนี้,
	khaang-nâ	ข้างหน้า
befriend	pen pheuan	เป็นเพื่อน
beg (ask for)	khaw; onn-wonn	ขอ, อ้อนวอน
begger	khaw-tharn	ขอทาน
begin	rerm-tonh	เริ่มต้น
behind	khaang-lang	ข้างหลัง
believe	sheua; waang-chai	เชื่อ, วางใจ
bell	krading; rakhang	กระดิ่ง, ระฆัง
belly	phoung	พุง
belong	penh-khong	เป็นของ
below	khaang-laang;	ข้างล่าง,
	tamh-kwâ	ต่ำกว่า
belt	khem-khad	เข็มขัด
bench	mâ-nang	ม้านั่ง
bend	khod; ngâw-tua	ขด, งอตัว
berth	thi-nonn	ที่นอน
beside	khaang	ข้าง
besides:	nawk chaak ni	นอกจากนี้
best	yawd-yiam; di-thisut	ยอดเยี่ยม, ดีที่สุด
better	di-kwâ	ดีกว่า

etween	ra-waang	ระหว่าง
everage	khreuang-duem	เครื่องดื่ม
iased	énh-iang	เอนเอียง
ig	yai	ใหญ่
ilingual	phoud dai sawng phasa	พูดได้สอง ภาษา
ill	bai keb-ngoen; prakaad	ใบเก็บเงิน, ประกาศ
ird	nok	นก
Bird's nest:	rang-nok	รังนก
irth	karn kerd	การเกิด
birthday:	wan kerd	วันเกิด
birth place:	thi kerd	ที่เกิด
birth rate:	attra kerd	อัตราเกิด
it(piece)	shin lek	ชิ้นเล็ก
	khong lek noi	ของ เล็กน้อย
it (of animal)	kadd	กัด
itter	khom	ขม
lack	damh	ดำ
lackmail	hak-lang	หักหลัง
lame	klao thod	กล่าวโทษ
leed	leuad awk	เลือดออก
lind	ta-bawd	ตาบอด
low (with mouth)	pow	เป่า
(to give a blow)	shok toi	ชกต่อย
lue	si faa	สีฟ้า
dark blue:	si nam ngern	สีน้ำเงิน
light blue:	si faa onn	สีฟ้าอ่อน
luff	tob-tâ; lawk-luang	ตุบตา, หลอกลวง
lunt	thue; mai-khom	ทือ, ไม่คม
oard	phaen kradaan	แผ่นกระดาน

boarding house	haw-phak	หอพัก
boast	oh-oad; khui-mô	โอ้อวด, คุยโม้
boat	reua	เรือ
motor boat:	reua tit khreuang	เรือติดเครื่อง
rowing boat:	reua phaai	เรือพาย
body	raang-kaai	ร่างกาย
everybody:	thouk-thouk khon	ทุก ๆ คน
boil(abscess)	fi	ฝี
(to bubble up)	deuad; tomh	เดือด, ต้ม
(to boil rice)	houng khao	หุง ข้าว
bolt (of door)	klonn-pratou	กลอนประตู
(of thunder)	fa-phâ	ฟ้าผ่า
bone	kradouk	กระดูก
book	nangsue	หนังสือ
boot	rong-thao houm khaw	รองเท้าหุ้มข้อ
border	shaai-daen	ชายแดน
borrow	yuem; khaw-yuem	ยืม, ขอยืม
both	thang-sawng	ทั้งสอง
bother	rob-kuan; ram-kharn chai	รบกวน, รำคาญใจ
bottle	khuad	ขวด
boundry	a-nâ-khet; phrom-daen	อาณาเขต, พรมแดน
bow	khong-khamnab	โค้งคำนับ
bowl	shaam	ชาม
box	heep	หีบ
(to box)	ban-chu	บรรจุ
boxer	nak-muai	นักมวย
boy	dek-shaai	เด็กชาย
brains	samong	สมอง
branch	king-mai; sa-khâ	กิ่งไม้, สาขา

brass	thong-leuang	ทองเหลือง
brave	klâ; klâ-harn	กล้า, กล้าหาญ
bread	khanom-pang	ขนมปัง
break	taek	แตก
breath	lom-haai-chai	ลมหายใจ
breathe	haai-chai	หายใจ
bribe	sin-bonh	สินบน
bride	chaw-sao	เจ้าสาว
bridegroom:	chow-bao	เจ้าบ่าว
bridge	saphaan	สะพาน
bright	sawaang-sawai	สว่างไสว
bring	aow-mâ; namh khow mâ	เอามา, นำเข้ามา
brittle	prawh	เพราะ
broad	kwaang	กว้าง
broadcast	krachaai siang	กระจายเสียง
broom	mai-kwaad	ไม้กวาด
brown	si narm-tarn	สีน้ำตาล
brush	praeng	แปรง
brute	hode-raai	โหดร้าย
bucket	thang	ถัง
buckle	hua khemkhad	หัวเข็มขัด
buffalo	krabue (or) khwaai	กระบือ, ควาย
bug	tua-reuad	ตัวเรือด
build (a house)	kaw-saang	ก่อสร้าง
bull	woa tuaphu	วัวตัวผู้
bullet	louk-puen	ลูกปืน
burn	phow; mai	เผา, ไหม้
bury	fang	ฝัง
bus	rot pracham-thaang	รถประจำทาง

bus stop:	thi chawd-rot pracham-thaang	ที่จอดรถประจำทาง
bus station:	sathani khon-song	สถานีขนส่ง
business	thura-kit; thurah	ธุรกิจ, ธุระ
busy (having much work to do)	mi thura maak	มีธุระมาก
but	tae	แต่
butterfly	phi-seua	ผีเสื้อ
button	kradoum	กระดุม
buy	sue	ซื้อ
by	doai	โดย
to go by boat:	pai thaang rena	ไปทางเรือ
by and by:	nai mai shâ	ในไม่ช้า

C

cabin (in ship)	hong cabin	ห้องเคบิน
cage	krong-nok	กรงนก
cable	saai thoralek	สายโทรเลข
cablegram:	thoralek	โทรเลข
cafeteria	hong a-harn	ห้องอาหาร
cakes	khanom	ขนม
call	riak; yiam-yian	เรียก, เยี่ยมเยียน
callgirls:	naang thaang thorasab	นางทางโทรศัพท์
camera	klong-thaai-roup	กล้องถ่ายรูป
calm (of water)	ngiap; sa-ngob	เงียบ, สงบ
can	daai; tham-daai; krapong	ได้, ทำได้, กระป๋อง
candle	thian	เทียน

candlestick:	thian-khai	เทียนไข
annon	puen-yai	ปืนใหญ่
annot	mai-daai; mai-samart	ไม่ได้, ไม่สามารถ
anteen	rong a-harn	โรงอาหาร
apital (town)	nakhorn-luang	นครหลวง
(money)	ngoen-thoun	เงินทุน
apitalist	nai-thoun	นายทุน
aptain (of European ship)	kaptan reua	กัปตันเรือ
apture	chab; chab-daai	จับ, จับได้
ar	rot	รถ
Motorcar:	rot-yont	รถยนต์
car park:	thi-chawd-rot	ที่จอดรถ
ards	phai	ไพ่
visiting card:	narm-bat	นามบัตร
are	aow-chai-sai; sonh-chai	เอาใจใส่, สนใจ
areless	phleu-rer; lern-lerr	เผลอเรอ, เลินเล่อ
arpenter	shaang-maai	ช่างไม้
aretaker	khon dou-lae	คนดูแล
areful	rob-khob; ramat-rawang	รอบคอบ, ระมัดระวัง
argo	sin-khâ	สินค้า
arpet	phrom	พรม
arry	thue; hiew; baek	ถือ, หิ้ว, แบก
artridges	krasoun-puen	กระสุนปืน
ase	kawrani	กรณี
In case:	nai kawrani	ในกรณี
(judicial)	khadi	คดี
ash	ngoen-sod	เงินสด
to pay cash:	chaai-sod	จ่ายสด

cashier	phanak-ngârn khaan ngoen	พนักงาน การเงิน
catch (to seize)	chab	จับ
(To catch an illness)	tit-roke	ติดโรค
caterer	phu rab-chad a-harn	ผู้รับจัดอาหาร
cattle	pasusat	ปศุสัตว์
cause	head; ton-head	เหตุ, ต้นเหตุ
cave	ou-mong, thamh	อุโมงค์, ถ้ำ
caviar	khai-plâ	ไข่ปลา (คาเวียร์)
ceiling	phé-darn	เพดาน
cell	hong-khang	ห้องขัง
cemetery	su-sarn; pâ-shâ	สุสาน, ป่าช้า
center	soon	ศูนย์
century	sattawat	ศตวรรษ
certificate	bai-rab-rong	ใบรับรอง
chain	sô; louk-sô	โซ่, ลูกโซ่
chair	kao-i	เก้าอี้
chamber of commerce	haw-karn-khâ	หอการค้า
chance (luck)	ô-kard	โอกาส
change (alter)	plian plian	เปลี่ยนแปลง
(of clothes)	plian seua-pha	เปลี่ยนเสื้อผ้า
channel (TV)	shong	ช่อง
character (alphabetical)	aksorn	อักษร
(nature)	nis-sai	นิสัย
haracteristics	lak-sanah	ลักษณะ
charcoal	tharn; tharn-maai	ถ่าน, ถ่านไม้
charity	karn ku-son	การกุศล
charm (magic drug)	ya-faëd	ยาแฝด
(amulet)	khreuang-raang;	เครื่องราง
(beauty)	sa-neh	เสน่ห์

charming	mi saneh	มีเสน่ห์
Charter (UNO)	kod-bat	กฎบัตร
cheap	rakhâ thouk; khong léow	ถูก, คนเลว
cheat	khon kong	คนโกง
cheek	kaem	แก้ม
chest	ok; nâ-ok	อก, หน้าอก
chew	khiao	เคี้ยว
chief	hua-nâ	หัวหน้า
child	dek; bout; louke	เด็ก, บุตร, ลูก
children	dek-dek	เด็ก ๆ
childish	tham-meuan-dek	ทำเหมือนเด็ก
chin	khaang	คาง
choose	leuak	เลือก
cinema	rong pharb-phyont	โรงภาพยนตร์
citizen	phola-meuang	พลเมือง
city	meuang	เมือง
civic center	sala	ศาลากลาง
class	shanh	ชั้น
clean	sa-ard	สะอาด
cleaning:	laang	ล้าง
cleaner	khon-tham khwaam sa-ard	คนทำความสะอาด
clear	shad chenn	ชัดเจน
	chaëm-chaëng	แจ่มแจ้ง
clerk	samian; phanak- ngârn	เสมียน, พนักงาน
clever	sha-lard	ฉลาด
climate	phumi-akaad	ภูมิอากาศ
clock	nalikâ	นาฬิกา
close (near)	klai	ใกล้
(to shut)	pid	ปิด

cloth	phâ	ผ้า
clothes	seua-phâ	เสื้อผ้า
cloud	mekh	เมฆ
cloudy	a-kaad mued-mua	อากาศมืดมัว
club	samo-sorn	สโมสร
clumsy	ngum-ngârm	งุ่มง่าม
coast	fang tha-lê	ฝั่งทะเล
coat	seua-nawk	เสื้อนอก
cock	kai-tuaphu	ไก่ตัวผู้
code	rahad-lab	รหัสลับ
coin	ngoen-rian	เงินเหรียญ
cold	yenh; nao	เย็น, หนาว
collaborate	ruam-mue	ร่วมมือ
collect	ruab-ruam; keb	รวบรวม, เก็บ
colony	a-nâ ni-khom	อาณานิคม
color	si	สี
colorfast	si mai-tok	สีไม่ตก
comb (for hair)	wi	หวี
(of cock)	ngawn-kai	หงอนไก่
combine	ruam; ruam-hua	รวม, รวมหัว
come	mâ	มา
comfortable	sabaai-di	สบายดี
command (order)	sang; kham-sang	สั่ง, คำสั่ง
commission (brokerage)	khâ puai- karn	ค่าป่วยการ
commode (bathroom)	thô-suam	โถส้วม
committee	khanah kamma-karn	คณะกรรมการ
communicate	tit-taw	ติดต่อ
communication	karn sue-sarn	การสื่อสาร
commune	prashakom	ประชาคม

mmunity	shoum-shon	ชุมชน
mpanion	pheuan	เพื่อน
mpany	borisat	บริษัท
company limited:	borisat chamkad	บริษัทจำกัด
mpare	priab-thiab	เปรียบเทียบ
mpel	cham-chai	จำใจ
mpensate	tham-khwanh	ทำขวัญ
mpensation	khâ-thot-thaën	ค่าทดแทน
mpete	khaëng-khan	แข่งขัน
mplain	bonh; rong-thouk	บ่น, ร้องทุกข์
mplete	set; tham-samret	เสร็จ, ทำสำเร็จ
mplicate	young; sab-sonh	ยุ่ง, สับสน
mpliments	aphinan-thanakarn	อภินันทนาการ
mply	yomm; yomm-tarm	ยอม, ยอมตาม
mponent	suan-prakobb	ส่วนประกอบ
mprise	prakobb-duai	ประกอบด้วย
mpromise	prani pranom	ประณีประนอม
ndition	ngeuan-khai	เงื่อนไข
ndom	thõung-yang a-namai	ถุงยางอนามัย
nductor (bus)	krapaow rot	กระเป๋า (รถ)
(music)	vathaya-korn	วาทยากร
nference	prashum; prueksa	ประชุม, ปรึกษา
nfess	sara-pharb	สารภาพ
nfidence	khwaam man-chai	ความมั่นใจ
ngratulate	sadaeng khwaam yindi	แสดงความยินดี
nnect	tit-taw; taw	ติดต่อ, ต่อ
nsider	phi-chara-nâ	พิจารณา
nstitution	rat-thamma-noun	รัฐธรรมนูญ
nsulate	satharn kongsun	สถานกงสุล

consultant	thi prueksa	ที่ปรึกษา
contract	sanya	สัญญา
contractor	phu tham sanya	ผู้ทำสัญญา
contrary	trong kan-kharm	ตรงกันข้าม
contribute	mi suan shuai	มีส่วนช่วย
control	khuab khum	ควบคุม
convenience	khwaam saduak	ความสะดวก
public convenience:	suam-satharanah	ส้วมสาธารณะ
conversation	karn sonthana	การสนทนา
cook	phaw-khrua; mae-khrua	พ่อครัว, แม่ครัว
cooking	prung a-harn	ปรุงอาหาร
cool	yenh	เย็น
co-ordinator	phu prasarn-ngârn	ผู้ประสานงาน
corner	moum	มุม
corpse	sark-sob; sob	ทรากศพ, ศพ
correct	thouk-tong-di	ถูกต้องดี
corrupt	dai sin-bonh	ได้สินบน
cosmetics	khreuang sam-âng	เครื่องสำอาง
cost	rakhâ thoun	ราคาทุน
costly:	phaëng	แพง
couch	kao-i nuam yao	เก้าอี้นวมยาว
cough	aye	ไอ
counsellor	thi-prueksa	ที่ปรึกษา
count	nabb	นับ
country	prathed	ประเทศ
(rural)	baan-nawk	บ้านนอก
courage	khwaam klâ	ความกล้า
court	sarn	ศาล
Supreme Court:	Sarn Dika	ศาลฎีกา

ousin	louk-phi louk-nong	ลูกพี่ลูกน้อง
:oward	khi-khlaad; khon-khlaad	ขี้ขลาด, คนขลาด
razy	bâ-khlang	บ้าคลั่ง
redit	sab-sin; sin-cheua; khwaam cheua-thue	ทรัพย์สิน, สินเชื่อ, ความเชื่อถือ
reditor	chao-ni	เจ้าหนี้
remation	karn tham-sob; chapana-kit	การทำศพ, ฌาปนกิจ
rematorium	thi-phaow-sob	ที่เผาศพ
rew	louk-ruea; kalasi	ลูกเรือ, กลาสี
rime	achaya-kam	อาชญากรรม
riminal	achaya-korn	อาชญากร
rook	khod-kong	คดโกง
ross-examine	tai-suan	ไต่สวน
rossroads	thaang yaek	ทางแยก
rowd	khon; foung-shon	คน, ฝูงชน
crowded:	khon-naën	คนแน่น
rown	mongkut	มงกุฎ
Crown Prince:	Makut Rajkumarn	มกุฎราชกุมาร
ruel	hode-raai	โหดร้าย
ry	song-siang rong; rong-hai	ส่งเสียงร้อง, ร้องไห้
uddle	kawd, kawd-radd	กอด, กอดรัด
ultivate	ob-rom; fuek-fonh	อบรม, ฝึกฝน
(agricultural)	phoh-plouk	เพาะปลูก
ulture	wathana-tham	วัฒนธรรม
ure	raksâ	รักษา
ustom	praphéni	ประเพณี
ustomer	louk khâ	ลูกค้า

cut	tat	ตัด
cut in half:	phâ khrueng	ผ่าครึ่ง
cut short:	tat-bot	ตัดบท

D

daily	thouk-thouk wan	ทุก ๆ วัน
dairy farm	farm-nom	ฟาร์มนม
dam	kheuan	เขื่อน
dance	fawn-ram	ฟ้อนรำ
danger	anta-raai	อันตราย
dare	klâ lawng-di	กล้าลองดี
dark	mued	มืด
darling	thi-rak	ที่รัก
date	wan-thi	วันที่
daughter	bout-sao; louk-sao	บุตรสาว, ลูกสาว
day	wanh	วัน
day time:	klaang-wanh	กลางวัน
dead	taai laew	ตายแล้ว
death	khwaam-taai; moranah-kam	ความตาย, มรณกรรม
dear (costly)	pheang; thi-rak	แพง, ที่รัก
debit	ni-sin	หนี้สิน
debt	ni	หนี้
(indebted)	pen-ni	เป็นหนี้
decay	now; phuh	เน่า, ผุ
deceive	luang; lawk-luang	ลวง, หลอกลวง
decide	tok-long chai	ตกลงใจ

eck	dard-fâ	ดาดฟ้า
eclare	prakaad	ประกาศ
eclaration	praka-sit	ประกาศิต
eep	luek; luek-sueng	ลึก, ลึกซึ้ง
efend	taw-sou; pong-kanh	ต่อสู้, ป้องกัน
efendant	cham-leui	จำเลย
elay	phlad-pai	ผลัดไป
elegate	phu-thaen	ผู้แทน
elicious	a-roi	อร่อย
elighted	yindi	ยินดี
eliver	chad-song	จัดส่ง
emand	riak-rong; tharm	เรียกร้อง, ถาม
emonstrate	sadaeng; sa-thit	แสดง, สาธิต
entist	maw-fanh; thanta-phaed	หมอฟัน, ทันตแพทย์
eny	patiset	ปฏิเสธ
emocracy	prasha thi-patai	ประชาธิปไตย
epartment	phanaek; krom	แผนก, กรม
department store:	haang sanpha sinkha	ห้างสรรพสินค้า
eparture	karn chack, awk-pai	การจาก, ออกไป
eposit	faak; faak-ngoen	ฝาก, ฝากเงิน
bank deposit:	ngoen-faak	เงินฝาก
epress	kod-long	กดลง
escend	long	ลง
escribe	ban-yaai	บรรยาย
esert	thalé-saai	ทะเลทราย
esire	tongkarn	ต้องการ
estroy	tham-laai	ทำลาย
estiny	boun-kamh	บุญกรรม
etective	nak-sueb	นักสืบ

develop	khayaai; phathanâ	ขยาย, พัฒนา
devil	phi; pi-saat	ผี, ปีศาจ
dialect	phasâ thawng-thin	ภาษาท้องถิ่น
dialogue	bot-sonthanâ	บทสนทนา
diamond	phed	เพชร
diamond ring:	waen-phed	แหวนเพชร
dictionary	phochana nukrom	พจนานุกรม
die (of living things)	taai	ตาย
(of plants)	lomh	ล้ม
difference	khwaam taek-taang	ความแตกต่าง
different	taang-kanh	ต่างกัน
difficult	yaak; lambaak	ยาก, ลำบาก
dig	khud	ขุด
dine	tharn a-harn	ทานอาหาร
dining car	rot sabiang	รถเสบียง
dinner	a-harn yenh	อาหารเย็น
dimension	khanard; mitih	ขนาด, มิติ
diplomat	nak karn-thout	นักการทูต
direct	moung; shi-thaang; amnuai-karn	มุ่ง, ชี้ทาง, อำนวยการ
directions	thit-thaang	ทิศทาง
dirt	founh; la-ong	ฝุ่น, ละออง
dirty	sok-kaprok; mom-maem	สกปรก, มอมแมม
disappear	haai pai	หายไป
disagree	mai hen duai	ไม่เห็นด้วย
disappoint	phid-wang	ผิดหวัง
disaster	hay-nah; khwaam lom-chom	หายนะ, ความล่มจม
disbelief	mai-sheua	ไม่เชื่อ

ischarge	ploi-tua	ปล่อยตัว
	plod-awk chaak ngarn	ปลดออกจากงาน
iscover	khon phob	ค้นพบ
iscount	suan-lod	ส่วนลด
iscuss	a-phi-praai	อภิปราย
isease	roke	โรค
isgust	rang-kiat	รังเกียจ
ish	shaam	ชาม
ishonest	mai seu	ไม่ซื่อ
islike	mai shobb	ไม่ชอบ
ismiss	lai awk; lerk-thaew!	ไล่ออก, เลิกแถว
isorder	yung; mai pen rabiab	ยุ่ง, ไม่เป็น ระเบียบ
ispleased	mai phaw-chai	ไม่พอใจ
isplay	sadaeng	แสดง
ispute	tô-thiang	โต้เถียง
issolve	la-laai	ละลาย
istance	rayah-thaang	ระยะทาง
istress	khwaam-thouk	ความทุกข์
istrict	tambon	ตำบล
istribute	chack	แจก
isturb	rob-kuan	รบกวน
ive	dam-narm	ดำน้ำ
ivide	baeng-pen-suan	แบ่งเป็นส่วน
ivision	kawng	กอง
ivorce	yâ	หย่า
izzy	wien hua	เวียนหัว
o	tham; kratham	ทำ, กระทำ
octor	nai-phaed; maw	นายแพทย์, หมอ
ocuments	ék-kasarn	เอกสาร

dog	su-nak	สุนัข
donate	borichaakngoen	บริจาคเงิน
done	set-laew	เสร็จแล้ว
door	pratu	ประตู
double	sawng-thow	สองเท่า
doubt	song-sai	สงสัย
down	long; long-pai	ลง, ลงไป
downstairs	khaang laang	ข้างล่าง
downtown	nai-meuang	ในเมือง
drag	krashaak; laak-pai	กระชาก, ลากไป
drawer	lin-shak	ลิ้นชัก
dream	khwaam-fanh; fanh	ความฝัน, ฝัน
dress (garment)	seua-pha; pha	เสื้อผ้า, ผ้า
(to be dressed in any thing)	taeng-tua	แต่งตัว
dressmaker	shaang-seua	ช่างเสื้อ
drink	duem	ดื่ม
drive (hunt away)	lai	ไล่
(drive an automobile)	khab rot	ขับรถ
driving licence	bai khab-khi	ใบขับขี่
drop (to fall)	tok	ตก
(a drop)	yod	หยด
(to fall in drops)	yawd	หยอด
drug	yâ	ยา
drunk	maow surâ	เมาสุรา
dry	haeng; taak	แห้ง, ตาก
to dry	taak hai haeng	ตากให้แห้ง
dumb	khon-bai; penh-bai	คนใบ้, เป็นใบ้
dummy	houn; tua-sherd	หุ่น, ตัวเชิด

uring	nai ra-waang	ในระหว่าง
ust	founh; la-ong; phong	ฝุ่น, ละออง, ผง
uty (work)	ngârn; nâ-thi	งาน, หน้าที่
(Customsduties)	ngoen-phasi	เงินภาษี
ye	si-yom-phâ	สีย้อมผ้า

E

ach	anh-lah; khon-lah	อันละ, คนละ
arly	tae-shao; konn	แต่เช้า, ก่อน
arn	hâ-dai	หาได้
arth	phi-phob; din	พิภพ, ดิน
asily	ngai-daai	ง่ายดาย
at	kin; rap-pratharn	กิน, รับประทาน
dit	riab-riang; kae-khai	เรียบเรียง, แก้ไข
ducate	sueksa	ศึกษา
ffect	phon; kerd-phon	ผล, เกิดผล
fficiency,	prasithi-pharb	ประสิทธิภาพ
ffort	khwaam phaya-yaam	ความพยายาม
ither	yaang-dai	อย่างใด
lbow	khaw-sawk	ข้อศอก
lder	khon-kai; khon tô	คนแก่กว่า, คนโต
lect	leuak-tang	เลือกตั้ง
lectricity	fai-fâ	ไฟฟ้า
levator	lift	ลิฟท์
lse	uen	อื่น
elsewhere:	thi-uen	ที่อื่น

embark	khow khreuang; long-reua	เข้าเครื่อง, ลงเรือ
embrace	kawd	กอด
embassy	satharn ek-akkhra-rajathout	สถานเอกอัครราชทูต
emergency	head shouk-shern	เหตุฉุกเฉิน
emotion	a-rom	อารมณ์
	khwaam satheuan-chai	ความสะเทือนใจ
employ	chaang	จ้าง
employer	nai-chaang	นายจ้าง
employment	ngârn, korn chaang	งาน, การจ้าง
empty	waang-plao	ว่างเปล่า
end	chob; tonn-plaai; tonn-chob	จบ, ตอนปลาย, ตอนจบ
endurable	thon-tharn	ทนทาน
enemy	khâ-suek; sattru	ข้าศึก, ศัตรู
engaged	mai-waang; mi-khon-laew	ไม่ว่าง, มีคนแล้ว
engine	khreuang-chak	เครื่องจักร
engineer	visavakorn	วิศวกร
enjoy	sanuk	สนุก
enlarge	khayaai suan	ขยายส่วน
energy	phalang-ngârn	พลังงาน
enormous	yai-tô	ใหญ่โต
enough	phaw, phaw-laew	พอ, พอแล้ว
enter	khow-pai	เข้าไป
enterprise	kich-karn	กิจการ
entertaining	phloed-phlern	เพลิดเพลิน
enthusiastic	kratue rue-ronh	กระตือรือร้น
entire	thang-mod	ทั้งหมด
entrance	thaang-khow	ทางเข้า

envelope	sawng chod-mai	ซองจดหมาย
equal	thao kap; thao-kanh	เท่ากับ, เท่ากัน
equality	thao-thiam kanh	เท่าเทียมกัน
equipment	karn chad triam	การจัดเตรียม
error	khwaam khlaad-khleuan	ความคลาดเคลื่อน
erupt	raberd awk-mâ	ระเบิดออกมา
escalator	bandai-leuan	บันไดเลื่อน
escape	ni pai dai	หนีไปได้
escort	phu pai-song;	ผู้ไปส่ง,
	phu-khuab khum	ผู้ควบคุม
especially	doai sha-phaw	โดยเฉพาะ
estimate	pramarn	ประมาณ
	khaad kha-neh	คาดคะเน
eternal	talawd	ตลอด
ethics	seen-tham	ศีลธรรม
etiquette	marayart	มรรยาท
even	sameu-kanh;	เสมอกัน,
	thueng-mae-wa	ถึงแม้ว่า
evening	véla yenh	เวลาเย็น
ever	kheui	เคย
forever:	talawd pai	ตลอดไป
every	thouk-thouk	ทุก ๆ
everyone:	thouk-khon	ทุกคน
everyday:	thouk-wan	ทุกวัน
everything:	thouk-sing	ทุกสิ่ง
everywhere:	thouk-haeng	ทุกแห่ง
evidence	phayarn lak-tharn	พยานหลักฐาน
exact	nae-nonn	แน่นอน
examine	truad-dou; truad-sobb	ตรวจดู, ตรวจสอบ

example	tua-yaang	ตัวอย่าง
excite	tuen-tenh	ตื่นเต้น
excellence	khwaam-di lerd	ความดีเลิศ
except	wenh-wai tae; nawk-chaak	เว้นไว้แต่, นอกจาก
exchange	laek-plian	แลกเปลี่ยน
exchange-rate	attra laek-plian	อัตราแลกเปลี่ยน
exercise	awk kamlang	ออกกำลัง
exhibition	nitasakarn	นิทรรศการ
exit	thaang-awk	ทางออก
expect	wang; wang-wa	หวัง, หวังว่า
expensive	phaeng	แพง
experiment	thod-long	ทดลอง
experience	prasob-karn	ประสบการณ์
explain	a-thibaai	อธิบาย
explanation	karn a-thibaai-khwaam	การอธิบายความ
explosives	watthu raberd	วัตถุระเบิด
export	song taang prathed	ส่งต่างประเทศ
express	sadaeng khwaam rou-suk	แสดงความรู้ สึก
extinguish	dab	ดับ

F

face	nâ	หน้า
fade	hiao, chaang	เหี่ยว, จาง
factory	rong-ngârn	โรงงาน
fair	ngârm; suai; yutti-tham	งาม, สวย, ยุติธรรม
fall	tok; hok-lom	ตก, หกล้ม
false	mai-ching; plomm	ไม่จริง, ปลอม

amily	khrob-khrua	ครอบครัว
amous	shue-dang	ชื่อดัง
an	phatt; khon-rak	พัด, คนรัก
ar	klai	ไกล
are	kha-doai-sarn	ค่าโดยสาร
arm	rai; nâ	ไร่, นา
armer	kasikorn	กสิกร
arther	klai awk-pai	ไกลออกไป
ascinating	na long lai	น่าหลงไหล
ashion	baeb samai niyom	แบบสมัยนิยม
ast	réow	เร็ว
asten	phouk	ผูก
at	ouan	อ้วน
ate	shôke-shâtâ; phrom-likhit	โชคชะตา, พรหมลิขิต
ather	phaw; bida	พ่อ, บิดา
ault	khwaam-phid	ความผิด
fault-finding:	chab-phid	จับผิด
ear	klua	กลัว
east	liang shalong	เลี้ยงฉลอง
ee	kha-thamniam	ค่าธรรมเนียม
eel (sensation)	rou-suek	รู้สึก
elicitate	yin-di	ยินดี
ell (to cut down trees)	khône-lom	โค่นล้ม
ellow (man)	khon; pheun	คน, เพื่อน
emale	ying	หญิง
(of animals)	tua-mia	ตัวเมีย
ence	rua	รั้ว
erry	reua rab-song	เรือรับส่ง

fertilizer	pui	ปุ๋ย
fever	khai	ไข้
few	song-sarm	สอง-สาม
fiancé	khou-manh	คู่หมั้น
field	thoung-nâ	ทุ่งนา
fierce	duh; duh-raai	ดุ, ดุร้าย
fight	taw-sou	ต่อสู้
(of animals)	shonh	ชน
figure(cypher)	tua-lekh	ตัวเลข
(appearance)	roup-raang	รูปร่าง
file	faem ekka-sarn	แฟ้มเอกสาร
film(camera)	film thaai roup	ฟิล์มถ่ายรูป
find	khon-hâ; hâ-daai	ค้นหา, หาได้
fine	di-maak	ดีมาก
(penalty)	khâ-prab	ค่าปรับ
(thin)	la-iat	ละเอียด
finger	niew	นิ้ว
fore finger:	niew-shi	นิ้วชี้
middle finger:	niew-klaang	นิ้วกลาง
ring-finger:	niew-naang	นิ้วนาง
little-finger:	niew-koi	นิ้วก้อย
finish	set; amret; chob	เสร็จ, สำเร็จ, จบ
fire	fai	ไฟ
firearms:	Avudh puen	อาวุธปืน
fire stations:	Sathani dab phloeng	สถานีดับ เพลิง
fish	plâ	ปลา
fisherman	shao pramong	ชาวประมง
fit	mawh; somh; khow-roupe	เหมาะ, สม, เข้ารูป
fix	tit; yuet; trueng	ติด, ยึด, ตรึง

flag	thong	ธง
flame	pléow-fai	เปลวไฟ
flat	a-kharn	อาคาร
flavor	rod	รส
flea	tua-mad; tua-rai	ตัวหมัด, ตัวไร
flesh	neuâ	เนื้อ
flirt	kiao-phâ râ-si; cheep	เกี้ยวพาราสี, จีบ
flood	u-thok-phai; narm-thuam	อุทกภัย, น้ำท่วม
floor	phuen; shanh	พื้น, ชั้น
flower	dorkmaai	ดอกไม้
fluent	khlong	คล่อง
fly	bin	บิน
fog	mawk	หมอก
follow	tit-tarm	ติดตาม
food	a-harn	อาหาร
fool	khon-ngô	คนโง่
foot	thao	เท้า
for	samrab; pheua	สำหรับ, เพื่อ
forbid	haam	ห้าม
force	kamlang; am-nart	กำลัง, อำนาจ
foreign exchange	ngoen-trâ taang-prathed	เงินตรา ต่างประเทศ
foreigner	taang-dao	ต่างด้าว
forest	pâ; pâ-maai	ป่า, ป่าไม้
forget	luem	ลืม
forgive	yok-thod; a-phai hai	ยกโทษ, อภัยให้
fork	somm	ส้อม
form	roup-raang	รูปร่าง
formality	rabiab; phi-thi	ระเบียบ, พิธี

former	tae-konh; anh-konh	แต่ก่อน, อันก่อน
fortune (luck)	shôke; laab	โชค, ลาภ
fortune-teller	maw-dou	หมอดู
forward	khaag nâ	ข้างหน้า
foundation	moun-nithi	มูลนิธิ
fountain	narm-phuh	น้ำพุ
fragile	taek-ngaai	แตกง่าย
fragrant	klin-homm; homm	กลิ่นหอม, หอม
freight	khâ-rawaang	ค่าระวาง
frequently	boi; thi; khwaam-thi	บ่อย, ถี่, ความถี่
fresh	sod; mai-mai	สด, ใหม่ ๆ
fried	thawd; phad	ทอด, ผัด
friend	sahaai; pheuan	สหาย, เพื่อน
friendship	mitttrapharb	มิตรภาพ
fright	tok-chai; klua	ตกใจ, กลัว
from	chaak	จาก
frozen	yenh; yen-chon-khaeng	เย็น, เย็นจนแข็ง
front	darn-nâ; khaang-nâ	ด้านหน้า, ข้างหน้า
frontier	shaai-daen	ชายแดน
fruit	phol-maai	ผลไม้
fuels	sheua-phloeng	เชื้อเพลิง
full	tem; imm	เต็ม, อิ่ม
fun	sanuk; khob-khan	สนุก, ขบขัน
function	nâ-thi; ngârn	หน้าที่, งาน
funeral	pithi sob	พิธีศพ
furnish	chad-ha-hai	จัดหาให้
furniture	khreuang-reuan	เครื่องเรือน
further	taw-pai	ต่อไป
fussy	chu-chi	จู้จี้
future	a-nakhot	อนาคต

G

gain	dai kamrai	ได้กำไร
gamble	lenh-phanan	เล่นพนัน
gambler	nak karn-phanan	นักการพนัน
garage	rong-rot; ou-somm-rott	โรงรถ, อู่ซ่อมรถ
garden	suan	สวน
gardener:	khon tham suan	คนทำสวน
gate	pratou rua	ประตูรั้ว
gather	ruab-ruam	รวบรวม
gay	suai-gay	สวยเก๋
gem	phed-phloi	เพชรพลอย
generally	thua-pai	ทั่วไป
generous	ob-omm ari	โอบอ้อมอารี
gentle	supharb	สุภาพ
gentleman:	supharb-burud	สุภาพบุรุษ
get	aow-mâ	เอามา
get in:	khow mâ	เข้ามา
get rid of:	kamchat	กำจัด
get off:	long-pai	ลงไป
gift	khong-khwan	ของขวัญ
girl	dek-ying	เด็กหญิง
ghost	phi	ผี
give	hai	ให้
glad	yin-di; dichai	ยินดี, ดีใจ
glass	krachok; kaew	กระจก, แก้ว
go	pai	ไป
go back:	klab-pai	กลับไป

go in:	khow-pai	เข้าไป
go out:	awk-pai	ออกไป
god	phra chao	พระเจ้า
gold	thawng	ทอง
goldsmith:	shang-thawng	ช่างทอง
good	di	ดี
government	ratthabarn	รัฐบาล
grain	med; maled	เม็ด, เมล็ด
grand	yai; yai-to	ใหญ่, ใหญ่โต
grant	a-nuyart	อนุญาต
grass	yâ	หญ้า
grateful	katan-you	กตัญญู
grave	loum sop	หลุมศพ
gray	si-thow	สีเทา
grease	khai; manh	ไข, มัน
great	ying-yai	ยิ่งใหญ่
green	si khiao	สีเขียว
grey	si thow	สีเทา
grocery	raan khaai-khong sham	ร้านขายของชำ
ground	phuen din; sanarm	พื้นดิน, สนาม
group	mou; kloum	หมู่, กลุ่ม
grow	terb-tô; plouk	เติบโต, ปลูก
guard	yarm raksa-karn	ยามรักษาการ
guess	dow	เดา
guest	phu rab-shern; khaek	ผู้รับเชิญ, แขก
guidance	karn nae-namh	การแนะนำ
guide	shi-thaang; makkhu-thed	ชี้ทาง, มัคคุเทศก์
guilty	mikhwaam-phid	มีความผิด
gulf	aôw; paak-aôw	อ่าว, ปากอ่าว
gun	puen	ปืน

habit	nissai	นิสัย
hair	phom; khon	ผม, ขน
haircut	tat-phom	ตัดผม
hairdresser:	shaang taeng phom	ช่างตัดผม
hall	hong-thong	ห้องโถง
	hong-prashum	ห้องประชุม
hand	mue	มือ
hand-made:	tham-due-mue	ทำด้วยมือ
handkerchief	pha-shed-nâ	ผ้าเช็ดหน้า
handsome	roup-law; roup-ngârm	รูปหล่อ, รูปงาม
hang	khwaen; hoi	แขวน, ห้อย
hanger	thi khwaen seua	ที่แขวนเสื้อ
happiness	khwam-souk	ความสุข
happy	mi khwam-sòuk; penh-souk	มีความสุข, เป็นสุข
harbor	thâ-reua	ท่าเรือ
hard (with difficulty)	yaak	ยาก
(quiality)	khaeng	แข็ง
harm	an-ta-rai	อันตราย
haste	reep-reng	รีบเร่ง
hat	muak	หมวก
hate	kliad	เกลียด
have	mi	มี
head	hua	หัว
head-line:	phaad-hua	พาดหัว
head-ache:	puad-hua	ปวดหัว

health	sou kha-pharb	สุขภาพ
hear	dai-yin	ได้ยิน
heart	hua-chai	หัวใจ
heat	khwam ronn; tham hai ronn	ความร้อน, ทำให้ร้อน
heel	sonh-thao	ส้นเท้า
hell	narok	นรก
help	shuai; shuai-leuâ	ช่วย, ช่วยเหลือ
hen	mae-kai	แม่ไก่
hide	sonn	ซ่อน
high	soung	สูง
highway	thaang-luang	ทางหลวง
hill	khow; doi	เขา, ดอย
hip	sa-phôke	สะโพก
hire	shaow	เช่า
hirer	phu-châng	ผู้จ้าง
history	pravat-saad	ประวัติศาสตร์
hit	ti; thoup; krathob	ตี, ทุบ, กระทบ
hobby	ngârn adirek	งานอดิเรก
hold	thue	ถือ
hole	rou	รู
holiday	wan-yout	วันหยุด
holy	sak sit	ศักดิ์สิทธิ์
home	baan; thi-you	บ้าน, ที่อยู่
homesick	khid thueng baan	คิดถึงบ้าน
honest	sue; sue-sat	ซื่อ, ซื่อสัตย์
honor	kiart; kiart-niyom	เกียรติ, เกียรตินิยม
hope	wang; khwaam-wang	หวัง, ความหวัง
horse	mâ	ม้า

horse racing	karn khaeng-mâ	การแข่งม้า
hospital	rong phaya-barn	โรงพยาบาล
host	chao-pharb	เจ้าภาพ
hot	ron	ร้อน
hotel	rong-raem	โรงแรม
hour	shua-mong	ชั่วโมง
house	baan	บ้าน
housekeeper	mae-baan	แม่บ้าน
how	yaang-rai	อย่างไร
humid	shuen	ชื้น
hunger	khwaam-hiew	ความหิว
hungry	hiew	หิว
hurry	reep-réng; réow!	รีบเร่ง, เร็ว
hurt	tham-raai; baad-cheb	ทำร้าย, บาดเจ็บ
husband	sami	สามี

ndoor	nai-romh	ในร่ม
ndustry	ut-saha-kam	อุตสาหกรรม
nfant	dek-daeng	เด็กแดง
nfectton	tit-rôke	ติดโรค
nfluence	itthi-phon	อิทธิพล
nform	chaeng hai saab	แจ้งให้ทราบ
nformal	pen-kanh-eng	เป็นกันเอง
nformation	khao; khwaam-rou	ข่าว, ความรู้
nhabitant	phola-meuang; shao-baan	พลเมือง, ชาวบ้าน

injection	karn shide-yâ	การฉีดยา
injury	baad-cheb	บาดเจ็บ
injustice	mai yutti-tham	ไม่ยุติธรรม
inland	nai prathed	ในประเทศ
ink	muek	หมึก
inn	rong-raem; thi-phak	โรงแรม, ที่พัก
inquire	tharm	ถาม
insecticides	yâ khâ malaeng	ยาฆ่าแมลง
inside	khaang-nai	ข้างใน
insist on	yuen-yanh	ยืนยัน
inspect	truad-trâ	ตรวจตรา
instead of	thaen-thi	แทนที่
institution	satha-ban	สถาบัน
insurance	karn rap-prakan	การรับประกัน
insure	rap-prakan	รับประกัน
intelligence	panya; shaow	ปัญญา, เชาวน์
intend	tang-chai	ตั้งใจ
intention	khwaam tang-chai	ความตั้งใจ
interest	khwaam sonh-chai	ความสนใจ
interesting	na-son chai	น่าสนใจ
interfere	saek	แทรก
internal	phaai-nai	ภายใน
international	sakon; rawaang prathed	สากล, ระหว่างประเทศ
interpreter	laam-plae	ล่ามแปล
interview	samphard; sonthana	สัมภาษณ์, สนทนา
interrupt	sawd-saek	สอดแทรก
introduce	nae-namh	แนะนำ
introduction	kham-nam	คำนำ
investment	karn long-thoun	การลงทุน

vestigate	sobb-suan	สอบสวน
vitation	karn shern	การเชิญ
vite	sheua-shern	เชื้อเชิญ
on	reed; reed-phâ	รีด, รีดผ้า
(metal)	lek	เหล็ก
land	koh	เกาะ
sue	pradenh	ประเด็น
ch	khan	คัน

J

il	khouk; ta-râng	คุก, ตะราง
w	kraam	กราม
alous	itsha	อิจฉา
welery	khreuang-phed	เครื่องเพชร
b	karn ngârn	การงาน
int	ruam-kanh	รวมกัน
ke	reuang talok	เรื่องตลก
urnalist	nak nang sue phim	นักหนังสือพิมพ์
ice	narm-pholamai	น้ำผลไม้
mp	kradode	กระโดด
st	phaw-moh; phow-di; pheung-chah	พอเหมาะ, พอดี, เพิ่งจะ
stice	khwaam yutti-tham	ความยุติธรรม

K

keep	keb; raksâ	เก็บ, รักษา
key	louk kounchae	ลูกกุญแจ
kick	teh	เตะ
kidneys	tai	ไต
kill	khâ	ฆ่า
kind	karuna; chai-di; mi-metta	กรุณา, ใจดี, มีเมตตา
king	phrachao-phaen-din; kasat	พระเจ้าแผ่น ดิน, กษัตริย์
kingdom	raj a-nachak	ราชอาณาจักร
kiss	choub	จูบ
kitchen	khrua	ครัว
kite	wao	ว่าว
knee	hua-khow	หัวเข่า
knife	mide	มีด
knock	ti; thoup; faad	ตี, ทุบ, ฟาด
know	rou; rou-chak	รู้, รู้จัก

L

ladies' room	hong-naam ying	ห้องน้ำหญิง
ladder	ban-dai	บันได
lady	supharb-satri	สุภาพสตรี
lake	thalé-saap	ทะเลสาบ

lamp	ta-kiang; khome fai	ตะเกียง,โคมไฟ
land	thi-din; phaen-din	ที่ดิน,แผ่นดิน
to land:	long chawd	ลงจอด
language	pha-sa	ภาษา
large	yai; tô	ใหญ่, โต
last	sud-thaai	สุดท้าย
late	shâ; saai; mai-thanh véla	ช้า, สาย, ไม่ทัน เวลา
laugh	hua-rawh	หัวเราะ
laundry	raan sak-reed	ร้านซักรีด
lavatory	hong naam	ห้องน้ำ
law	kod-maai	กฎหมาย
lawyer	thanaai-khwaam	ทนายความ
lazy	khi-kiad	ขี้เกียจ
lead	namh; phâ-pai	นำ, พาไป
leader	phu-namh	ผู้นำ
leaf	bai-mai; bai; phaën	ใบไม้, ใบ, แผ่น
leak, leaky	rua; thaluh	รั่ว, ทะลุ
lean(thin)	phomm	ผอม
(to lean upon)	phing	พิง
leap	kradode	กระโดด
learn	rian	เรียน
lease	hai shaow	ให้เช่า
leather	nang-fawk	หนังฟอก
leave	lâ; awk-chaak	ลา, ออกจาก
lecture	kham ban-yaai	คำบรรยาย
left	daan saai	ด้านซ้าย
leg	khâ	ขา
legacy	moradok	มรดก

legal	thouk kod-maai	ถูกกฎหมาย
leisure	véla-waang	เวลาว่าง
lend	hai yuem	ให้ยืม
length	khwaam yao	ความยาว
lesson	bot-rian	บทเรียน
let	ploi hai; hai shaow	ปล่อยให้, ให้เช่า
letter	aksorn; tua nangsue; chodmai	อักษร, ตัวหนังสือ, จดหมาย
level	radab	ระดับ
liable	ard-chah	อาจจะ
liaison	prasarn ngârn	ประสานงาน
library	hong samud	ห้องสมุด
license	bai anu-yart	ใบอนุญาต
lie	phoud-pod	พูดปด
liar	khon ko-hok	คนโกหก
life	shivid	ชีวิต
lift	yok; yok-khuen	ยก, ยกขึ้น
light	bao; saeng-sawaang	เบา, แสงสว่าง
head-lights:	fai-nâ	ไฟหน้า
side lights:	fai khâng	ไฟข้าง
lighter	thi chud fai	ที่จุดไฟ
lightning	fâi-laeb	ฟ้าแลบ
like	shob	ชอบ
line	sen; naew	เส้นแนว
lip	rim fi-paak	ริมฝีปาก
liquor	laow	เหล้า
list	banshi	บัญชี
listen	fang	ฟัง
little	lek; lek-noi	เล็ก, เล็กน้อย

live	you a-sai; yang-you	อยู่อาศัย, ยังอยู่
loan	ngoen-kou; ngoen-yuem	เงินกู้, เงินยืม
long	yao; naan	ยาว, นาน
lonely	ngaw; wawê	เหงา, ว้าเหว่
loud	dang	ดัง
look	dou; mong-dou	ดู,มองดู
look after:	du lae	ดูแล
look back:	liao-lang	เหลียวหลัง
look at:	truad-dou	ตรวจดู
look for:	mawng-hâ	มองหา
look over:	samruad	สำรวจ
look upon:	phi-charana	พิจารณา
look down:	dou-thouk	ดูถูก
look into:	sobb-suan	สอบสวน
look forward:	tangchai khoi	ตั้งใจคอย
oose	luam	หลวม
ose	lost, haai	หาย
otion	narm-homm	น้ำหอม
ovely	nâ-rak	น่ารัก
ow	tam	ต่ำ
ck	shoke	โชค
cky	shoke di	โชคดี
ggage	heep	หีบ
nch	a-harn klaang-wan	อาหารกลางวัน
ng	pord	ปอด

machine	khreuang-chak kon	เครื่องจักรกล
mail	praisani-phan	ไปรษณียภัณฑ์
mailbox	tou-chodmaai	ตู้จดหมาย
main	sam-khan	สำคัญ
majority	suan-maak	ส่วนมาก
make	tham	ทำ
male	phed-shaai	เพศชาย
man	phu-shaai	ผู้ชาย
manager	phu chad-karn	ผู้จัดการ
manner	mara-yart	มรรยาท
many	maak; laai	มาก, หลาย
map	phaen-thi	แผนที่
mark	khanaen; khreuang-maai	คะแนน, เครื่องหมาย
market	talaad	ตลาด
marry	taeng-ngarn	แต่งงาน
marvelous	di-ching; yiam-ching	ดีจริง, เยี่ยมจริง
massage	nuad	นวด
massage parlor	rong-nuad	โรงนวด
master	chao naai	เจ้านาย
match	mai khide fai	ไม้ขีดไฟ
mattress	fouke; thi-nonn	ฟูก, ที่นอน
material(raw)	watthu-dib; art-chah	วัตถุดิบ, อาจจะ
may	art	อาจ
maybe	art-pen-daai	อาจเป็นไปได้
meal	a-harn	อาหาร
mean	maai-khwaam-wâ	หมายความว่า
meat (beef)	neua	เนื้อ

mechanic	shang chak kol	ช่างจักรกล
medicine	yâ	ยา
medium	klaang	กลาง
meet	phob	พบ
member	samashik	สมาชิก
memorandum	banthuek	บันทึก
mend	somm; kae	ซ่อม, แก้
mention	phoud-thueng	พูดถึง
message	khao	ข่าว
messenger	phanak-ngarn song-ekkasarn	พนักงานส่งเอกสาร
metal	lo-hah	โลหะ
meter	khreuang-wat	เครื่องวัด
metropolis	nakorn luang	นครหลวง
middle	klaang; tawn klaang	กลาง, ตอนกลาง
midnight	thiang-khuen	เที่ยงคืน
might	am-nart; art-chah	อำนาจ, อาจจะ
milk	nom-sod	นมสด
military	karn thaharn	การทหาร
mill (rice)	rong-si khao	โรงสีข้าว
mind	chit-chai	จิตใจ
mine	khawng-shan	ของฉัน
mineral	raë	แร่
minute	na-thi	นาที
mirror	krachok ngao	กระจกเงา
misfortune	shôke-raai	โชคร้าย
miss	naangsao; khid thueng	นางสาว, คิดถึง
mistress	nai phuying	นายผู้หญิง
miss, missing	haai-pai; khaad	หายไป, ขาด

mistake	phid; khowchai-phid	ผิด, เข้าใจผิด
mix	ponh; pha-som	ปน, ผสม
mobile	khleuan-thi	เคลื่อนที่
model	baeb	แบบ
modern	thanh-samai	ทันสมัย
modest	supharb	สุภาพ
moment	véla; khanah	เวลา, ขณะ
money	ngoen	เงิน
monk	phra	พระ
month	deuan	เดือน
monument	anusawari	อนุสาวรีย์
moon	duang chand	ดวงจันทร์
mount	doi	ดอย
more	maak-kwâ	มากกว่า
morning	véla shao	เวลาเช้า
mosquito	yung	ยุง
most	suan-yai	ส่วนใหญ่
mother	mae; marn-dâ	แม่, มารดา
motor	khreuang-yont	เครื่องยนต์
mountain	phu-khao	ภูเขา
mouth	paak	ปาก
move	khleuan yaai	เคลื่อนย้าย
movie	pharb-phayon	ภาพยนตร์
Mr.	Naai; Khun	นาย, คุณ
Mrs.	Naang; Khun-naai	นาง, คุณนาย
much	maak	มาก
mud	khlône	โคลน
murderer	khata-korn	ฆาตกร
muscle	klaam neua	กล้ามเนื้อ

museum	phiphitphaphan-sathaarn	พิพิธภัณฑ์สถาน
mushroom	hed	เห็ด
music	don-tri	ดนตรี
musician	nak-dontri	นักดนตรี
must	tong	ต้อง
my	khong-shan	ของฉัน
myself	tua-shan-eng	ตัวฉันเอง

N

nail	tapou; leb	ตะปู, เล็บ
nail file	tabai leb	ตะไบเล็บ
naked	plueai	เปลือย
name	shue	ชื่อ
napkin	phâ-ched-paak	ผ้าเช็ดปาก
narrow	khaeb	แคบ
nation	shaat	ชาติ
national	haeng shaat	แห่งชาติ
natural	thammashaat	ธรรมชาติ
naughty	souk-sonh	ซุกซน
near	klai; mai-klai	ใกล้, ไม่ไกล
nearly	keuab; keuab-pai	เกือบ, เกือบไป
ecessary	cham-penh	จำเป็น
eck	khaw	คอ
ecklace	soi-khaw	สร้อยคอ
ecktie	thai; nek thai	ไท, เนคไท
eeds	cham-penh; khwaam tong-karn	จำเป็น, ความต้องการ

needle	khém	เข็ม
neighbor	pheun-baan	เพื่อนบ้าน
neighborhood	thi klai baan	ที่ใกล้บ้าน
nephew	laan-shai	หลานชาย
nerve	pra-saat	ประสาท
never	mai-kheui	ไม่เคย
nevertheless	theung-yaang-rai	ถึงอย่างไร
new	mai	ใหม่
news	khao	ข่าว
newspaper	nangsue-phim	หนังสือพิมพ์
next	taw-pai; tad-pai	ต่อไป, ถัดไป
nice	di; ngârm; a-roi	ดี, งาม, อร่อย
nickname	shue-lenh	ชื่อเล่น
night	klaang-khuen	กลางคืน
nobody	mai-mi khrai	ไม่มีใคร
noise	siang	เสียง
noisy	uek-ka-thuek	อึกทึก
none	mai-mi	ไม่มี
noodles	senh-mi	เส้นหมี่
noon	thiang; thiang-wanh	เที่ยง, เที่ยงวัน
north	thit-neua	ทิศเหนือ
nose	cha-mouk	จมูก
notebook	samudban-thuek	สมุดบันทึก
nothing	mai-mi arai	ไม่มีอะไร
notice	prakaad; sangket	ประกาศ, สังเกต
notify	chaeng-hai-saab	แจ้งให้ทราบ
novel (book)	nangsue ann-lenh	หนังสืออ่านเล่น
now	diao-ni	เดี๋ยวนี้
nowhere	mai-mi thi-nai	ไม่มีที่ไหน

number	maai-lekh; lekh-thi	หมายเลข, เลขที่
nun	naang-shi	นางชี
nurse	naang phayabarn; phi-liang	นางพยาบาล, พี่เลี้ยง

O

obey	sheuâ-fang	เชื่อฟัง
obliged	cham-chai	จำใจ
obstacles	upa-sak	อุปสรรค
occasionally	pen khrang-khrao	เป็นครั้งคราว
occupation	a-sheep	อาชีพ
occupied	khow you	เข้าอยู่
ocean	maha-samud	มหาสมุทร
offence	khwaam-phid	ความผิด
offer	khaw-saneu	ข้อเสนอ
office	samnak-ngârn	สำนักงาน
official	khâ rajakarn	ข้าราชการ
often	sameu-sameuh	เสมอ ๆ
oil	narm-manh	น้ำมัน
old	kae; mi-ayuh; khow	แก่, มีอายุ, เก่า
once	khrang-diao	ครั้งเดียว
one-way	thaang-diao	ทางเดียว
onion	hua-homm	หัวหอม
only	thow-nanh	เท่านั้น
open	perd	เปิด
operation	karn phâ-tat	การผ่าตัด
opinion	khwaam-henh	ความเห็น

opportunity	ô-kard	โอกาส
opposite	trong-khârm	ตรงข้าม
optician	chaksu-phaed	จักษุแพทย์
orange	som	ส้ม
order	kham-sang; awk khamsang	คำสั่ง, ออกคำสั่ง
ordinary	thamma-da	ธรรมดา
organization	ong-kârn	องค์การ
oriental	tawan-awk	ตะวันออก
original	khong-derm	ของเดิม
ornament	khreuang pradab	เครื่องประดับ
other	uen	อื่น
ought	khuan	ควร
out	awk-pai	ออกไป
out-of-date:	mod samai	หมดสมัย
outlaw:	nawk kod-maai	นอกกฎหมาย
outdoor:	nawk-baan	นอกบ้าน
outside:	khaang-nawk	ข้างนอก
over	kern pai; khaang-bonh	เกินไป, ข้างบน
overcharge	khid-phaeng koen pai	คิดแพงเกินไป
overcooked	souk-pai	สุกไป
overhaul	prab khreuang	ปรับเครื่อง
overhead	khaang-bonh	ข้างบน
oversea	khaam tha-lé	ข้ามทะเล
overtime	luang véla	ล่วงเวลา
owe	penh-ni	เป็นหนี้
own	tonh-eng; pen chao-khong	ตนเอง, เป็นเจ้าของ
owner	chow-khong	เจ้าของ

P

pack	haw	ห่อ
page	nâ nangsue	หน้าหนังสือ
paid	chamrah-laew	ชำระแล้ว
pain	cheb; cheb-puad	เจ็บ, เจ็บปวด
paint	si tha-baan; thâ-si	สีทาบ้าน, ทาสี
painting	pharb khian duai si	ภาพเขียนด้วยสี
pair	khou	คู่
palace	phra rajawang	พระราชวัง
pale	seed-siao	ซีดเซียว
pants	kang-keng nonn	กางเกงนอน
pantry	hong keb aharn	ห้องเก็บอาหาร
paper	kradaad	กระดาษ
parcel	haw phassadu	ห่อพัสดุ
pardon	a-hosih; a-phai	อโหสิ, อภัย
parents	phu pok-khrong	ผู้ปกครอง
park	suan sathara-nah	สวนสาธารณะ
parking space	tthi chawd rot	ที่จอดรถ
part	shin-suan	ชิ้นส่วน
participate	khow ruam	เข้าร่วม
parts (component)	suan prakobb	ส่วนประกอบ
partner	houn-suan	หุ้นส่วน
party	ngârn-liang; khanah; phak karn-meuang	งานเลี้ยง, คณะ, พรรคการเมือง
pass	phaan; sobb-lai dai	ผ่าน, สอบไล่ได้
passenger	phu-doai-sarn	ผู้โดยสาร
passport	nangsue dern thaang	หนังสือเดินทาง
past	a-dite	อดีต

path	thaang-dern	ทางเดิน
patient	khon-khai; od-thon	คนไข้, อดทน
pattern	baeb-phaen	แบบแผน
pay	chaai; chaai-ngoen	จ่าย, จ่ายเงิน
payment	karn chamrah-ngoen	การชำระเงิน
payee	phu rab-ngoen	ผู้รับเงิน
peace	santipharb	สันติภาพ
peaceful	sa-ngob ngiab	สงบเงียบ
peak	yawd; yawd khao	ยอด, ยอดเขา
pen	paakka	ปากกา
pencil	din-saw	ดินสอ
people	prasha-shon; foung shon; phu-khon	ประชาชน, ฝูงชน, ผู้คน
per	taw	ต่อ
Per day:	taw-wanh	ต่อวัน
performance	karn sadaeng	การแสดง
perfect	dee; somboon	ดี, สมบูรณ์
perfume	narm-homm	น้ำหอม
perhaps	baang-thi	บางที
period	kam-nod	กำหนด
permanent	thavorn	ถาวร
permission	a-nuyart	อนุญาต
person	buk-khon;khon	บุคคล, คน
personality	buk-khlik-pharb	บุคคลิกภาพ
petrol (gasoline)	narm-manh	น้ำมัน
pharmacist	phésash-korn	เภสัชกร
photograph	pharb thaai	ภาพถ่าย
photographer	shang-pharb	ช่างภาพ
photography shop	raan thai-roup	ร้านถ่ายรูป

pick	leuak	เลือก
Pick up:	keb	เก็บ
picture	roup-pharb	รูปภาพ
piece	shin; anh	ชิ้น, อัน
pier	tha-khârm	ท่าข้าม
pill	med	เม็ด
pillow	mawn or monn	หมอน
pilot	nak-bin	นักบิน
pin	khem-moud	เข็มหมุด
pitiful	nâ song-sarn	น่าสงสาร
place	satharn-thi	สถานที่
plain	riab-riab; thi-raab	เรียบ ๆ, ที่ราบ
plan	khrong-karn; phaen	โครงการ, แผน
plate	chaan	จาน
platform	shaan-shala	ชานชาลา
play	lenh; sadaeng	เล่น, แสดง
pleasant	arom di	อารมณ์ดี
please	karuna; proad	กรุณา, โปรด
pleasure	khwaam yindi	ความยินดี
plenty	maak; somboun	มาก, สมบูรณ์
pledge	hai sanya	ให้สัญญา
pocket	krapow;	กระเป๋า,
pickpocke:	luang krapow	ล้วงกระเป๋า
point	choud prasong	จุดประสงค์
	khanaen	คะแนน
poison	ya-phid	ยาพิษ
poisonus	pen-phid	เป็นพิษ
police	tamruat	ตำรวจ
traffic police:	tamruat chara chorn	ตำรวจจราจร

polish	khad; thou	ขัด, ถู
political	karn-meuang	การเมือง
politician	nak karn meuang	นักการเมือง
pond	baw-nârm	บ่อน้ำ
pool	sa; sa waai-nârm	สระ, สระว่ายน้ำ
poor	yaak-chon	ยากจน
popular	kwaang-khwaang; pen thi niyom	กว้างขวาง, เป็นที่นิยม
port	tha-reua	ท่าเรือ
porter	khon yok khong	คนยกของ
portrait	pharb-thaai	ภาพถ่าย
position	tamnaeng	ตำแหน่ง
positive	nae thi-diao	แน่ทีเดียว
possible	penh-dai	เป็นได้
post card	praisani-bat	ไปรษณียบัตร
post office	samnak-ngarn praisani	สำนักงานไปรษณีย์
powder	paeng; phong	แป้ง, ผง
power	kamlang; am-nart	กำลัง, อำนาจ
powerful	mi am nart	มีอำนาจ
practical	shai-daai	ใช้ได้
practice	karn-fuek	การฝึก
precious	mi khâ	มีค่า
prefer	shob maak kwa	ชอบมากกว่า
pregnant	tang-khanh; mi thawng	ตั้งครรภ์, มีท้อง
prepare	chad-triam	จัดเตรียม
prescription	bai-sang yâ	ใบสั่งยา
present	khong-khwan	ของขวัญ
presentation	karn namh saneu	การนำเสนอ
present	patchu-banh	ปัจจุบัน

press	kod; beep	กด, บีบ
pressure	khwaam-kod danh	ความกดดัน
pretty	ngârm; suai	งาม, สวย
prevent	pong-kanh	ป้องกัน
previous	tae-konn	แต่ก่อน
price	ra-khâ	ราคา
priest	phra-song	พระสงฆ์
primary	pathom	ปฐม
principles	lak-kârn	หลักการ
prison	khuk; ta-raang	คุก, ตะราง
prisoner	nak-thode	นักโทษ
private	suan-tuâ; suan buk-khon	ส่วนตัว, ส่วนบุคคล
prize	raang-wanh	รางวัล
probable	penh-pai-daai	เป็นไปได้
probably	baang-thi	บางที
problem	pan-hâ	ปัญหา
process	kam-vithi	กรรมวิธี
produce	phlid awk mâ	ผลิตออกมา
production	phlid-phnl	ผลิตผล
profession	a-sheep	อาชีพ
professor	sastra-charn	ศาสตราจารย์
profit	kam-rai	กำไร
program	raai karn	รายการ
progress	khwaam kao-nâ	ความก้าวหน้า
prohibit	haam	ห้าม
project	khrong-karn	โครงการ
promise	sanyâ	สัญญา
prominent	denh	เด่น
promote	songserm	ส่งเสริม

pronunciation	karn awk siang	การออกเสียง
proof	khaw phisout	ข้อพิสูจน์
propaganda	karn khosanâ	การโฆษณา
property	sab-sin	ทรัพย์สิน
prosper	mang-khang; somboun	มั่งคั่ง, สมบูรณ์
protect	khum-kanh; pok pong	คุ้มกัน, ปกป้อง
proud	ying; phoom chai	หยิ่ง, ภูมิใจ
provide	chad ha hai	จัดหาให้
province	changwad	จังหวัด
public	sathara-nah; prasha-shon	สาธารณะ, ประชาชน
publish	phim khosanâ	พิมพ์โฆษณา
pull	dueng awk mâ	ดึงออกมา
pump	pump	ปั๊ม
punish	long-thode; tham-thode	ลงโทษ, ทำโทษ
purchase	sue	ซื้อ
pure	sa-ard	สะอาด
purple	si-muang	สีม่วง
purpose	wathu-prasong	วัตถุประสงค์
purse	krapow sai-ngoen	กระเป๋าใส่เงิน
push	phlak; danh khow pai	ผลัก, ดันเข้าไป
put	sai; waang-long	ใส่, วางลง

Q

quality	khuna-phaab	คุณภาพ
quantity	pari-marn	ปริมาณ
quarrel	thalaw-vivaad	ทะเลาะวิวาท

ueen	rajini	ราชินี
uestion	tharm	ถาม
uick	réow; wai	เร็ว, ไว
uiet	ngiab	เงียบ
uite	thidiao	ทีเดียว

R

ace	sheua-shaat	เชื้อชาติ
adio	vithayu	วิทยุ
ailroad	rot-fai	รถไฟ
ain	fonh	ฝน
ainbow	saai-roung	สายรุ้ง
aincoat	seua-fonh	เสื้อฝน
aise	yok khuen; pherm	ยกขึ้น, เพิ่ม
apidly	doai-réow	โดยเร็ว
are	ha-yark	หายาก
ash	phuen-khan	ผื่นคัน
ate	attra	อัตรา
ate of exchange	attra laek-plian	อัตราแลกเปลี่ยน
ather	khonn-khaang chah	ค่อนข้างจะ
aw	dib	ดิบ
azor	mide-kône	มีดโกน
each	mide-kône	มาถึง
ead	ânn	อ่าน
eady	phrom-laew	พร้อมแล้ว
eal	thae-ching	แท้จริง
eally	doai thae-ching	โดยแท้จริง
ear	khaang-lang	ข้างหลัง

reason	head-phon	เหตุผล
reasonable	som head-phon	สมเหตุผล
receipt	bai-rab	ใบรับ
receive	rab	รับ
receiver	khreung-rab	เครื่องรับ
recent, recently	meua réow-réow-ni	เมื่อเร็ว ๆ นี้
recognize	yomm-rab; cham dai	ยอมรับ, จำได้
remove	yaai; khleuan-yaai	ย้าย, เคลื่อนย้าย
renew	tham-mai; taw a-yuh	ทำใหม่, ต่ออายุ
rent	shaow; kha-shaow	เช่า, ค่าเช่า
repair	somm-saem	ซ่อมแซม
repeat	phoud sam	พูดซ้ำ
replace	plian; thaen kan dai	เปลี่ยน, แทนกันได้
reply	kham-tobb	คำตอบ
report	raai-ngârn	รายงาน
republic	satharana-rat	สาธารณรัฐ
reputation	shue-siang	ชื่อเสียง
request	raai-ngârn	ขอร้อง
rescue	shuai shi-wit	ช่วยชีวิต
reserved	sam-rong wai	สำรองไว้
residence	thi-you	ที่อยู่
responsible	rab-phid shop	รับผิดชอบ
respect	nab- thue	นับถือ
rest	phak-phonn; yout-phak	พักผ่อน, หยุดพัก
restaurant	phatta-kharn	ภัตตาคาร
restroom	hong naam	ห้องน้ำ
result	phon	ผล
return	klab mâ	กลับมา
return ticket:	tua pai-klab	ตั๋วไป-กลับ

review	phi-charana	พิจารณา
reward	raang-wan	รางวัล
rice	khao; khao-chao	ข้าว, ข้าวเจ้า
rich	mang-mi; ram-ruai	มั่งมี, ร่ำรวย
ride	khi; khab-khi	ขี่, ขับขี่
right	thouk-tong; khwâ mve	ถูกต้อง, ขวามือ
ring (for finger)	waen	แหวน
(to ring a bell)	sanh krading	สั่นกระดิ่ง
(hoop)	wong-waen	วงแหวน
ripe	souk	สุก
rise	khuen	ขึ้น
river	mae-nârm	แม่น้ำ
road	thanon	ถนน
roast	ping; yaang	ปิ้ง, ย่าง
rob	lak; khamoai	ลัก, ขโมย
robber	khamoai	ขโมย
rock (stone)	hinh	หิน
(to rock)	khayaow	เขย่า
roll	muân	ม้วน
roof	lang-khâ	หลังคา
room	hong	ห้อง
rope	sheuak	เชือก
rose	dork kularb	ดอกกุหลาบ
rough	yarb; khru-khrah	หยาบ, ขรุขระ
round	moun-robb; klom	หมุนรอบ, กลม
round-trip:	pai lae klab	ไปและกลับ
routine	ngârn pracham	งานประจำ
rub	thou	ถู
rubber	yaang	ยาง

rubbish	kha-yah	ขยะ
rude	yarb-khaai	หยาบคาย
rule	kod; ra-biab	กฎ, ระเบียบ
rumor	khao lue	ข่าวลือ
run	wing	วิ่ง
runway	thaang-wing	ทางวิ่ง

S

sad	saow; saow-soke	เศร้า, เศร้าโศก
safe	plawd-phai	ปลอดภัย
sail	laen-reua	แล่นเรือ
sailor	kalasi reua	กลาสีเรือ
salary	ngoen-deuan	เงินเดือน
salesman	khon dern talaad	คนเดินตลาด
salt	kleua	เกลือ
same	meuan-kanh	เหมือนกัน
sample	tua-yaang	ตัวอย่าง
sand	saai	ทราย
sanitary	suk-khapharb; a-namai	สุขภาพ, อนามัย
sanitary napkins	pha-ana-mai	ผ้าอนามัย
satisfy	phaw chai	พอใจ
save	prayad; sah-som	ประหยัด, สะสม
say	phoud; klao	พูด, กล่าว
scales	ta-shang	ตาชั่ง
(of fish)	kled-plâ	เกล็ดปลา
scar	phlae-penh	แผลเป็น
scarce	ha-yaak	หายาก

scare	tham hai klua	ทำให้กลัว
scarf	pha phan khaw	ผ้าพันคอ
schedule	tarang kamnod	ตารางกำหนด
school	rong-rian	โรงเรียน
science	vithaya-saat	วิทยาศาสตร์
scientist	nak vithaya-saat	นักวิทยาศาสตร์
scissors	kan-krai	กรรไกร
scratch	thalawk; khuan	ถลอก, ข่วน
scrub	khad; thou	ขัด, ถู
sea	tha-lé	ทะเล
sea-water:	narm tha-lé	น้ำทะเล
seafood:	a-harn tha-lé	อาหารทะเล
search	khon; khon-hâ	ค้น, ค้นหา
seasick	mao-khluen	เมาคลื่น
season	ruedoo	ฤดู
seat	thi-nang	ที่นั่ง
secret	khwaam-lab	ความลับ
secretary	lékhâ-nukarn	เลขานุการ
section	phanaek; muad	แผนก, หมวด
security	khwaam plawd-phai	ความปลอดภัย
see	dou; henh	ดู, เห็น
select	leuak	เลือก
sell	khaai	ขาย
send	song-hai; song-pai	ส่งให้, ส่งไป
seniority	a-wu-sô	อาวุโส
sense	prasard; samong	ประสาท, สมอง
sensible	rob-khob; mi satih	รอบคอบ, มีสติ
sentence	kham phi-phaak-sâ	คำพิพากษา
seperated	yaek-kanh	แยกกัน

serious	aow-ching aow-chang	เอาจริงเอาจัง
servant	khon-shai	คนใช้
serve	borikarn; rab-shai	บริการ, รับใช้
set (to place)	waang	วาง
(to set down)	tang	ตั้ง
settle (of disputes)	ra-ngab; tok-long	ระงับ, ตกลง
several	laai-laai	หลาย ๆ
severe	roun-raeng	รุนแรง
sex	phed	เพศ
sew	yeb	เย็บ
shade (of tree)	rom-maai	ร่มไม้, ชายคา
shadow	ngaow	เงา
shape	roup raang lak-sanah	รูปร่างลักษณะ
share (to divide)	baeng-suan	แบ่งส่วน
sharp	khom	คม
sharpen (knives)	lab-mide	ลับมีด
(pencils)	laow din-saw	เหลาดินสอ
shave	kône	โกน
sheet	phaën; phuen	แผ่น, ผืน
shelf	hing; shanh	หิ้ง, ชั้น
shine	song-saeng	ส่องแสง
ship	reua-yai	เรือใหญ่
(of war)	reua-rob	เรือรบ
(steam)	reua kon-fai	เรือกลไฟ
(sailing)	reua bai	เรือใบ
shoe	rong-thao	รองเท้า
shoot	ying	ยิง
shop	raan; raan-khâ	ร้าน, ร้านค้า
shopping center	soun karn-khâ	ศูนย์การค้า

shore	fang	ฝั่ง
short	sanh; tia	สั้น, เตี้ย
should	khuan; khuan-chah	ควร, ควรจะ
shoulder	lai	ไหล่
show	sadaeng hai dou	แสดงให้ดู
show off:	ouad	อวด
shower (bath)	ab-narm fak-bua	ฝักบัวอาบน้ำ
shut	pid	ปิด
shy	kradaak; aye	กระดาก, อาย
sick	cheb; mai-sabaai; puai	เจ็บ, ไม่สบาย, ป่วย
side	khaang; daan	ข้าง, ด้าน
sight (eyesight)	saai-ta	สายตา
signal	san-yarn	สัญญาณ
sign	khreuang-maai	เครื่องหมาย
signature	laai-senh	ลายเซ็น
silent	ngiab; mai-phoud	เงียบ, ไม่พูด
silk	mai; phrae	ไหม, แพร
silly	ngô; rai sara	โง่, ไร้สาระ
silver	ngoen	เงิน
similar	meuan; khlaai	เหมือน, คล้าย
simple	ngaai	ง่าย
since	tang-tae	ตั้งแต่
sing	rong-phleng	ร้องเพลง
single	diao	เดี่ยว
(unmarried)	sode	โสด
sit	nang	นั่ง
size	khanard	ขนาด
skill	khwaam chamnarn	ความชำนาญ
skin	phiew-nang	ผิวหนัง

skirt	kra-prong	กระโปรง
skull	kraloke sisah	กระโหลกศรีษะ
sky	thong-fâ	ท้องฟ้า
slap	tob; tob-nâ	ตบ, ตบหน้า
sleep	nonnlab	นอนหลับ
sleeve	khaen-seua	แขนเสื้อ
slice	shin	ชิ้น
(to slice)	hanh-pen-shin	หั่นเป็นชิ้น
slipper	rong-thao taeh	รองเท้าแตะ
slippery	luen	ลื่น
slow	shâ	ช้า
slowly:	shâ-shâ	ช้า ๆ
small	lek	เล็ก
smart	phueng-chai; chalard	พึงใจ, ฉลาด
smell	dom; dai-klin	ดม, ได้กลิ่น
smelly	klin mai-di	กลิ่นไม่ดี
smile	yim	ยิ้ม
smoke	khwan-fai;	ควันไฟ,
(to smoke)	soup	สูบ
smooth	riab	เรียบ
snack	a-harn waang	อาหารว่าง
snake	ngoû	งู
snore	kronh	กรน
so	dang-nan	ดังนั้น
soap	sabu	สบู่
social	sangkhom	สังคม
society	samakhom	สมาคม
soft	onn; noum	อ่อน, นุ่ม
soil	phuen-din	พื้นดิน

sold	khaai	ขาย
solid	khaeng; naën-nâ	แข็ง,แน่นหนา
soldier	tha-harn	ทหาร
some	baang; baang-khon	บาง, บางคน
sometimes	baang-khrang	บางครั้ง
son	bout-shaai	บุตรชาย
song	phléng	เพลง
soon	mai-shâ; réow	ไม่ช้า, เร็ว
sore	cheb-saeb; ak-sek	เจ็บแสบ,อักเสบ
sorry	sia-chai	เสียใจ
soul	duang vin-yarn	ดวงวิญญาณ
sound (noise)	siang	เสียง
soup	narm-kaeng	น้ำแกง
sour	priao	เปรี้ยว
(spoiled)	boude	บูด
souvenir	khong thi-ra-luek	ของที่ระลึก
space	a-wa-kard	อวกาศ
speak	phoud	พูด
spectacles	waen-ta	แว่นตา
special	phised	พิเศษ
speed	khwaam-réow	ความเร็ว
spend	shai-ngoen	ใช้เงิน
spicy	phed; phed-ronn	เผ็ด, เผ็ดร้อน
split	taek-yaek	แตกแยก
spoiled	sia; now	เสีย, เน่า
spoon	shonn	ช้อน
sport	kilâ	กีฬา
spot	choud; tombon	จุด, ตำบล
spouse	khou som-rod	คู่สมรส

spray	shide; phon	ฉีด, พ่น
spread	phrae, khachaai	แพร่, กระจาย
square	si-yaek	สี่แยก
squeeze	khan; beep	คั้น, บีบ
stab	thaeng	แทง
stain	roi-peuan	รอยเปื้อน
stairs	ban-dai	บันได
stand	yuen	ยืน
star	duang dao; dara	ดวงดาว, ดารา
starch	paeng	แป้ง
start	rerm; rerm-tonh	เริ่ม, เริ่มต้น
stay	phak-you; asai-you	พักอยู่, อาศัยอยู่
statistics	sathitih	สถิติ
steal	khamoai	ขโมย
steel	lek-klâ	เหล็กกล้า
steep	soung; shan	สูง, ชัน
step	kaô; kaô-khâ	ก้าว, ก้าวขา
stick	maai-thao	ไม้เท้า
stiff	khaeng	แข็ง
still	yang-ik	ยังอีก
sting	toi; kad	ต่อย, กัด
stomach	thawng	ท้อง
stone	konn-hin; konn-kruad	ก้อนหิน, ก้อนกรวด
stop	yout; lerk	หยุด, เลิก
store	raan-khâ	ร้านค้า
storm	phayu	พายุ
story	nitharn; reuang-rao	นิทาน, เรื่องราว
straight	trong-pai	ตรงไป
strange	plaek	แปลก

stranger	khon-plaek-nâ	คนแปลกหน้า
street	tha-non	ถนน
string	sheuak	เชือก
strong	khaeng-raeng	แข็งแรง
stubborn	due	ดื้อ
student	nak-rian; nak-sueksa	นักเรียน, นักศึกษา
study	rian; sueksa	เรียน, ศึกษา
stupid	ngô	โง่
style	tha-thaang; baeb; vithi	ท่าทาง, แบบ, วิธี
subject	reuang; hua-khoh	เรื่อง, หัวข้อ
submit	yom chamnon	ยอมจำนน
such	shen-ni; shen-nan	เช่นนี้, เช่นนั้น
succeed	tham samret	ทำสำเร็จ
suck	doud	ดูด
sudden	than-thi	ทันที
suffer	thon thawra-marn	ทนทรมาน
sugar	narm-tarn	น้ำตาล
suggest	nae-nam	แนะนำ
suicide	kha-tua-taai	ฆ่าตัวตาย
summer	na ronn	หน้าร้อน
sun	duang athit; saeng-daed	ดวงอาทิตย์, แสงแดด
sunny	daed-dee	แดดดี
supply	song hai	ส่งให้
support	sanab-sanun	สนับสนุน
suppose	sommut	สมมติ
sure	nae-chai	แน่ใจ
surgeon	salya-phaed	ศัลยแพทย์
surname	narm sakun	นามสกุล
surprise	pralard-chai	ประหลาดใจ

surrender	yom chamnon	ยอมจำนน
survive	yang-you; rawd-taai	ยังอยู่, รอดตาย
suspect	song-sai	สงสัย
suspend	phak-wai-konn	พักไว้ก่อน
swallow	kluen	กลืน
sweat	ngeuâ	เหงื่อ
sweep	kwaad	กวาด
sweet	waan; (sweets)	หวาน
swim	waai-narm	ว่ายน้ำ
sword	krabi; darb	กระบี่, ดาบ
syllable	phayaang	พยางค์
syringe	khem shide yâ	เข็มฉีดยา
system	vithi; rabob	วิธี, ระบบ

T

table	toh	โต๊ะ
tail	haang	หาง
tailor	shaang tat-seua	ช่างตัดเสื้อ
take	aow; rab-aow	เอา, รับเอา
talk	phoud	พูด
tall	soung	สูง
tank	thang-narm	ถังน้ำ
target	pow; pow-maai	เป้า, เป้าหมาย
taste	rod; rod-chart	รส, รสชาติ
(totaste)	shim	ชิม
tax	phasi akorn	ภาษีอากร
tea (tea leaves)	shâ	ชา

teach sonn สอน
teacher khru; acharn ครู, อาจารย์
tear narm-tâ น้ำตา
telegram thoralek โทรเลข
telephone thorasab โทรศัพท์
elevision thorathat โทรทัศน
ell bawk บอก
emperature oun-ha-phoum อุณหภูมิ
emple wat วัด
emporary shua-khrao ชั่วคราว
ender noum; onn; baow นุ่ม, อ่อน, เบา
errible na-klua น่ากลัว
est thod-long ทดลอง
hankful khob-khun ขอบคุณ
heater rong-lakhorn โรงละคร
heft khamoai ขโมย
herefore phraw shanan เพราะฉนั้น
ick nâ หนา
in baang บาง
ink khid; nuek คิด, นึก
irst krahaai narm กระหายน้ำ
read daai ด้าย
reat khou ขู่
roat khaw คอ
rough talawd ตลอด
row khwaang; pâ; yône ขว้าง, ปา, โยน
umb niew hua mae-nue นิ้วหัวแม่มือ
under fâ-rong ฟ้าร้อง
ket tuâ ตั๋ว

tidy	pen rabiab	เป็นระเบียบ
tie	phouk; madd	ผูก, มัด
tiger	seuâ	เสือ
time	véla; khrang; samai	เวลา, ครั้ง, สมัย
timid	khi-aye	ขี้อาย
tin	di-bouk; krapong	ดีบุก, กระป๋อง
tip	plaai	ปลาย
tire (tyre)	yaang-rot	ยางรถ
title	shue-reuang; tamnaeng	ชื่อเรื่อง, ตำแหน่ง
to	thueng	ถึง
toe	niew-thao	นิ้วเท้า
together	duai-kanh	ด้วยกัน
toilet	hong-narn	ห้องน้ำ
tongue	linh	ลิ้น
too	duai; meuan kan	ด้วย, เหมือนกัน
tool	khreuang-mue shaang	เครื่องมือช่าง
tooth	fanh	ฟัน
total	ruam thang-mod	รวมทั้งหมด
touch	taeh; taeh-tong	แตะ, แตะต้อง
tour	thong-thiao; thasanachorn	ท่องเที่ยว, ทัศนาจร
town	meuang	เมือง
trade	karn khâ	การค้า
train	fuek-hadd; rot-fai	ฝึกหัด, รถไฟ
transit	dern-thaang phaan	เดินทางผ่าน
transport	karn khon song	การขนส่ง
travel	dern-thaang	เดินทาง
trick	kol-med; louk-mai	กลเม็ด, ลูกไม้
trouble	lam-baak, yung-yaak	ยุ่งยาก, ลำบาก
true	ching	จริง

truth	khwaam ching	ความจริง
trust	wai-waang-chai	ไว้วางใจ
try	phaya-yaam; lawng-dou	พยายาม,ลองดู
tune	siang phléng	เสียงเพลง
turn	moun; hanh-klab	หมุน, หันกลับ
type	phim	พิมพ์

ugly,	na-kliad; khireh	น่าเกลียด, ขี้เหร่
umbrella	rom	ร่ม
under	tai; khaang-taai; tam kwa	ใต้, ข้างใต้, ต่ำกว่า
understand	rou; khow-chai	รู้, เข้าใจ
university	maha vithayalai	มหาวิทยาลัย
unless	wen-tae; nawk-chaak	เว้นแต่, นอกจาก
unit	nuai	หน่วย
until	chon krathang	จนกระทั่ง
unusual	phid pokkatih	ผิดปกติ
up	bonh; khaang-bonh	บน, ข้างบน
upper	neua khuen pai	เหนือขึ้นไป
upstairs	shan-bonh	ชั้นบน
urgent	duan	ด่วน
use	shai	ใช้
usually	tarm pokkatih	ตามปกติ
useful	mi prayode	มีประโยชน์
useless	mai mi prayode	ไม่มีประโยชน์
utensil	pha-shanah	ภาชนะ

vacant	waang	ว่าง
vacation	wan youd	วันหยุด
valuable	mi rakha	มีราคา
value	kha	ค่า
vehicles	yuad-yarn	ยวดยาน
venture	karn siang phai	การเสี่ยงภัย
veterinarian	satava-phaed	สัตวแพทย์
very	thae-ching; maak	แท้จริง, มาก
view	pharb	ภาพ
village	mou-baan	หมู่บ้าน
virgin	borisut	บริสุทธิ์
visa	visa	วีซ่า
visit	yiam-yian	เยี่ยมเยียน
visitor	khaek; a-khan-tukah	แขก, อาคันตุกะ
voice	siang-phoud; siang-rong	เสียงพูด, เสียงร้อง
voluntary	doai samak-chai	โดยสมัครใจ
vomit (to)	a-chian	อาเจียน
voyage	karn dern-thaang	การเดินทาง

waist	sa-éw	สะเอว
wait	raw-khoi; khoi	รอคอย, คอย
wake	tuen; plouk hai tuen	ตื่น, ปลุกให้ตื่น
walk	dern	เดิน

wall	fâ-phanang; kamphaeng	ฝาผนัง, กำแพง
wallet	krapow ngoen	กระเป๋าเงิน
want	tong-karn	ต้องการ
war	songkhram	สงคราม
warm	oun	อุ่น
warn	teuan	เตือน
wash	laang; shamrah	ล้าง, ชำระ
wash basin	âng samrab laang	อ่างสำหรับล้าง
watchman	yarm	ยาม
water	narm	น้ำ
waterfall:	narm-tok	น้ำตก
wheel	law; kong-law	ล้อ, กงล้อ
when	meuâ	เมื่อ
where	thi-nai	ที่ไหน
whether	rue mai	หรือไม่
which(relative)	sueng; doai	ซึ่ง, โดย
(interrogative)	nai; anh-nai	ไหน, อันไหน
while	kha-nah thi	ขณะที่
white	si-khao; khao	สีขาว, ขาว
who (interrogative)	khrai	ใคร
whoever	khrai koh taam	ใครก็ตาม
whole	thang-mod	ทั้งหมด
why	tham-mai; phraw a-rai	ทำไม, เพราะอะไร
wide (spacious)	kwaang	กว้าง
widow	penh maai	เป็นหม้าย
wife	mia	เมีย
(politely)	phanraya	ภรรยา
wild (of land)	pâ-pliao	ป่าเปลี่ยว
(savage)	pâ-theuan	ป่าเถื่อน
wild animals:	satt pâ	สัตว์ป่า

willing	tem-chai	เต็มใจ
win	sha-nah	ชนะ
wind	lom	ลม
window	na-tâng	หน้าต่าง
wine	laow	เหล้า
wing	peek	ปีก
wipe	shed; thou	เช็ด, ถู
wire	luad	ลวด
wise	chalard; sukhum	ฉลาด, สุขุม
wave	khluen	คลื่น
way	vithi; thaang	วิธี, ทาง
weak	mai-mi raeng; onn-ae	ไม่มีแรง, อ่อนแอ
wear	suam-sai	สวมใส่
weather	din-fâ- a-kard	ดินฟ้าอากาศ
weight	narm-nak	น้ำหนัก
welcome	shern; yindi tonn-rab	เชิญ, ยินดีตอนรับ
well	sabaai di; thouk-tong	สบายดี, ถูกต้อง
wet	piak	เปียก
what	a-rai	อะไร
with	duai; kab	ด้วย, กับ
withdraw (money)	thawn	ถอน (เงิน)
without	pras-sa-chaak	ปราศจาก
witness	pha-yarn	พยาน
woman	phu-ying	ผู้หญิง
wonder	pralard-chai	ประหลาดใจ
wonderful	nâ phis-sa-wong	น่าพิศวง
wood (timber)	maai	ไม้
(forest)	pâ	ป่า
wool	khon-sat	ขนสัตว์

ord	kham; kham-phoud	คำ, คำพูด
ork (business)	thura-kit	ธุรกิจ
(to labor)	tham-ngarn	ทำงาน
orld	lôke	โลก
orm	tua-non; pha-yard	ตัวหนอน, พยาธิ
orry	nak-chai	หนักใจ
worried:	rob-kuan; kuan-chai	รบกวน, กวนใจ
orse (inferior in quality)	léow	เลว
(morally worse)	marayart saam	มรรยาททราม
orship	bushâ	บูชา
orth (value)	rakhâ	ราคา
(use)	mi-khâ	มีค่า
ould	art; art-chah	อาจ, อาจจะ
ound (injury)	baad-phlae	บาดแผล
rap	haw	ห่อ
rinkle	yonh; roi-yonh	ย่น, รอยย่น
rist	khaw-mue	ข้อมือ
wristwatch:	nalikâ khaw-mue	นาฬิกาข้อมือ
rite	khian	เขียน
rong	phid	ผิด

ard (of length)	lâ	หลา
awn	hao	หาว
ell	ta-kône	ตะโกน
ear	pi	ปี
new year:	Pi mai	ปีใหม่

yellow	si leuang	สีเหลือง
yes	chah; khah; khrap; khrap-phom	จ้ะ, ค่ะ, ครับ ครับผม
yet	yang; yang konn kra-nanh	ยัง, ยังก่อน กระนั้น
you	thanh; khun; theu	ท่าน, คุณ, เธอ
young	noum; sao; on-yao	หนุ่ม, สาว, อ่อนเย

Z

zinc	sang-ka-si	สังกะสี
zipper	zip route	ซิปรูด
zone	phark	ภาค
zoo	suan-sat	สวนสัตว์